HENRIK VON SCHEEL | CIPRIAN POPA | JOS

Strategy
IN THE
AGE OF DISRUPTION

A Handbook to Anticipate Change and Make *Smart Decisions*

WILEY

Published by John Wiley & Sons, Inc., Hoboken, New Jersey.
Published simultaneously in Canada.

The logos and trademarks of the company featured in this publications are owned by those respective organizations and are used under license or permission from the respective mark owners. The authors are independent of are not affiliated with such companies.

For general information on our other products and services or for technical support, please contact our Customer Care Department within the United States at (800) 762-2974, outside the United States at (317) 572-3993 or fax (317) 572-4002.

Wiley also publishes its books in a variety of electronic formats. Some content that appears in print may not be available in electronic formats. For more information about Wiley products, visit our web site at www.wiley.com.

Library of Congress Cataloging-in-Publication Data is Available:

ISBN 9781394210268 (Paperback)
ISBN 9781394210275 (ePub)
ISBN 9781394210282 (ePDF)

Cover Design and Illustrations: © Henrik von Scheel

Printed and bound in Great Britain by Bell & Bain Ltd, Glasgow

Thou shall not pass!

You hold a handbook that is a call to action for

    . . . Executives, who want to learn to lead in constant changes

    . . . Experts, who need to deliver on promise

    . . . Consultants, who want to capitalize on new approaches

    . . . Entrepreneurs, who want to invent the future

    . . . Game changers, who challenge outdated thinking

    . . . Visionaries, who demand a bigger horizon

    . . . Students of life, who crave to see everything in brighter colors

    . . . Pretenders, who need to move beyond the hype and get real

An invitation to think differently and revise how you learn, unlearn, and relearn to thrive in a constant changing world.

It is only when a mosquito lands on your testicles that you realize there is a way to solve problems without using violence.

Confucius

Disclaimer

This work is not meant, in any way, to offend or otherwise hurt anybody.

The authors may be excused as they have self-diagnosed themselves to suffer from Dyslexia, Attention Deficit Hyperactivity Disorder, Alien Hand Syndrome, Münchausen Syndrome, and a dose of bad humor.

Münchausen Syndrome by proxy

If our jokes offend you

1. We are sorry.

2. It won't happen again.

3. It doesn't mean you are right.

4. It's your choice to be offended.

5. 1+2 are lies.

Foreword

Expressive drawing by Gloria Popa, 4 years.
She is so adorable and a force to be reckoned with.

Zeal of Appreciation

Thank you to the Chairman who provides abundantly.
I am in you and you are in me in divine love.

To the strongest and most beautiful person I know - *my wife*
After 30 years you are still my heroine. I can't get enough of you.

To my biggest critics and best friends - *my sons*
When I grow up, I want to be just like you. Yes, you are right,
I would have made a terrible doctor. People would have died
(for a good cause).

To the future - *our grandchild*
You are the brim of light, that the future looks bright.

To my *mother*, who gave me life
Mom, I am not a drug dealer. Yes, I travel a lot and earn well, but

I work in IT. No, I can't fix your PC; I am not that type of IT guy.

Dedications

To my *teacher,* who ignited a flame in a dyslexic and stuttering boy.

To *Didier*
You are the most amazing guy, but I am married, so I think we should just be friends.

To *those who inspired it* and will not read it.

To *everyone,* who only hears from me when I need something.

To those who always wanted a book dedicated. Let's fix that.
This book is dedicated to: _____

Contents

Anatomy Chart

We create great ideas that sometimes others take the credit for

ATTENTION ASSHOLE!

8th commandment

"thou shalt not steal or copy"

God is watching

You thieving degenerate

INTRODUCTION

Chapter One

Welcome to the most disruptive period in human history. The next 20 years will bring more changes than the previous 300 years.

We live in a radically changing world, called the 4th Industrial Revolution, which fundamentally alters every aspect of our human experience, from our lives, work, business to the economy, the environment, and social interactions at a global level.

In its scale, scope, and complexity, the transformation will modify everything that we know beyond recognition across industries and borders, unlike anything humankind has experienced before.

Yet it remains poorly understood, and most do not know how we should respond.

This book holds the promise to have a deep impact on your life, your work, and your organization.

It is written for YOU, as a practical guide to help you

> **See the big picture**
> Focus on what matters
> Make **smarter** decisions

It will help you get started from where you stand, exploit what's available to you, and take action to meet the biggest challenges of our times.

That, my friends, is why this book exists.

The structure of the book is focused around YOU. To build a good understanding of what the changes are, how you can respond and benefit from it.

Latest insight on Industry 4.0

The book is written as a practical guide on what Industry 4.0 is, what this means for YOU, and how YOU as a leader, manager, expert, entrepreneur, or investor capitalize and put it into practice.

Great shifts that slip our attention

Today, the news cycle is filled with doomsday prophecies that paint a dark and hopeless future. The authors are eternal optimists and believe in humanity's ability to adopt to change and collaborate for a better future. For this reason, we dedicated chapter 4 on our great human accomplishment of the past 100 years to shine light on what we as humans can handle of the challenges ahead.

Handbook on strategy execution

You hold a complete handbook on strategy, part of an Executive MBA program. Designed as a guided step-by-step from a strategic position, strategic choices to strategy execution.

Designed for doers

In the words of Herman Hesse: "Theory is knowledge that does not work. Practice is when everything works and you do not know why." If you are a practical person, this book is designed for you with all the latest management practices, techniques, visual memory effects, and reusable templates that enable immediate hands-on use.

You will learn how to systematically guide and approach how to manage the present and create the future.

Checklist of what you can get out of this book

- ✓ Get fresh insight on the 4th Industrial Revolution from the originator.
- ☐ Learn how to spot trends and exploit disruption.
- ☐ Understand the how, where, and when to adopt to changes or disrupt.
- ☐ Uncover what strategy is and how to apply it.
- ☐ Become a strategy hero!
- ☐ Build a new business!!
- ☐ Exploit how to strategy in a step-by-step guide.
- ☐ Benefit from the latest management disciplines.
- ☐ Learn how to manage the present operations while creating the future.
- ☐ Profit from change.
- ☐ Evolve into game changers in your field.
- ☐ Find new ways to make a living.
- ☐
- ☐
- ☐

Some people are
worth melting for.

Henrik von Scheel

The Godfather

Best known as the originator of the "4th Industrial Revolution" and the Global Digital themes of today.

Named the "leading authority on strategy" and recognized as "the most influential management thinker of our times."

His work has shaped the performance of the fastest-growing companies and is applied to 24 national economies.

A sought-after speaker, iconic futurist, and advisor, he has evolved the mainstream thinking and practices on the toughest and most important issues in business today.

Honored with the Knowledge Award viz. the Nobel laureates of knowledge sharing in 2019.

He is a Professor at the Arthur Lok Jack Global School of Business.

Henrik does not work for ฿$€ – he is compensated by his self-realization.

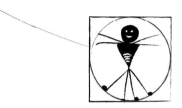

Ciprian Popa

Man of Magic

If you meet Ciprian, you enter a world of magic. He radiates positive energy and manifests endless impossibilities.

He is one of the most influential blockchain personalities in supply chain and a pioneer in financial engineering.

His thought is action in rehearsal that solves complex problems with a unique ability to create new insights to better meet demand.

His sweet spot is applying technology to digitalize assets.

Ciprian specializes in visual strategy positioning and strategic decision-making.

Ciprian delivers! A driven people person who is realistic about his own capabilities and insightful about others.

Joshua **von Scheel**

The Pilot

A creative problem solver who is obsessed with simplifying the complexity of strategy execution through visual thinking, business logic, and design.

Joshua designed the book based on his experience as a Business Architect and his natural gift to think strategically.

His trademark is strategic thinking - his unique ability is to rethink outdated business practices and evolve the mainstream practices of today.

Joshua has a natural talent for strategy + execution and asks the right questions.

He is a passionate commercial pilot and describes flying as "learning how to throw yourself at the ground and miss."

ALWAYS BE YOURSELF

UNLESS YOU CAN BE A
CHIEF STRATEGY OFFICER

Co-authors

John A. Zachman

Father of Business Architecture

John is the *inventor* of our modern Enterprise Architecture thinking of today.

He is the author of the famous Zachman Framework, which is a global Enterprise Architecture standard for integrative framework, an ontology for descriptive representations for Enterprises.

John is known for his ability to enable executives to link strategy with operational execution.

Dr. Douglas van den Berghe

The Problem Solver

One of the world's most influential and iconoclastic business thinkers on foreign direct investment and special economic zone. His official nickname is "FDI Guru."

He asserts that economic development models must continually reinvent themselves, and not just in times of crisis. He has worked with leading governments, companies, and investors across the globe, and is a dynamic and sought-after advisor and speaker.

Jamal Bin Huwaireb

The Historian

Jamal is the cultural advisor to the Government of Dubai and the CEO of Mohammed Bin Rashid Al Maktoum Foundation, and serves as a Board member of the UNESCO Institute for Lifelong Learning.

He is a passionate historian and prolific writer of Nabataean poetry, and has documented the cultural and creative movement of the Emirate of Dubai, the rest of Emirates of the country, and the Persian Gulf region. He has documented Arab and Islamic heritage, presented in the TV show "Al Rawi" during the month of Ramadan for more than 8 years.

Gabriel von Scheel

The Creative Brain

A big-scale thinker who loves the details just as much. Recognized for his business logic and design thinking that simplifies complexity and problem solving through visual thinking.

Gabriel is the creative designer that has triggered most of the concepts in the book.

Through his mix of unique visual, analytical strategic skills, and attention to detail, he is a rising star in the making and ONE TO WATCH.

Chandana Wagal Pai

The Powerhouse

There is no other way to describe Chandana than a *Powerhouse*, and a maestro Business Developer.

Chandana is a compelling storyteller who can captivate leaders with her passion, clarity of thought, and intelligence.

She puts people first and sees potential in every individual, which makes her a natural "Skill Builder." She is a pro at finding and harnessing opportunities for business growth.

Chandana makes a difference. She is a big thinker who loves the details.

Gert Jansson

The Bohemian Guru

Award-winning entrepreneur and innovator with deep experience helping businesses transform.

A trendsetter with big, bold ideas. Best known as the "Bee-Man" who masters the art of creating innovative solutions for a sustainable economy.

Gert is a smart worker, and an extremely social and networking junkie.

Driven by an elemental force spiced with an extreme curiosity, to learn to fail is to learn to grow.

Yige Dai

Master of Mindfulness

A big picture translator into operational execution.

Yige is known for his ability to help you change the way you look at things so that things you look at change.

He made a career as Chief Strategy Officer; he is responsible for driving Qbank's growth strategy through acquisitions, strategic partnerships, investments, co-development, and innovation.

Yige has previous experience in managing more than $5 billion venture capital investment portfolio with a focus on fostering innovation and leading market transitions.

Phil McCleenon

The Doer

Known for his ability to advise executives on how to tackle *their blind spots*.

He made a career of supporting business leaders on how to tackle the "change gap" by discovering the why, defining the what, and delivering the how.

Renowned for his ability to solve complex problems through his visual thinking in workshops and hands-on projects.

Acknowledgment of Contributors

No book of this kind can be written without help. Let us take a moment to give credit and appreciation to the many people who made this possible with their contributions as critics, sparring partners, colleagues, influencers, clients, or a dedicated Industry 4.0 and digitalization community of practitioners. Thank you!

Nobody really sees, how many times we have tried and failed until we got the right balance. This book is a kudos to you. Special recognition goes to you. . .

Those Who Believe
Confidants and friends who have inspired, scrutinized, given input, or contributed.

Those Who Invest
Visionary Financiers, financial moguls, and HNIW, who adopt to design and capitalize on the future.

Those Who Influence
Marketers who nudge our opponents on what we think and consume.

Those Who Engage
Maverick Experts who applied the concepts in real life. The heroes who push the frontline; the *backbone of* Industry 4.0 and digitalization practitioners with an indefatigable commitment to shaping a bright global future, one project at a time.

Those Who Dare
Thought leaders, colleagues, and authorities who research, examine, dialogue, and influence the latest practices with us.

Those Who Inspire
The Philanthropist who seeks to promote the welfare of others.

Those Who Lead
The Pioneers and Leaders of the world who influenced our lives. They have implemented and shared the lessons learned in the latest management practices on the biggest challenges of our times.

Those Who Rise
The Rising Stars in the making, that are poised to influence our future. They are the ones to watch and invest in.

#THOSE WHO BELIEVE

#THOSE WHO DARE

Benjamin Lee
Camelia Popa
Christian (Hitsch) Bolt
Danielle Jensen Rusch
Didier Schluchter
Eric Bushman
Gabriel von Scheel
Guido Uchtdorf
Hanne Foss Nørrung
Helena Mølgaard
James Mangan
Jesper & Mette Paulsen

Prof. Abderrahmane Leshob
Prof. Adams Coates
Assoc. Prof. Akram Awad
Prof. Alain Aspect
Allan N. Gjerding
Prof. Allen Stretton
Prof. Amy C. Edmondson
Prof. Arastou Khatibi
Prof. Ardavan Amini
Prof. August Wilhelm Scheer
Prof. Bent Grev
Bent Raymond Jørgensen

Geoffrey Hinton
Geoffrey Sparks
Prof. Georg Sørensen
Prof. Gerald C. Kane
Gerd Leonhard
Prof. Guoli Chen
Prof. Hajo Reijers
Hal Gregersen
Prof. Dr. Harald Welzer
Prof. Dr. Hasso Plattner
Prof. Dr. Henning Kagermann
Jamal Bin Huwsire

Prof. Philipp Schröder
Prof. Pinar Ozcan
Ram Charan
Dr. Ray Kurzweil
Prof. Richard D. Aveni
Prof. Dr. Richard David Precht
Prof. Rich Hilliard
Dr. Richard McCarthy
Dr. Richard Soley
Prof. Richard Whittington
Prof. Rita McGrath
Prof. Robert Kaplan

The future belongs to those who can IMAGINE IT, DESIGN IT, and EXECUTE IT.

H.H. Sheikh Mohammed bin Rashid Al Maktoum

Justin Tomlinson
Lisa Emelie von Scheel
Maik and Lars Cziesla
Marco de Savigny
Marianne Fonseca
Paul Peterson
Ro Gerta von Rosing
Sebastian Stenholm Paulsen
Shanaya Fischer
Stein Hugo Hansen

Bernard Marr
Prof. Björn-Ola Linnér
Prof. Brian Scassellati
Chan Kim & Renée Mauborgne
Dr. Carl Diver
Prof. Chris Starr
C. K. Prahalad
Prof. Clayton Christensen
Dr. Con Kenney
Prof. Daniel T. Jones
Prof. David Coloma
Prof. David P. Norton
Prof Didier Bonnet
Prof. Dirk Draheim
Prof. Erik Proper
Prof. Frank Gertsen
Prof. Fei-Fei Li
Gary Hamel

Prof. Jan Emmanuel De Neve
Prof. Jan vom Brocke
Prof. Johan Vernaillen
Prof. John McAfee
Johan Goossens
Prof. Jürgen Jung
Prof. Laurence Capron
Prof. Karel Cool
Prof. Manfred Reichert
Prof Marlon Dumas
Marshall Goldsmith
Prof. Michael E. Porter
Prof. Michael von Kutzschenbach
Dr. Michio Kaku
Prof. Dr. Monika Möhring
Prof. Niels Egelund
Prof. Pankaj Ghemawat
Prof. Paul M. W. Hackett

Prof. Salman AlQahtani
Prof. Samir EL-MASRI
Dr. Selin N. Şenocak
Sheila A. Cane
Prof. Per Kongshøj Madsen
Dr. Stefanie Auge-Dickhut
Steve Durbin
Prof. Steve Giggs
Prof. Thomas Rønde
Prof. Tom Lawrence
Tom Peters
Prof. Ulf Seigerroth
Prof. Venkat Ramaswamy
Vijay Govindarajan
Vitalik Buterin
Prof. Yvonne Dittrich
Prof. Zakaria Maamar
Prof. Zohar Ben-Ashe

#THOSE
#WHO INVEST

Abigail Johnson	Gautam Adani	Laurene Powell Jobs	Stephen Schwarzman
Alain Wertheimer	Gerard Wertheimer	Lee Shau Kee	Steve Ballmer
Alexey Mordashov	German Larrea	Len Blavatnik	Susanne Klatten
Alessandro Chiesa	Gina Rinehart	Leonard Lauder	Tadashi Yanai
Alfred Gantner	Giovanni Ferrero	Leonardo Del Vecchio	Takemitsu Takizaki
Anatoly Yakovenko	Guillaume Pousaz	Leonid Mikhelson	Thomas Frist
Arnaud Barray	Harold Hamm	Lloyd Blankfein	Thomas Peterffy
Alice Walton	He Xiangjian	Li Ka-shing	Vladimir Lisin
Aliko Dangote	Henry Cheng	Lukas Walton	Vladimir Potanin
Alisher Usmanov	Huang Shilin	Ma Huateng	Wang Chuan-Fu
Amancio Ortega	Iris Fontbona	MacKenzie Scott	Wang Wenyin
Andrew Forrest	Jack Ma	Mark Zuckerberg	Warren Buffett

Those who are unwilling to invest in the future haven't earned one.

Harold Lewis

Andrey Melnichenko	Jacqueline Badger Mars	Michael Bloomberg	William Ding
Azim Premji	James Dyson	Michael Dell	Yang Huiyan
Bernard Arnault	James Simons	Michael Hartono	Zeng Yuqun
Bill Gates	Jeff Bezos	Miriam Adelson	Zhang Yiming
Budi Hartono	Jensen Huang	Mohammed bin Rashid Al Maktoum	Zhong Shanshan
Carl Icahn	Jiang Rensheng	Mukesh Ambani Pallonji	
Carlos Slim	Jim Walton	Mistry Pang	
Changpeng Zhao	John Mars	Kang Peter Woo	
Charles Koch	John Menard	Ray Dalio	
Dan Gilbert	Jorge Paulo Lemann	Radhakishan Damani	
Dieter Schwarz	Julia Flesher Koch	Rob Walton	
Donald Bren	Ken Griffin	Robert Kuok	
Elaine Marshall	Klaus-Michael	Sergey Brin	
Eric Schmidt	Kuehne Lakshmi Mittal	Shiv Nadar	
Ernesto Bertarelli	Larry Ellison	Shai Agassi	
Francois Pinault	Larry Page	Stefan Quandt	
Francoise Bettencourt Meyers	Laurence Fink		

#THOSE WHO INFLUENCE

Alessandra Bellini
Alex Aiken
Alex Schultz
Alessandra Bellini
Aline Santos
Angela Zepeda
Ann Lewnes
Amy Fuller
Arjan Dijk
Benjamin Braun
Brie Carere
Britta Seeger

Marc Pritchard
Marisa Thalber
Octavio Fernandez
Oliver Stoldt
Raja Rajamannar
Rachel Ferdinando
Russell Wager
Ryan Selkis
Sara Bennison
Sally Susman
Sarah Franklin
Stephanie McMahon

#THOSE WHO RISE

Abdullah Salah
Ahmet C. Bozer
Brigadier General Ethud Schneerson
David J. O'Reilly
Flemming Elbæk Mortensen
Hans Vestberg
Imtiaz Murshed
Jan Plovsing
Jo-Ann Boodoosingh
Johan Dennelind
Jørgen Buhl Rasmussen
Jørgen Vig Knudstorp

#THOSE WHO INSPIRE

Cornelia Gantner
Dan Ariely
Didier Schluchter
Dr. Joe Dispenza
Esther Perel
Malcolm Gladwell
Marianne Fonseca von Scheel
Melinda Gates
Gregory Mihalcheon
Peter Diamandis

People don't buy what you do; they buy why you do it.
Simon Sinek

Bozoma Saint John
Carla Hassan
Charlotte De Brabandt
Chris Capossela
Christian R Andersen
Conny Braams
Colin Murphy
Dara Treseder
Sir David Attenborough
Deborah Wahl
Detlev von Platen
Diego Scotti
Enrico Galliera
Eric Lempel
Hildegard Wortmann
Janine Pelosi
Jens Thiemer
Jonathan Auerbach

Julia Goldin
Julia White
Lars Løkke Rasmussen
Leslie Berland
Lorenzo Bertelli
Lorraine Twohill
Lynne Biggar
Michael Bloomberg
Morgan Flatley
Nick Tran
Ukonwa Kuzi-Orizu Ojo
William White

Ralf Schneider
Rashid bin Mohammed bin Rashid Al Maktoum
Samuel Gantner
Satoshi Nakamoto
Silvia Thibodean
Tom Johnstone

#THOSE
#WHO LEAD

Abigail Johnson	Bob Iger	Dilma Rousseff	Hugo Ansker	John Legere
Adalberto Netto	Bob van Dijk	Doug McMillon	Imran Khan	John Seifert
Akio Toyoda	Brian Chesky	Douglas L. Peterson	Imtiaz Murshed	John T. Stankey
Al Monaco	Brian Cornell	Elon Musk	Ivan Menezes	Jørgen Mads Clausen
Alan Jope	Brian J. Porter	Emma Walmsley	Jack Bowles	Jørgen Tang-Jensen
Albert Bourla	Bruce Flatt	Enrique Salem	Jack Dorsey	Jose Ignacio Sanchez Galan
Alex Gorsky	Dr. C.C. Wei	Eric Emerson Schmidt	Jack Ma	Joseph Tucci
Alexander Dreiling	Carlos A. Rodriguez	Ernest Scott Santi	Jacob L. Gammelgaard	Julie Sweet
Alexey Miller	Carsten Dilling	Ernie Herrman	Jakob Stausholm	Karenann Terrell
Alfred F. Kelly Jr.	Charles J. Meyers	Eugene Kaspersky	James M. Foote	Kay Sallee
Amin H. Nasser	Charles W. Scharf	Evan G. Greenberg	James P. Gorman	Kelly S. King
Anand Mahindra	Chee Mun Foong	Fabrizio Freda	James Quincey	Kenichiro Yoshida
Anders Opedal	Christian Klein	Faisal Omar al-Sakkaf	Jamie Dimon	Kenneth Frazier

Everything is possible. The impossible just takes longer.
Dan Brown

Andrew Cecere	Christian Nicholas Stadil	Francesco Milleri	Jane Fraser	Kevin A. Lobo
Andy Jassy	Christine Lagarde	Francesco Starace	Jay A. Brown	Kevin Johnson
Angela Merkel	Christopher J.Kempczinski	Francois-Henri Pinault	Jean-Claude Juncke	Khalifa bin Zayed Al-Nahyan
Antonio Guterres	Chuck Robbins	Frank Bisignano	Jean-Laurent Bonnafe	Kim Fournais
Arvind Krishna	Craig Menear	Frank Slootman	Jean-Pascal Tricoire	Kjeld Johannesen
Axel Dumas	Cristiano Amon	Gary E. Dickerson	Jeffrey C. Sprecher	Klaus Schwab
Barack Obama	Dan Schulman	Gary Nagle	Jeffrey Preston Bezos	Klaus Vitt
Belen Garijo	Daniel O'Day	Gary S. Guthart	Jensen Huang	Kosai Alabdulkarim
Ben van Beurden	Daniel S. Glaser	Geoffrey S. Martha	Jerome Lambert	Kristin C. Peck
Benjamin Netanyahu	Daniel Zhang Dara	Ginni Rometty	Jesper Kasi Nielsen	Krzysztof Skurzak
Benoit Potier	Khosrowshahi	Gita Gopinath	Jim Clifton	Larry Ellison
Bernard Looney	Darius Adamczyk	Gregory J. Hayes	Jim Farley	Larry Fink
Bernd Montag	Darren Woods	Guillaume Faury	Jim Taiclet	Larry Page
Bill Clinton	Darryl White	H. Lawrence Culp Jr.	Jim Umpleby	Lars Fruergaard Jorgensen
Bill Gates	Dave Calhoun	Hamid Moghadam	Joaquim Silva e Luna	Lars Rebien Sørensen
Bill McDermott	David Cordani	Hans Vestberg	John C. May	Leo Apotheker
Billy Gifford	David I. McKay	Henrik Poulsen	John Chambers	Leonard Schleifer
Bjorn Rosengren	David M. Solomon	Herbert Diess	John Donahoe	Lindsey Rivera
Bob Chapek	David S. Tayler	Hossam Wazzan	John G. Morikis	Lloyd Blankfein

#THOSE
#WHO LEAD

Lloyd Blankfein
Lotte Tange
Louie Ehrlich
Louwrence D. Erasmus
Luiz Inácio Lula da Silva
Lynn Good
Ma Huateng
Manmohan Singh
Marc Benioff
Mario Greco
Mark Hurd
Mark Zuckerberg
Martin Brudermuller

Ola Kallenius
Oliver Bate
Oliver Bussmann
Oliver Zipse
Pablo Isla
Pascal Soriot
Patrick Pouyanne
Paul Hudson
Paul Maritz
Paul Otellini
Paul Perreault
Peter Wennink
Peter Woudsma

Sanjiv Mehta
Sashidhar Jagdishan
Satya Nadella
Scott Charlton
Sergey Brin
Severin Schwan
Shantanu Narayen
Sheik Khalifa bin Zayed al-Nahyan
Sheikh Mohamed bin Zayed bin Sultan Al Nahyan
Shemara Wikramanayake
Sri Shivananda
Stephen A. Schwarzman
Stephen Gold

Tom Rutledge
Ulf Mark Schneider
Vasant Narasimham
Vincent Roche
Volker Rebhan
Waleed A. Al-Mogbel
Walid Farghal

Walter Craig Jelinek
Walter W Bettinger II

The best way to predict the future is to create it.
Abraham Lincoln

Marvin Ellison
Mary Barra
Masayoshi Son
Mats Rahmstrom
Matt Comyn
Michael Dell
Michael Wirth
Michel Doukeris
Michele Hunt
Mike Henry
Mike Roman
Mukesh Ambani
Narendra Modi
Nathan Fullington
Niall O'Connor
Nick Jeffery
Nicolas Hieronimus
Noel Paul Quinn
Noel R. Wallace

Pietro Beccari
Piyush Gupta
Rajesh Gopinathan
Ramon Laguarta
Randy Mott
Reed Hastings
Richard Edelman
Robert A. Bradway
Robert M. Davis
Roksana Ciurysek
Roland Busch
Ron Moskovitz
Ryan Lance
Safra Catz
Salil Parekh
Samuel N. Hazen
Samuel Palmisano
Sandeep Bakhshi
Sanjay Mehrotra

Stephen Squeri
Steve Ballmer
Steve Jobs
Sundar Pichai
Tan Hock Eng
Ted Sarandos
Terrence A. Duffy
Theresa May
Thomas Boosz
Thomas Buberl
Thomas Christian Olsen
Thomas H. McInnerney
Thomas Piketty
Thomas Polen Becton
Tim Cook
Timotheus Hottges
Timothy Archer
Tobias Lutke
Tom Bartlett

Wang Jianlin
William Jefferson Clinton
William S. Demchak
Xi Jinping
Yousef A. Al-Wably
Yousef Al-Benyan
Yukio Hatoyama
Yurii Pyvovarov
Zach Nelson

#THOSE
#WHO ENGAGE

Aaron Bozeman
Aatif Umar Khalil
Abdallah Al Hadidi
Abdul Azeem Uqaili
Abdul Manan
Abdul Mateen Mahmood
Abdul Samie
Abdulla Al Ajmi
Abdulla Al Sumaiti
Abdullah Al Azemi
Abdullah Almajed
Abdullah Alsaleh
Abdullah Omar Al Midfa

Ahmad Al Eidan
Ahmad Al Jemaz
Dr. Ahmad Farag
Dr. Ahmed Dabbagh
Ahmed Diry
Ahmed Hafez
Aidan McCullen
Akini Cobbler
Aksel Bjørn Møller
Alaa Abdulaal
Alain Benichou
Alain Dehaz
Alain Donzeaud

Alexey Krasin
Alexey Smirnov
Alexis Ferraris
Alfonso Esteve
Dr. Alhussein Banuson
Ali Al-Ali
Ali Bakhsh
Ali Shehab
Ali Tauaha
Alice Chen
Alistair Davidson
Allan Tang
Allison Watson

Andrew Harvie
Andrew Matler
Andrew McGregor
Andrew McLean
Andrew Pfeiffer
Andrew Ross
Andrew Woodyatt
Andrew Yuhas
Andy McFarlane
Aneel Khan
Anette Falk Bøgebjerg
Angus Marshall
Anil Lutchman

Bastian Bach
Bavani Yunassogaram
Ben Stormer
Ben Watkins
Benny Boye Johansen
Berk Ozturk
Bernard Fernandes
Bertrand Blancheton
Bertus Zuijdgeest
Bettina Danielsen
Bharti Goyal Maan
Bidesh Dwarka
Bob Storms

It is not the best strategy that wins, but the best executed one that does.

Elon Musk

Abdulmajeed Alzahrani
Abdulrahman Al-Harbi
Abdulwahhab Alzaidan
Aboobakar Shahjahan
Acolla Lewis-Cameron
Ad Voogt
Adalberto Netto
Adam Monsterin
Adam R. Leggett
Addie Rooij
Adel Alfalasi
Adel Tawfiqi
Adelle Cachia
Adnan Munir Rajput
Adonis Zachariades
Adrian Wright
Aftab Ahmad
Agnete Rokkedal
Agnieszka Marszynska

Alan Trefler
Alastair Edwards
Albert Hirsch
Albert Mavashev
Aleksandra Markov
Alena Siuta
Alessandro Carone
Alex Taylor
Alexa Castlunger
Alexander Chechetkin
Alexander Chukhlantsev
Alexander Gaunares
Alexander Hemdorff
Alexander Kravets
Dr. Alexander v. Preen
Alexandru Petrescu
Alexei Anokhine
Alexei Chirokikh

Alya Alshamsi
Amadeus von Neuman
Amanda Nthati Chembezi
Amin Zoufonoun
Amine Tazi
Amirul Noor Azmi
Ana Maria Pesantes Salazar
Anat Weinstock
Anders Fransson
Anders Lydeen
Andre Attale
Andrea Bhagwandeen
Andréa Cozzi Machado
Andreas Andreopoulos
Andreas Kluehmichael
Andreas Perelman Glezer
Andrei Merkolov
Andres Penaloza
Andrew Dennis

Anita Joos
Anjanie Sammy
Anjanie Seenarine
Ann O'Connell
Anna Carlsson
Antje Amrhein
Anton Otto
Antonis Iliadis
Antony Dicks
Anvita Varshney
Aris Dimitriadis
Arnoud Roebers
Ashley Griffitts
Ashraff Ali
Atif Noor Khan
Aurelio Alarcón Celaya
Ayushya Mishra
Bappy Sharker
Basem Al Issa

Bogi Eliasen
Bonnie Urquhart
Braam Greeff
Brandy Pafford
Breen Coyne
Brent Coutain
Brent Stutz
Brian Copeland
Brian Ecker
Brian Harrison
Brian Riddell
Brian Roberts
Brian Solis
Brodey A. Dover
Bruce Porter
Bruce Sabatta
Bruno Bouchard
Caleb Zipperstein
Callie Smit

#THOSE
#WHO ENGAGE

Caressa Naicker
Carlo Beaudoin
Caroline Harvey
Carsten Dilling
Catherine Long
Cay Clemmensen
Cecilie Eilskov Norrung
Cezanne Maherali
Charlie McGee
Charlotte de Brabandt
Chiara Palieri
Chris Belk
Chris Booker

Corne du Plooy
Costantino Fattore
Curt Wellington
Cynthia Mothelesi
Dakpa Gyeltshen
Dale Maxima
Damion Fusco
Dan Boudria
Dan Buckley
Dan McBride
Dan Moorcroft
Dan Omahony
Dan Smith

David Wynd
Davlin Thomas
Debbie Harner
Debbie Rogina
Declan F. Magee
Deepak Seshadri
Denys Bousquet
Derek Luk Pat
Derek Walsh
Dhanraj Singh
Dick de Kok
Dickson Hunja Muhita
Didi Horn

Ellen Richards
Elma Marks
Elon Musk
Emad Sultan
Enerelt Enkhbold
Enric Pijuan
Ephraim Kentse
Erez Vigodman
Eric Duffaut
Eric Le Breton
Eric Nakamoto
Éric P. Bélanger
Erik Bushman

Felix Hartmann
Fihliwe M.Sikhulile
Fiona Martin Nieves
Francesca Gualtieri
Francia Díaz Del Valle
Francis John
Francisco Medina Castro
Frank Flosbach
Frank Rørtvedt
Freek Stoffel
Gábor Györfi
Gaetan Japy
Gaitree Deodat

PLAN your execution, EXECUTE your plan.
Angela Dorothea Merkel

Chris Dufala
Chris Govender
Chris Hopkins
Chris Nokkentved
Christel Hendricks
Christian Enghave
Christian Joly
Christian Vasino
Christopher Swierczynsk
Ciprian Cioaza
Claas Hansen
Claudio Thiago de Avila Menezes
Claus Stenholm Paulsen
Clay Costa
Clay Rowland
Clemens Utschig-Utschig Clodoaldo Tomazelli
Cody Nelson
Conor Harty

Daniel Brambilla
Daniel Jones
Daniel Oriesek
Daniella Dimitrov
Danny Christ
Darin Michael
Darin Morris
Darren Allen
Darren McHugh
Darrielle Wattie
Darryl Rondganger
Daryl Rooseboom
David Maraj
David Causi
David Hill
David James
David Johnson
David Reilly
David V. Salazar

Dirk Kotze
Divyang Yadav
Doljinsuren Jambal
Don Sturdivant
Donald Austin
Duarte Goncalves
Duncan Saunders
Dung Nguyen
Dwayne Pierre
Ebrahim Molla
Eddie Andre Lie
Edison Alvares
Edmond Goon
Eduard Harbuzyuk
Edward J. Maddock
Ekkehard Ernst
Eldridge Bravo
Elizabeth O'Callaghan
Elizabeth Stuart

Erik Verbon
Erik Weber
Erika Zuza
Erin Montanemi
Erin Perry
Erwin Van Eyndhoven
Eva Boušková
Eva Werther
Evangelos Pastras
Ewa Szymanska
Fabian Westmaas
Fadi Hamwi
Fahad Al Daihany
Faheem Mohammed
Faheem Rehman Usmani
Fakher-i-Alam Sahibzada
Farah Al Sayegh
Fareena Mazhar
Fatima Ledbar

Gary Dunlap
Gholamreza Ghanimi
Glen Fry
Greg Jones
Guilherme Machado
Gustavo Godinho
Hadeer Magdy
Harley Reiss Slaven
Hasan Abu El Rub
Hatem Azzam
Heather Taylor Strauss
Helge Nørrung
Helwig Larsen
Henk Kuil
Henning Isager Troelsen
Henrik Naundrup Vester
Herb Berger
Hind Alowais
Hisaka Kimura

#THOSE
#WHO ENGAGE

Howaida Nadim
Hugo Mello
Ian John
Ibrahim Al Musiateer
Igor Jiang
Intiaz Khairudin
Ionel Moise
Iqbal Baksh
Ivars Sauka
Jacco Kooij
Jack Benton
Jack Nolan
Jamie Dimon

Jochen B. Sutterer
Joe Compton
Joe Frodsham
Joel Jack
Johan Borkent
Johan Coetzee
Johan H. Benthin
Johanne D. LeBel
John Bertram
John Campagino
John Gaffney
John Golden
John Ravan

Karen Tobiassen
Karen Tom Yew
Karin Kousgaard
Karma Tenzin
Karsten Hede
Kassem Younes
Kathy Campbell
Kathy McCosh
Katia Bartels
Katie Evans
Katja Mühleman
Kausar Shabbir
Kees Haring

Kristina Lukacova
Krzysztof Skurzak
Kuldeep Kaushik
Lakhan Mohammed
Lal Dino
Lame Sharon Simon
Lance Boyer
Lani Scholtz
Lanny Tucker
Lars Berg
Lary Becessar
Laura Cuesta
Lawrence Dinga

Louise Pridham
Louwrence Erasmus
Luca Binazzi
Lucie Leipnik
Luke Fisher
Dr. M. Aman Ullah
M. Faisal Khokhar
Maarten Hofs
Maarten Ploemen
Madalein Young
Mahendra Singh
Mahmood Tufail
Mahmoud Adullah

Where your attention goes, your energy flows.
Dr. Joe Dispenza

Jane Feng
Jawaid Iqbal Karim
Jean Bérubé
Jeff Greer
Jeff Winter
Jem Pagán
Jennifer Martin
Jens Bjørn Andersen
Jens Theodor Nielsen
Jesper Lindhardt
Jhon Chacin
Jill Smart
Joachim Janert
Joan Ferrer Frigola
Joanne Griffin
Joanne Paul
Jobit George
Jocelyn Boyer
Jocelyne Rochefort

John W. Hart
John Yates
Johnny White
Joke van der Pol
Jonas Gudjonsson
Jonn Nolitt
Jonnro Erasmus
Jose Recinos
Joseph Seshabela
Joshua Derek
Joyce Westerdahl
Judith Hurwitz
Julie Harris
Julie Sweet
Jürgen Eberhardt
Kamil Reddy
Kanari Kurayim
Kandace Phillip
Karen Rohde

Kees van Tiggelen
Keld Viftrup Møller
Kemi Anthony
Kenneth A. Carraher
Kenneth D. Teske
Kenrick Attale
Kerry Whiteside
Kester Siewlal
Kevin Cornell
Khaled Al Qaoud
Kim Muller
Kim Scott
Kim Zelders
Kimberly Rahamut
Kirk Sookram
Kirsten Schmidt
Kishaun Jagdeo
Klaus Holse
Koray Yilmaz

LeAnne Spurrell
Legakwa Seema
Leo van Heijden
Leonardo Furtado
Lesang Dikgole
Leslie Bentley
Levi Dick
Lewis Cobb
Liam Curham
Likotsi Morienyane
Lillian Barnard
Lilly Sebake
Linda Dodd
Lise Chartrand
Lloyd Ashby
Lord Wei of Shoreditch
Lori Havlovitz
Lori L. Gildersleeve
Loriann Deschamps

Maite Rico
Maj Britt Andersen
Majid Almughaimedh
Malcolm Campbell
Malcom Nkalanga
Malik Muhammad Afaq
Manal Almadi
Mandar Mhaskar
Manfred Ender
Manie Mountany
Manon Boucier
Manuela Richter
Marc Weber Bång
Marcel Boulianne
Marcello Marcellini
Marcia Maja
Marco Tasoni
Mareen Mcdonald
Margarida Bento

#THOSE #WHO ENGAGE

Margit Kolb
Maria Christina Perez de la Sala
Maria Eugênia Trannin
Maria Hourani
Maria Johnson
Maria Koch
Marian Lamos
Mariano Browne
Marie Kissane
Marilia Oliveira Martins
Marinella Andaloro
Marius Hărătău
Marius Haratau

Max Tari
Maxim Arzumanyan
Maxim Stoudennikov
Mayank Pandya
Medhat Elmasry
Megan Schwab
Mehboob Ul Haq
Mehdi Hashemi
Mejbel Al Shammer
Mel Torrie
Meletia Hossanah
Melina Costa
Mfundisi Calvin Ncube

Mohamad A. Hossein
Mohamed Al Musharrak
Mohamed Rahayem
Mohammad Ali Khan
Dr. Mohammed Alenezi
Mohammed Khair Fallaha
Molapo Jonathan
Mona Itani
Monica Rancati
Monika Walker
Mooketsi Benndict Telete
Moritz von Stosch
Mshari Al-Onaizy

Neshon Frederick
Nesreen Abdelghafar
Nic Rose
Nicholas Chazapis
Nicholas Pearson
Nicholas Rodopoulos
Nick Ayton
Nick Szabo
Nicklaus A. Rhodes
Nicolas Celier
Nicolas Neysen
Norbert Hies
Nour Al Mutawa

Failure is not the opposite of success; it is part of success.
Arianna Huffington

Marius Snel
Mark Bednarski
Mark Boyd
Mark Diamond
Mark McClennon
Mark Roopnarine
Mark Singh
Mark Soden
Mark Stanford
Markus Bussen
Marlon Mason
Martin Oberholster
Martyn Anstey
Mary Meehan'
Mary Roberts
Maryse Jackman
Matt Shelley
Matthew Gardiner
Maurice de Feijter

Michael Blom
Michael D. Tisdel
Michael McDonald
Michael Melvill
Michael Nyman
Michael O'Kane
Michale Hilton
Michelle Darceuil
Michelle Trotman
Miguel Muñoz de Rivera González
Miguel Oliver Delma
Miguel Silveira
Mika K. S. Tienhaara
Mikael Munck
Mikael Stelander
Mike Tisdel
Mirza Ali-Mohammed
Mitha Vivek
Moayad Alshaar

Muhammad Asif Khan
Muhammad Azeem Iqbal
Muhammad Bilal Khokhar
Muhammad Khashih-ur-Rehman
Muhammad Mazhair
Dr. Muhammad Riaz
Muhammad Zakaria
Mukarram Jah Ansari
My Hanh Dinh
Nadira Lyder
Nagesh Tummapudi
Namale Shilla
Narisha Khan
Nasser Alhunmaid
Natalie Mansoor
Naval Ravikant
Dr. Naveen Aggarwal
Naveen Ragoonan
Nei Pontes

Nour Algabal
Ntsholetsang Ikgopoleng
Nurjemal Jalilova
Nyron Mohammed
Obakeng Kokwe
Octave Descours
Octavio Fernandez
Octavio Pitaluga Neto
Olav Hermes
Oliver Bäte
Oliver Wenzel
Olympios Vratimos
Otis Murray
Otto Heer
Pablo Flores
Paddy Trikilis
Palloma Diniz
Pankaj Ballal
Patrícia Antunes de Paula

#THOSE
#WHO ENGAGE

Patricia Autayo
Patricia Hajali
Patrick Sweeney
Patrik Hallen
Paul Hunt
Paul Kurth
Paul Maxwell
Paul Okpurughre
Paula Salgado
Paulo Garcia
Penelope Bradshaw-Niles
Per-Allan Karlsson
Pernille Kofoed

Pini Kamari
Piyush Goel
PJ Moloney
Pramod Prabhu
Prashant Odhrani
Precious Piper-Derrick
Rafat Hamud
Rainer Bauer
Ralph Jean-Poix
Dr. Rami Shaheen
Ramon Freire Garcia
Randy Adkins
Ranjeeve Moonan

Rob Tollenaar
Robert Argyle
Robert E. Klein
Robert E. Renaud
Robert Hamilton
Robert Thacker
Roberta Robertson
Robin Grünbirchler
Rod Peacock
Rodney Mabuza
Rodney Payne
Roger Young
Rohit Coonjah

Samuel Felicio
Sanaa Habib
Sander van Pelt
Sandip S. Shimpi
Sara Bassi
Sara Bennison
Sarah Allen
Sarah Black-Smith
Sarah M. Lee
Scott Seymour
Sean Somair
Sean Strong

Simone Griffith
Simone Oostwijk
Sonam Lhamo
Sonia Ganpat
Stacy Thomas-Lewis
Stan Barter
Stanimir Ninovski
Stanton Gomes
Stefan Hessenbruch
Steffen Strzygowski
Stephen Barclay
Steve Stidhem
Steve Willoughby

Nature does not hurry, yet everything is accomplished.
Lao Tzu

Perry Gillis
Pete Grazaitis
Peter Gramskov
Peter Horwing
Peter McCord
Peter Robb
Peter Saeman
Peter Woodhull
Petros Michelakakis
Philip Morris
Philip Steenekamp
Philippe Thibault
Phillipp Gysler
Pierre Jacobs
Pierre Stander
Pieter Erasmus
Pieter Vanderbeeken
Pieter Walraven
Pilar Madrigal

Raul A. Castillo Jr.
Ravi Lalla
Raymond Mohlala
Reinhard Mallow
Renata Chaielen Tres
Rentia Barnard
Resh Patel
Riah Dass-Mungal
Rich Hilliard
Richard Cash
Richard Champion
Richard Kriek
Richard Lightbound
Richard McCarthy
Richard O'Connor
Ricky Klint Gangsted-Rasmussen
Rifat Parvez
Ritendra Banerjee
Rob Geary

Ron Batdorf
Ron Monhiet
Ron Moskovitz
Rosangela Santos
Ruaan Ras
Rudolf Fehlmann
Rukshini Etheldred
Rukshini Etheldred
Russel Dhill
Ryan Hutchinson
Saba Ejaz
Sabrina Borde-Ferreira
Sachin Saini
Sadiq Hssain
Saji Oommen
Sajjad Hussain
Saken Algiev
Sam Wadekar
Sami Astan

Sebastian Ponceliz
Shai Agassi
Shaima Al Ghunaim
Shane Hicks
Shane Hogan
Shane Pearce
Shannon Laughlin
Shaun Ferreira
Shavonte Evans
Shawn Smith
Sheik Shabiulla Makbool
Sheila Cane
Sherma Jack
Shin Ohinata
Shyroz Ratanshi
Sicelo Njeje
Sidar Ok
Simon Reid

Steven Barr
Steven Bednikoff
Steven Melcher
Stuart Schreiber
Subash Balakrishnan
Surel Aucamp
Dr. Suresh Kumar
Suriya Jamal
Sven Vollbehr
Swagath Bhat
Tackoor-Add Ludmila
Taj Muhammad Khan
Tala Al Ansari
Talmadge Eyre
Tamara Edward
Tamara Nedela
Tammy D. Draper
Tanja Marthur
Tapan Mishra

#THOSE
#WHO ENGAGE

Tashi Dorji
Tasos Gkamaris
Tawanda Matewu
Thabo Sereko
Tharina de Wet
Thomas Bartlett
Thomas Buberl
Thomas Christian Olsen
Thomas Fisker Engbjerg
Thomas Nel
Thomas Preston
Throwa Tenzin
Thuso Manale

Torben Claus Dahl
Torben Dyrholm
Tracey Banks
Trent Ryan
Trisha Robinson
Ulrich Schumann
Umesh Sookoo
Unathi Petros
Urs Keim
Venessa Snel
Verena Cantin
Victor Abele
Vijay Krishna

Zack Love
Zayd Maniar
Zita Verbenyi
Zuhfran Qasim
Zulfiqar Ali

If I can see it and believe it, then I can achieve it.
Arnold Schwarzenegger

Tiago De Benedicto
Tiffany Dial
Tim Diack
Tim Hoebeek
Tim Vermaak
Tina Bello-Williams
Tina Kristensen
Titose Chembezi
Titus Monageng
Tobias Hess
Todd Ireland
Tom Christensen
Tom Clancy
Tom Ding
Tom Kindermans
Tom Matheussen
Tomasz Dziechciarz
Tommy Andorff
Tony Oliver

Vincent Snels
Vinnie de Oliveira
Vishodie Bhagwandin
Wagner Moll
Walaa Maher
Waleed Al Bbaderi
Walter Loertscher
Walter Longwe
Wayne Herbert
Weeke Erik
Wendy Swash
Weng Tatt Chan
Werner Wortmann
Willy Salt
Wim Laurie
Xiaowen Wang
Yasin Janjua
Yury Orlov
Zabeeda Nazir

If you fart in space,
you move forward.

#COMPANIES
#THAT ENGAGE

Firms that worked with the authors (i.e., 34% of the Fortune 500 and 11 of the G20)

Put employees first; they will take care of your clients and the bottom line will follow.

Louis V. Gerstner

#COMPANIES
#THAT ENGAGE

Firms that worked with the authors (i.e., 34% of the Fortune 500 and 11 of the G20)

The greatest achievement is to outperform yourself.

Denis Waitley

#GOVERNMENTS
#THAT ENGAGE

Governments (11 of the G20), Non-Profit-Organizations, and Foundations that worked with the authors that impacted the national economies, influenced GDP growth, and triggered digitalization and innovation index improvement.

The greatest countries are those that produce great people.

Benjamin Disraeli

#ORGANIZATIONS
#THAT SET THE STANDARD

In collaboration, the authors have set various standards on software development, quality, ERP implementation, Service, Governance, and compliances that have evolved the mainstream thinking and practices on the toughest and most important issues in business today.

A man is just a woman´s strategy for making other women.
My wife

To unlock the power 2 think differently!

Ask yourself the following

What do you want?

What is true?

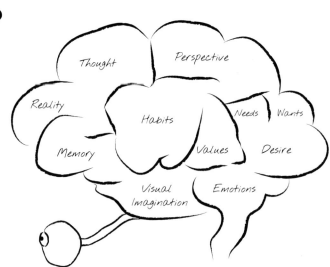

What will you do about it?

The illiterate of the 21st century will not be those who cannot read and write, but those who cannot *learn, unlearn,* and *relearn.*

Make a list of what you believe you need to *unlearn.*

Complement that with a list of what you intend to *relearn.*

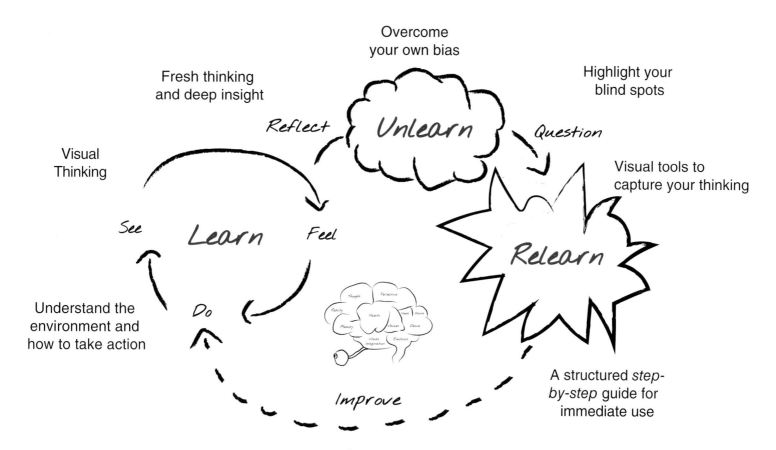

Overcome
your own bias

Fresh thinking
and deep insight

Highlight your
blind spots

Reflect *Unlearn* Question

Visual
Thinking

Visual tools to
capture your thinking

See *Learn* Feel

Relearn

Understand the
environment and
how to take action

Do

A structured *step-by-step* guide for
immediate use

Improve

Realize how to
create value

How to sequence thinking differently!

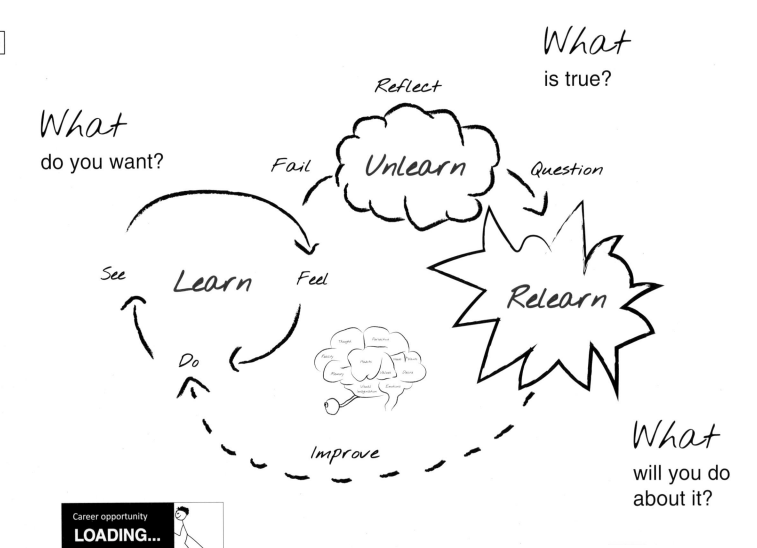

What
is true?

What
do you want?

Reflect

Fail

Unlearn

Question

See

Learn

Feel

Relearn

Do

Improve

What
will you do
about it?

When we don't
Learn, Unlearn, and *Relearn*

The average lifetime of Standard & Poor's Fortune 500 companies has declined from 93 to 15 years

- 89% of the original Fortune 500 companies from 1955 are gone!

- 40% from the Fortune 500 you know today will not be on the list in 10 years.

- 35% of the Fortune 500 companies represented 64% of the US GDP in 2012.

- By 2025, 46% of all Fortune 500 corporations will come from China.

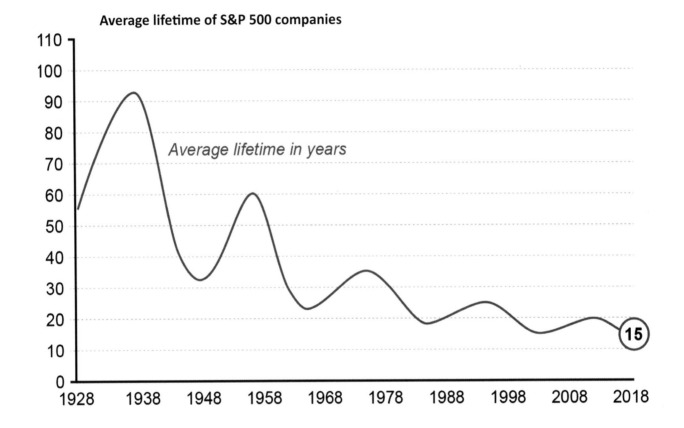

Average lifetime of S&P 500 companies

Average lifetime in years

Change is constant

If you have not noticed it by now, we live in one of the most disruptive, fast-changing environments ever in human development history.

The only constant today is change.

In disruptive times, the power comes from people. Often underestimated, it is the people who make the difference. People make up the companies, government, teachers, entrepreneurs, and investors. People have a unique ability to adapt to their environment.

Our intelligence is rooted in the ability to adapt to change by learning, unlearning, and relearning. In the words of Charles Darwin: "It is not the strongest of the species that survives, nor the most intelligent. It is the one that is most adaptable to change."

So, certainty is the enemy of change.

The only constant in life is change. In the next chapter we will look at the rate of change and trends that disrupt our lives as a result of the 4th Industrial Revolution.

I'd flex but I don't
want to hurt your eyes.

We are all in love with the future and nobody knows what it will bring.

The reality is that the future influences the present just as much as the past. Therefore, our future starts today, not tomorrow.

Henrik von Scheel
Ordinary Futurist that ignited 2 global themes

The *Art* of
Strategy + Execution

Move beyond the hype to deliver impact, and make it stick

Chapter Two

Myth-busters
on Strategy

What is the challenge with putting any strategy into execution?

Let's look at the biggest symptoms and explore the root causes to identify a solution.

Losing
the WAR?

9 out of 10

strategies are declared a success

Perception

7 out of 10

projects are declared a success

70%

of strategy initiatives are never successfully implemented

Reality

72%

of projects fail to deliver on time, budget, and value

Why strategies fail

The most common reason why 70% of strategies fail boils down to the inability to take design decisions to gain an advantage in the present and future. The 70% failure reason is rated based on the critical biases of the strategic initiates throughout the organizational development stages.

The result is devastating, to say the least, with 72% of projects that run 45% over budget, 7% behind schedule, and 56% less functional when delivered than predicted. *Holy macaroni!*

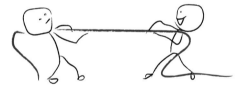

F.A.I.L: First Attempt In Learning

1. Not having a strategy at all.

2. No real choice. Many strategies are not actually strategies - just presentations, reports, and a set of actions with no real choices. Poor design stems from confirmation bias (9%).

3. Turning faulty and not applicable worst practices into best practices, called *anchoring bias* (6%).

4. Inability to move from strategy formulation to execution, known as the *top-down process*. Lack of follow-through that comes from emotional bias (14%).

5. Letting selection happen organically, called the *bottom-up implementation. Often based on* confirmation bias (9%).

6. Leadership's inability to see and adapt to changes, called the *blind spot* Rooted in overconfidence bias (4%).

7. Overestimating strengths, also called chronic meta-cognition (11%).

8. Mistaking transformation for innovation. Opportunity misinterpretation or the availability bias (10%).

9. Not able to define differentiation that leads to competency misalignment. Often derives from the overconfidence bias (7%).

Strategy failure reasons rated based on the critical biases

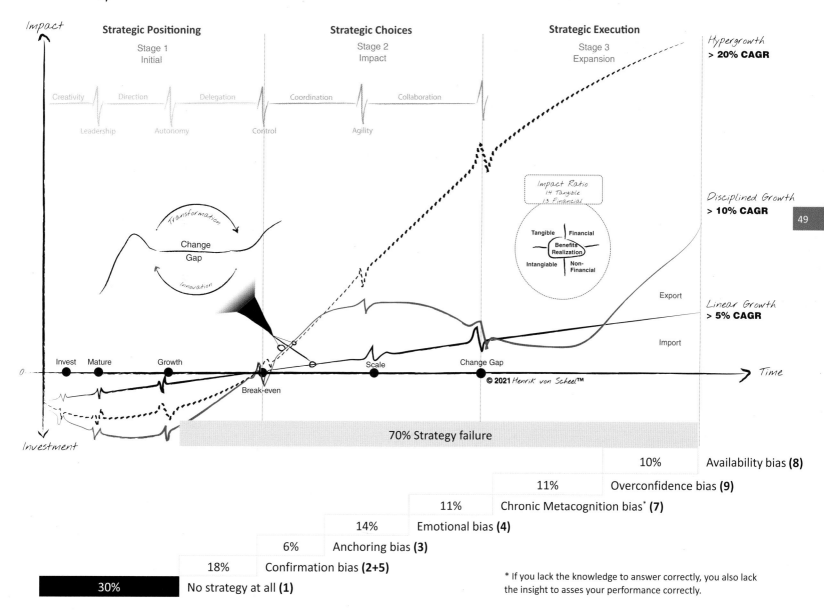

Strategic Positioning — Stage 1 Initial

Strategic Choices — Stage 2 Impact

Strategic Execution — Stage 3 Expansion

Impact

Time

Investment

0

Creativity — Direction — Delegation — Coordination — Collaboration

Leadership — Autonomy — Control — Agility

Transformation — Change Gap — Innovation

Invest — Mature — Growth — Break-even — Scale — Change Gap

Hypergrowth > 20% CAGR

Disciplined Growth > 10% CAGR

Export

Linear Growth > 5% CAGR

Import

Impact Ratio
14 Tangible
13 Financial

Tangible | Financial
Benefits Realization
Intangible | Non-Financial

© 2021 Henrik von Scheel™

70% Strategy failure

10%	Availability bias **(8)**
11%	Overconfidence bias **(9)**
11%	Chronic Metacognition bias* **(7)**
14%	Emotional bias **(4)**
6%	Anchoring bias **(3)**
18%	Confirmation bias **(2+5)**
30%	No strategy at all **(1)**

* If you lack the knowledge to answer correctly, you also lack the insight to asses your performance correctly.

Outsmart your own biases

It happens to the best of us. We don't realize that some of our decisions are affected by cognitive and organizational biases.

Our thought process often conceals the reality behind biases. Biases have a variety of forms and appear as cognitive ("cold") biases, such as mental noise, or motivational ("hot") biases, such as when beliefs are distorted by wishful thinking. Both effects can be present at the same time.

There are three techniques to outsmart behavioral strategy biases:

1. Decide which decisions justify the effort

2. Identify the biases likely to affect critical decisions

3. Embed practices to counter the most relevant biases

Left unchecked, subconscious biases will undermine strategic decision-making. Here's how to counter them and improve corporate performance.

Consider the following:

1 *Don't steer your strategy by wrong stars*. Leaders' plans may falter if they're relying on superficial analogies to find answers to their biggest problems.

2 *Spot strategy alternatives in the momentum case*. A momentum case can reveal what could happen if a company takes no, or only limited, strategic action.

3 *Lifting your head from the sand*. Business conversations work better when business leaders actively acknowledge potentially unpleasant information rather than run from it.

I AM AN ECONOMIST, to save time,
let´s just assume that I am never wrong.

4 *Avoid snap decisions*. When making important business decisions, it's critical to put first impressions aside and explore the facts.

7 *Be smart at the start*. Does the requirement meet the value impact expected in a project? Conducting a pre-mortem can help teams anticipate project failure—and head it off.

5 *Breaking the silence*. How can the Executive break employees' silence and get the critical input needed to make the right strategic moves?

8 *Strategy decisions are interdependent decisions*. Don't forget to anticipate competitors' moves when making your own.

6 *Less is more*. Do you know when to kill a project? You're keen on encouraging innovation and letting a thousand flowers bloom, but how do you sort the weeds from the seeds?

9 *Up-front contingency planning*. When making staged-investment decisions, you are focused on expected future returns from their investments more than the costs associated with previous investments. Avoid throwing good money after bad by developing "contingent road maps"—plans for updating your investment strategy based on unbiased feedback from the market.

The building blocks of
Strategy

Strategy is like rock and roll, and we like it.

"Strategy requires a strong mental mindset to visualize change, imagine the impossible, and is propelled by a termination to dare.

Henrik von Scheel
Compulsive Mind Masturbator on
Thinking Functionally and Acting Strategically

The nature of strategy

Strategy is the big picture of how the organization is to win in its environment.

In a nutshell, strategy is about strategic positioning, strategic choices, and strategy execution of the following three choices: What not to do, where to be different, and what to focus on. In that order.

This chapter will provide a guided approach on how to apply strategy to

> *Being the best at the game to win.*
>
> *Perfect to anticipate.*
>
> *Strong in defense to push and pull.*
>
> *Fast adaption to outplay, outperform, and outcompete the game.*
>
> *When the game gets tough –*
> *disrupt to rewrite the rules or*
> *change the game.*

Strategy is in many ways a mind game.
The best at it have the aptitude to communicate or build a culture round it.

As I often say: *"You can't win on the outside if you are losing on the inside."*

Strategy requires a strong mental mindset to visualize change, imagine the impossible, and is propelled by a termination to dare.

Today, in a disruptive environment, it is more important than ever before to take design decisions based on options of what not to do, what to do less, where to differentiate to gain an advantage, what do more off, where to innovate, and when to transform.

In my experience, the most successful strategies are based on models of understanding to align executive teams to take design decisions on managing the present business, while creating the future business.

This is the only way the authors have been able to make strategy execution work with an outcome driven approach.

Personally, I have been creating the strategies that shaped the performance of over 23% of the Fortune 500 companies, was applied to 21 national economies, triggered Global Digital and Industry 4.0 themes, and influenced the GDP of 5% in Europe with the Digital Agenda.

In essence, strategy is about getting clarity in strategic positioning, giving focus on strategic choices, and obtaining accountability in strategy execution.

Henrik von Scheel
Unworthy Apprentice of Sun Tzu

Seeing strategy as an end-to-end lifecycle

Today, strategy should be seen as a lifecycle that needs to be managed. From an organizational point of view, a strategy works with different objectives across business, services, competencies, and IT layers' domains.

This refers to an ingrained nervous system present in an organization that operates on the interrelationships between strategic objectives, known as meta-objectives. This system is dependent on semantics or ontology.

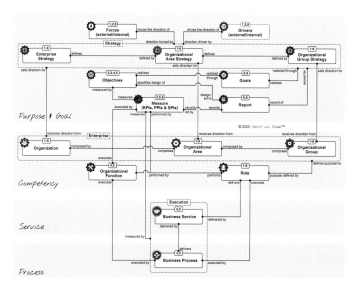

This creates a guiding principle how to link, for example, strategic objective with critical success factor. Acting like a skeleton for the nervous system to connect strategy with operational exception to increase the level of re-usability and replication.

A strategy consists of the following

1. **Strategic Positioning**
   - Understand, Analyze, & Develop
   - Market & Brand
   - Purpose with Mission & Vision
   - Forecast & Plan
   - Control & Monitor
   - Culture
   - Capabilities
   - Policies, Rules, & Guidelines

2. **Strategic Choices**
   - No 1. What not to do
   - No 2. Where to differentiate
   - No 3. What to focus on

3. **Strategy Execution**
   - Report & Measure
   - Portfolio, Project, & Programs
   - Maturity & Change Management
   - Best Practices
   - Services, i.e., Work Flows & Processes
   - Execution, Delivery, & Processing

4. **Strategy Governance**
   - Oversight & Audits
   - Maturity & Change Management

5. **Continuous Improvements**
   - Oversight & Audits
   - Maturity & Change Management

"Know thyself, know thy enemy.
  A thousand battles, a thousand victories."
    Sun Tzu

"The art of strategy" is a modern visual interpretation of the *Art of War* from Sun Tzu by Henrik von Scheel. Know thyself and know thy enemy rest on the sequence of the Strategic Positioning, Strategic Choices, and Strategy Execution to deliver victory.

As a golden rule with *"The art of strategy,"* 40% of time spent on strategy should be used in strategic positioning to understand the drivers and forces of the inside-out and outside-in view that identifies the visual options and scenario thinking. Twenty percent should be used on the Strategic Choice of what not to do, how and where to differentiate, and what to focus on. Focus is often on scenario thinking and prototyping. The remaining 40% should be dedicated to a diligence strategy execution of the plan.

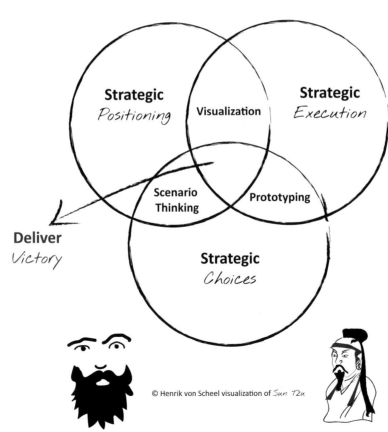

© Henrik von Scheel visualization of *Sun Tzu*

Building blocks of Strategy

If you haven't had a great deal of experience with formulating a strategy for your business or unit, you're in good company. It's not an everyday activity. Some firms coast along for years with the same strategy and address that strategy only when it is obviously obsolete.

Even then, many turn to strategy consultants to do the job. Strategic thinking is not a core managerial competence at most companies. Executives hone their management capabilities by tackling problems over and over again, and changing strategy; however, strategy is not usually a task that managers face repeatedly. Once companies have found a strategy that works, they want to use it, not change it. Consequently, most management teams do not develop a competence in strategic thinking.

So if you are not highly practiced at formulating strategy or you want to give a helping hand to someone on your team who is tackling strategy for the first time - here are steps to follow.

A strategy consists of strategic positioning, strategic choices, and strategy execution that should be seen as a lifecycle and needs to be managed. A strategy involves looking both outside and inside the organization since the market to be served is outside the organization and the capabilities for making the strategy work are within it.

As the business environment becomes more complex, strategic management is gaining in importance. Few words are as commonly used in management as *strategy*.

In simple terms, strategy means looking at the long-term future to determine what the company wants to become, and putting in place a plan of getting there.

Strategy is both art and science. Strategy is an art because it requires creativity, intuitive thinking, and an ability to visualize the future and inspire and engage those who will implement the strategy. Strategy is science because it requires analytical skills, the ability to collect and analyze information, and make well-informed decisions.

Without a strategy, an organization is directionless and vulnerable to the changes of the business environment. Strategy acts as some kind of a guidepost for a company's ongoing evolution. Strategy provides a direction for the company and indicates what must be done to survive, grow, and profit. Strategy addresses the questions who the customer is, what product or services are offered, what the value is, and if the company can do it efficiently. With the average lifecycle of the Fortune 500 company decreasing, one has to look at strategy and tweak it in periodic intervals.

Hi, have you been working out?

 People are not disturbed by things,
but by the views they take of them.

Epictetus

Strategic *Positioning*

If you change the way you look at things, the things you look at change

Chapter Three

How to think strategically

Take an outside-in view

Look outside for strategic positioning to identify threats and opportunities. At the highest level, strategy is concerned with the external market and how the organization's resources should be allocated to create an exploitable advantage.

There are always emerging trends in the form of drivers, disruptive forces, and threats: new entrants, competitive forces, regulation, globalization, economic, workforce, market, consumer and demographic changes, suppliers who might cut you off, substitute products that could undermine your business, and macroeconomic trends that may reduce your customers' ability to pay.

The business may be threatened by a competitor that can produce the same quality goods at a much lower price or a much better product at the same price.

A strategy must be able to cope with these threats. The outer environment also harbors opportunities: new technologies, emerging competitors, an unserved customer base, and so forth.

Thus, the first job of strategists is to scan the outer environment for threats and opportunities. Here's a proven approach: Form a team of executives, a department manager, and individuals with special insights.

The team's job is to identify the core threats and opportunities. Avoid having anyone on the team who appears complacent or wedded to the status quo.

Gather the views of customers, suppliers, and industry experts. These outside views can be powerful. Some firms, particularly those in technological fields, enlist teams of scientists and engineers to look outward to markets, competitors, and technical developments. It's their job to find anything that could threaten a firm's current business or point toward new directions in the industry or market.[2]

Understanding the voice of the customer is not just the job of the sales and marketing team, but of each and every person in the organization.

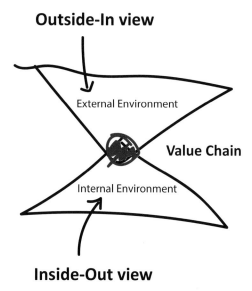

Outside-In view

External Environment

Value Chain

Internal Environment

Inside-Out view

62

The most essential model of understanding for a strategic positioning is the outside-in and inside-out view of your value chain.

Henrik von Scheel
Toilet Paper Messiah

Inside-Out view

Look inside at resources, capabilities, and practices. Resources and internal capabilities can constrain your choice of strategy.

A strategy to exploit an unserved market in the electronics industry might not be feasible if your firm lacks the necessary financial capital and human know-how.

Likewise, a strategy that would require substantial entrepreneurial behavior on the part of employees, for example, would seem doomed from the beginning if your people practices reward years of service over individual performance.

These internal capabilities – especially the human ones – matter greatly and are too often overlooked by strategists. A strategy can succeed only if it has the backing of the right set of people and other resources; these must be properly aligned with the strategy.

Consider strategies for addressing threats and opportunities. The strategy teams first prioritize the drivers of opportunities and forces of disruption, and then discuss each in broad strokes.

As you follow this advice when developing strategies that focus on each core threat and opportunity, be sure to do the following:

- Create many alternatives. There is seldom one way to do things. In some cases, the best parts of two different strategies can be combined to make a stronger third strategy.

- Check all facts, and question all assumptions.

- Look for missing information; there is bound to be some.

- Determine what data you need to better assess a particular strategy. Then get it.

- Vet the leading strategy choices among the wisest heads you know. Doing so will help you avoid "biases group think" within the strategy team.

- Once you have come to the final strategy road map, try explaining it to the junior-most person in the organization.

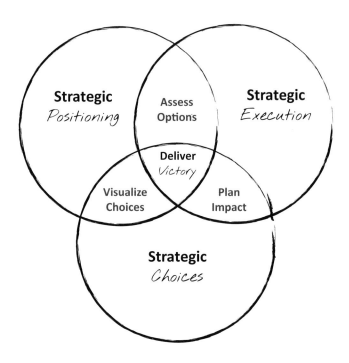

The importance of a Business Model

Simply put, a business model is a representation of a business to take informed choices.

A business model is the most powerful way to describe how an organization creates, delivers, and captures value.

A business model is the most important executive decision and design tool to manage the present and shape the future of an organization.

It is the only way today: strategic positioning, strategic choices, and strategy execution.

The building blocks of an organization are competencies, i.e., resources, skills, and capabilities.

Competencies describe where, how, and who creates and delivers value. In a business model, this is represented through the functional areas, groups, tasks, services, business processes, flows, lifecycles, roles, systems, projects, maturity level, measurements, etc.[3]

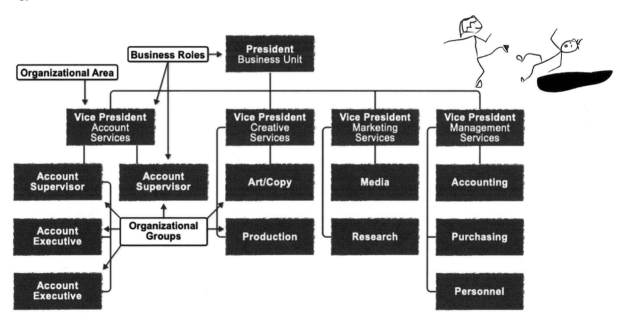

The nervous system that delivers business value

Value Chain 4.0 – Strategic Positioning (Level 1)

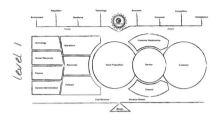

The value chain 4.0 is all about strategic positioning. It represents the highest-level view of an organization's functional areas and the cost, revenue, and service flow of activities that generate value for the customer. It is a transparent look at how forces and drivers affect and influence the organization.

Business Model 4.0 – Strategic Choices (Level 2)

The business model 4.0 describes how an organization creates, delivers, and captures value.

The focus is on Strategic Positioning and how to model the organization.
It represents an accountability view with functional areas and groups classified into strategic, tactical, and operational tiers.

Operating Model 4.0 – Strategy Execution (Level 3)

The operating model 4.0 focuses on how the organization executes. It describes the detailed relationship and correlations of how an organization operates to deliver.

It represents a comprehensive view of functional areas, groups, tasks, activities, people, processes, projects, systems, information, data, flows, and other types that are all classified into strategic, tactical, and operational tiers.

Decisions made at this level

- Trendspotting of emerging forces and drivers.

- Business and Service Design.

- Competitive Intelligence.

- High-level financial anatomy of revenue- and cost-flow.

- Strategic Positioning on what not to do, where to differentiate, and what to focus on.

- Resource distribution, culture, and environment.

- Strategic choices on what not to do, where to differentiate, and what to focus on.

- Capability & Accountability modeling.

- Decision notation for Value, Cost, Revenue, Service, Operating, and Performance.

- Measurements.

- Align Portfolio, Program, and Project.

- Opportunities for Transformation & Innovation, i.e., bottlenecks, integration, standardization, automation, optimization, alignment, and maturity.

- Service, workflow, information, process, and data flow.

- Strategy Execution: monitor, measure, report, evaluate, execute, govern operational practices, program, project and portfolio, change management and processes.

- Apply notation for better decision-making, i.e., information flow, critical systems, policy, and requirements.

- Analyze and develop the operating maturity levels, and create a development path.

- Data flow and critical systems.

- Steps and activities.

Originality is merely an illusion.

M.C. Escher

Think Functionally, Act Strategically

Rethink how to work with competencies to take design decisions

The nervous system that manages the present and future

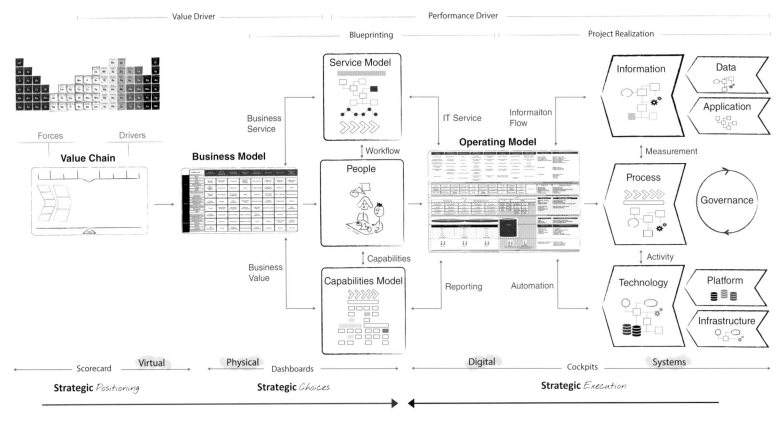

Think Functionally and Act Strategically with capabilities to compete, deliver innovative services and product, and new business models.

Think Functionally and Act Strategically with competencies to transform performance, operation, and costs models.

A business model is the blood that enables the central nervous system of business to function.

The evolution of the Value Chain

The value chain was developed by Michael Porter and used throughout the world for nearly 30 years.[4] The value chain is a powerful tool, a static model of understanding that disaggregates a company into its strategically relevant activities in order to focus on the sources of competitive advantage, i.e., the specific activities that result in higher prices or lower costs.

A company's value chain is typically part of a larger value system that includes companies either upstream (suppliers) or downstream (distribution channels), or both.

The idea of a value chain is based on the process view of organizations, the idea of seeing a manufacturing (or service) organization as a system, made up of subsystems each with inputs, transformation processes, and outputs. Inputs, transformation processes, and outputs involve the acquisition and consumption of resources, money, labor, materials, buildings, land, administration, and management.

How value chain activities are carried out determines costs and affects profits. Most organizations engage in hundreds, even thousands, of activities in the process of converting inputs to outputs. These activities can be classified generally as either primary or support activities that all businesses must undertake in some form.

The primary activities are:

- **Inbound Logistics** - involves relationships with suppliers.

- **Operations** - all the activities required to transform inputs into outputs.

- **Outbound Logistics** - all the activities required to collect, store, and distribute the output.

- **Marketing and Sales** - activities inform buyers about products and services, induce buyers to purchase them, and facilitate their purchase.

- **Service** - all the activities required to keep the product or service working effectively for the buyer after it is sold and delivered.

The secondary activities are:

- **Procurement** - the acquisition of inputs, or resources, for the firm.

- **Human Resources** - consists of all activities involved in Human Resource Management.

- **Technological Development** - pertains to the equipment, hardware, software, procedures, and technical knowledge brought to bear in the firm's transformation of inputs into outputs.

- **Infrastructure** - serves the company's needs and ties together its various parts; it consists of functions or departments.

A value chain is defined by the first action that creates value for a customer and the following actions that support the execution of the first action.

Henrik von Scheel
Toilet Paper Messiah

The Value Chain 4.0

This perspective about how value is created forces managers to consider and see each activity, not just as a cost, but as a step that has to add some increment of value to the finished product or service.

In the words of one of the greatest strategists, Sun Tzu: "Simulated disorder postulates perfect discipline; simulated fear postulates courage; simulated weakness postulates strength."

The Value Chain 4.0 takes the traditional view of a value chain to the next level with an integrated visual, simulation, and modeling tool for making design decisions, relating both the external and internal forces and drivers that enable alignment of the current operating performance and value indicator. Furthermore, it becomes a whiteboard to outline scenario thinking of various options to create the future of the company.

The Value Chain 4.0 is the most powerful decision toolbox for scenario thinking and alignment of the executive team to make informed choices.

It puts a 30-year-old static value chain concept on steroids and quantum leaps it into today. It differs in the unique setup with core and non-core competencies, links mapping of trends, forces and drivers to each section, and decision cockpit of the six business model areas disciplines.

The Value Chain 4.0 represents the highest-level view of an organization's functional areas and the flow (cost, revenue, services) of activities that generate value for the customer.

The Value Chain 4.0 – the strategy positioning decision board

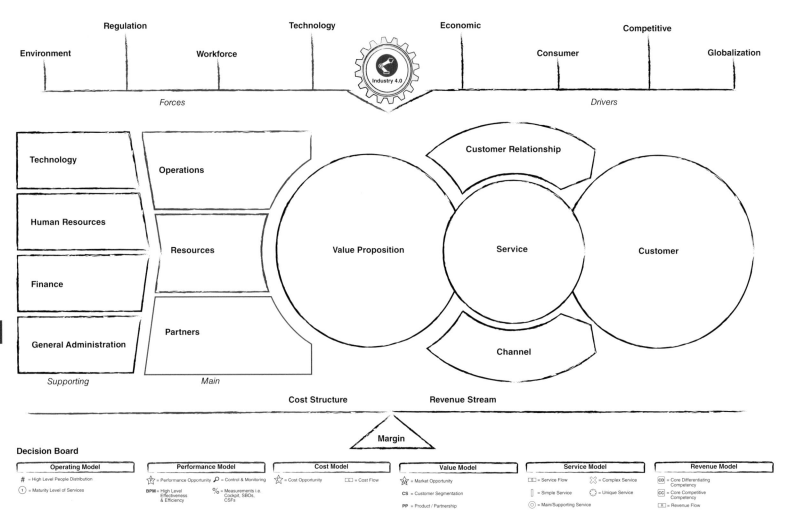

Environment · **Regulation** · **Workforce** · **Technology** · Industry 4.0 · **Economic** · **Consumer** · **Competitive** · **Globalization**

Forces · *Drivers*

Technology
Human Resources
Finance
General Administration

Supporting

Operations
Resources
Partners

Main

Value Proposition
Customer Relationship
Service
Channel
Customer

Cost Structure · Revenue Stream

Margin

74

Decision Board

Operating Model	Performance Model	Cost Model	Value Model	Service Model	Revenue Model
# = High Level People Distribution	☆ = Performance Opportunity ρ = Control & Monitoring	☆ = Cost Opportunity ⬓ = Cost Flow	☆ = Market Opportunity	⬓ = Service Flow ✕ = Complex Service	CD = Core Differentiating Competency
① = Maturity Level of Services	BPM = High Level Effectiveness & Efficiency % = Measurements i.e. Cockpit, SBOs, CSFs		CS = Customer Segmentation	▯ = Simple Service ⬠ = Unique Service	CC = Core Competitive Competency
			PP = Product / Partnership	◎ = Main/Supporting Service	⬓ = Revenue Flow

Forces & Drivers

That impact the current
and future business

Step 4

Value Chain

How you operate
to deliver value

Steps 1 and 2

Financial Anatomy

Revenue income
and expenses

Step 3

Decision Board

Making informed decisions
and taking action

Step 5

The Value Chain identifies all the essential activities in the company that generate value. It can also be used to have a high-level overview of the business model to create a common understanding and create a view that enables innovative thinking.

Value chains are also used to identify the activities that create value and are core differentiating, core competitive competencies and no-core competencies. This will assist in making better-informed decisions and strategies with each competency. The value chain consists of end-to-end support and key activities that together are what deliver the value for the customer.

Key Activities deliver the value received by the customer, and thereby also create the competitive advantage and differentiation. Key activities are the physical production of the product/service and the following activities such as channel, sales, and marketing.

Supporting Activities sustain and support the key activities in their execution. These activities are necessary for the general management and administration of the organization.

Customer 4.0 is the one who receives and consumes the value. The value chain is always adapted according to the customer. One company can have multiple value chains depending on its range of customers. The value chain is the chain of events that a company does in order to serve and deliver that value to a specific customer segment.

In a complex world, visual clarity always wins.

Nothing cuts through complexity like visual thinking.

Visual thinking creates clarity on what really matters and a layout of why, where, when, and with what to focus.

Henrik von Scheel
Certified Elf Spotter

The most powerful decision cockpit today

A decision is a power in having a choice, but you can only choose if you can see the possibility that led to questions, and scenario thinking that provides choice.

The Value Chain 4.0 is the most powerful decision cockpit for executives today to manage the present while creating scenarios for future business.

It is like a visual representation of a chair on paper that you model. It is a transparent look at how forces and drivers affect and influence the organization.

If you don't ask the right questions, *you don't get the right answers*.

Choices in a Value Chain 4.0

- High level of business design for strategic options to run and develop the business.

- Where and how the forces (trends) disrupt the present business.

- Whether and whence emerging drivers (trends) can affect the future business.

- Competitive forces:
    1. Competition in the industry
    2. Potential of new entrants
    3. Power of suppliers
    4. Power of customers
    5. Threat of substitute products.

- Direct and indirect cost and revenue flow.

- Customer Segmentation.

- Map core differentiating, core competitive and non-core competencies.

- Delivery services.

- Innovation opportunities within the areas of revenue, value, and service.

- Transformation opportunities within cost, operations, and performance areas.

- Alliance, partners, and complementors.

Understanding the change and spotting the trends are rare skills, but two of the most important in strategy.

This chapter will provide the latest thinking and in-depth insight on the 4th Industrial Revolution by the originator himself.

It is an essential discipline for everybody who wants to stay ahead in strategy.

the
4th
INDUSTRIAL
REV⬜LUTI⬜N

Chapter Four

Industrial Revolution History

An industrial revolution is a period that radically changes and effects societies, businesses, economies, and environments. There are various moments throughout human history where new technological advancements collide at new heights or set a new bar, typically due to new technological advancements or discoveries. The industrial revolutions have shaped our world today into a global interconnected society that currently fuels the exponential growth thereof.

The 1st industrial revolution began in Britain in the late 18th century with the mechanization of the textile industry. The invention of mechanical production powered by water and steam started the first mechanical automation to create a huge breakthrough in productivity and consistency of production.

The 2nd industrial revolution began in the United States in the early 19th century with electricity and mass production. It was fueled by the start of mass production powered by electricity and combustion engines to power machines. The first assembly lines were introduced, the use of new materials and chemicals became possible, and communication was getting easier.

| Economy |
| Transport |
| Energy |
| Water |

Mechanization

1st Revolution
Water & Steam Power

1784

| Communication |
| Economy |
| Transport |
| Energy |
| Fossil |

Electrification

2nd Revolution
Electric Power

1913

Linear Innovation

The 3rd industrial revolution began in the United States in the middle of the 20th century with the harness of electronics and information technology to automate production.

In 1969, the introduction of automation and robotics ushered a new era, the Industry 3.0.

Electronics and IT such as the internet, mobile phones, computers, the cloud, and big data merged into a digital era of the information age.

The 4th industrial revolution began in Germany at the beginning of the 21st century around the fusion of the digital, physical, and virtual world with a focus on the planet, people, and prosperity, in that order.

It represents the biggest structural change in the past 250 years and is upon us. It is disrupting every aspect of our lives, economy, industry, and society.

In its scale, scope, and complexity, the transformation will be unlike anything humankind has experienced before.

| Communication |
| Economy |
| Transport |
| Energy |
| Fossil |

Digitalization

3rd Revolution
Automation

1969

Cyber Physical Systems

4th Revolution
Planet, People & Prosperity

2011

Exponential Innovation

Inception of the 4ᵗʰ Industrial Revolution

The 4th Industrial Revolution (4IR) was triggered by Germany's national strategy in 2009 called the "Digital Agenda." Henrik von Scheel was one of the masterminds behind Germany's Digital Agenda, which evolved into the 4IR and ignited the Global Digital (2009) and Industry 4.0 (2011) themes of today.

Beginning of the Global Digital theme

As part of the Advisory Council at the Federal Ministry of Economy & Technology, Henrik von Scheel played a significant role to define Germany's future digital strategy in 2009.

The "Digital Agenda" was adopted by the European Commission in 2010, resulting in the "Digital Agenda Europe 2020" that ignited the European Digital Revolution. The "Digital Agenda" is one of Europe's seven flagships - responsible for 5% of GDP, with a market value of €660 billion annually.[5]

Origin of the 4ᵗʰ Industrial Revolution

As one of the masterminds and driving forces behind this Industry 4.0, Henrik von Scheel was an Advisory Group member of the Federal Ministry of Education & Research - inter-ministerial innovation policy initiatives tasked to define the high-tech strategy for Germany. The final "Industry 4.0" report was announced in April 2013.

There are two options: adapt and evolve, or get replaced.

The 4th Industrial Revolution alters every aspect of human experience.

It fundamentally changes the way we live, consume, work, and relate to one another, reshaping our reality, sensory, dietary, and body - unlike anything humankind has experienced before.

It will transform every aspect of our economy, every industry, and all aspects of society on a scale and complexity never seen before.

Henrik von Scheel
Godfather of Industry 4.0

Exponential Disruption

The Industry 4.0 is exponential in nature. Exponential effects are difficult for human minds to comprehend.

To relate it to our lives, the Covid-19 pandemic was exponential in nature. It shut down a world within 3 months.

At its core, the exponential fuels both a disruption or the inability to adapt, and an exponential innovation or the ability to adapt and improve.

Normally, an industrial revolution is a period of radical changes that affect societies, industries, economies, and environments. There are various moments throughout human history where new technological advancements collide to new heights and set the bar higher, typically due to new advancements or discoveries.

The industrial revolutions have shaped our world today into a globally interconnected society that currently fuels the exponential growth thereof.

A revolution usually emerges as an evolution, but the 4IR evolutions are exponential in nature. The exponential effect is difficult to comprehend.

Let's try a "Gedanken-Experiment" to grasp the exponential effect. If you want to travel to the moon by foot and every step you take will double in length, how many steps until you reach the moon? Your 29th step will bring you to the moon. Step 30 will bring you back to Earth again.

It is critical that we understand the power of exponential disruption and opportunities as they are the lenses through which we must see our world today.

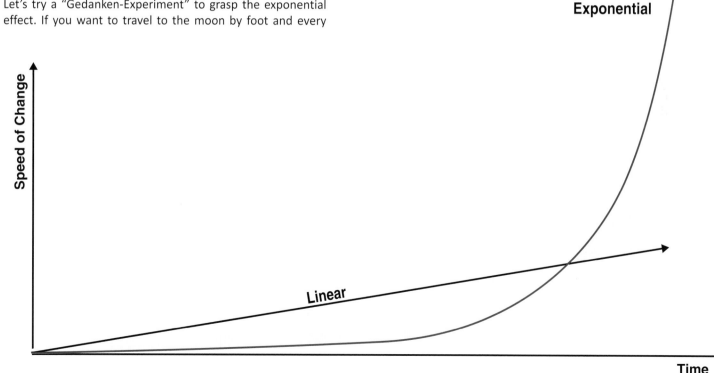

The exponential disruption changes every human experience

When compared with previous industrial revolutions, the 4th one is evolving at an exponential rather than a linear pace.

77 Megatrends that merge

The exponential effect in the 4IR is accelerated by the collision of 77 megatrends. The trends merge in various forms and manifest in form of disruptive forces and emerging drivers. Drivers are always a window of innovation opportunities that require proactivity, and forces are transformation opportunities that you must adapt or evolve toward.

The forces and drivers of the Industry 4.0 Periodic Table are comprised of 77 Megatrends, categorized into eight Groups according to their characteristics.

Three Worlds Collide

The merging of the 77 megatrends ignites a paradigm shift that erupts in the collision of the digital, virtual, and physical worlds. It is fundamentally altering everything we experience as human beings.

The fusion of the three worlds are manifested as the *Augmented Reality, Cyber-Physical Systems, Metaverse, and Miniverse.* They deliver unparalleled opportunities for growth and productivity. They will reset the competitive landscape on a scale never seen before with innovative service models, smart products, next generation of operational excellence, and truly end-to-end integrated value chains.

Groups

● Technology   ○ Regulatory   ◎ Workforce   ○ Enviroment
◌ Globalization   ◍ Demographic   ● Economic   ● Consumer

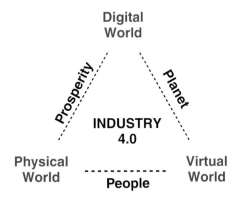

Eight stages of (R)evolution

As with any revolution, it is more of an evolution consisting of four stages that will change everything.

In essence, it affects every aspect of our lives: how we consume, work, and interact with each other, reshaping every facet of our society, economy, business, and environment at a pace and impact not seen before.

The tectonic plates of our economy, government systems, and wealth distribution are shifting, while the competitiveness and industry borders are eroding.

The pace of change and the threat of disruption creates tremendous opportunities. There has never been a time of greater promises, opportunities, and challenges.

Every industrial (r)evolution brings along a learning revolution and leapfrogs society. For many people, their first smartphone is the first and only computer they have. The 4IR extends the ladder of opportunity to anyone who is willing to adapt to changes by building skills, developing new capabilities, and competing on competencies.

It is important to note that the 4IR is not just about the technology or business, it is about society, the economy, and the environment.

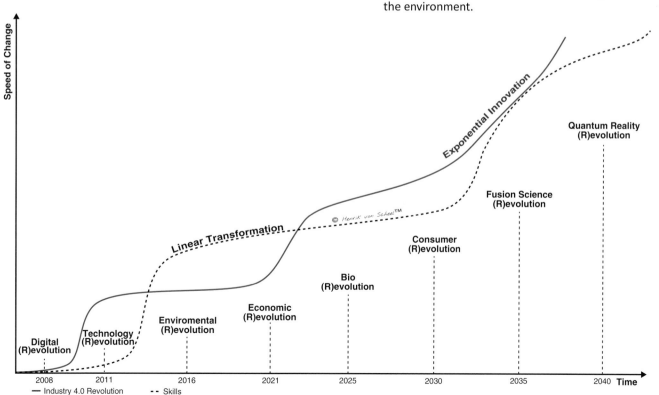

Periodic Table of the 4th Industrial Revolution

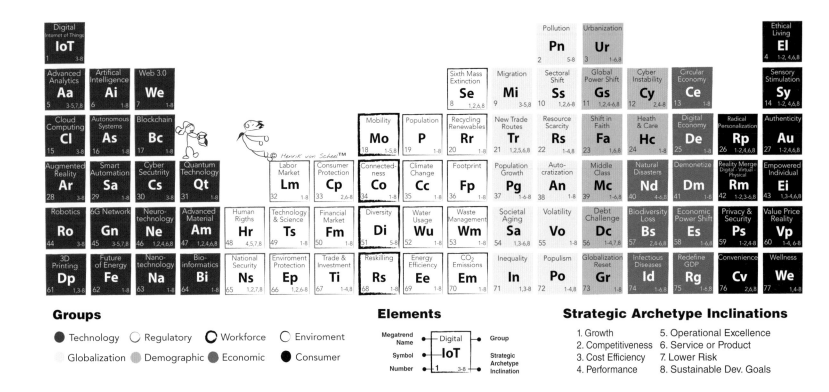

© Henrik von Scheel™

Groups

- ● Technology
- ○ Regulatory
- ◎ Workforce
- ○ Enviroment
- ▨ Globalization
- ◐ Demographic
- ● Economic
- ● Consumer

Elements

Megatrend Name — Digital — Group

Symbol — **IoT**

Number — 1 — 3-8 — Strategic Archetype Inclination

Strategic Archetype Inclinations

1. Growth
2. Competitiveness
3. Cost Efficiency
4. Performance
5. Operational Excellence
6. Service or Product
7. Lower Risk
8. Sustainable Dev. Goals

The forces and drivers of the Industry 4.0 Periodic Table are comprised of 77 megatrends categorized into six groups according to each one's characteristics.

Each megatrend's element is classified in line with the strategic inclination of the potential impact delivered.

Technology megatrends (19)

- Advanced Analytics
- Augmented Reality
- Cloud Computing
- Digitalization (IOT)
- Robotics
- 3D Printing
- Artificial Intelligence
- Autonomous Systems
- Blockchain
- Smart Automation
- 6G Communications
- Web 3.0
- Advanced Material
- Bioinformatics
- Cybersecurity
- Fusion Science
- Nanotechnology
- Neurotechnology
- Quantum Technology

Regulatory megatrends (8)

- Human Rights
- National Security
- Environment Protection
- Technology & Science
- Labor Market
- Consumer Protection
- Financial Market
- Trade & Investment

Workforce megatrends (4)

- Mobility
- Diversity
- Reskilling
- Connectedness

Environmental megatrends (9)

- Population
- Climate Changes
- Water Usage
- Energy Efficiency
- Sixth Mass Extinction
- Recycling Renewables
- Footprint
- Waste management
- CO_2 emission

Globalization megatrends (11)

- Migration
- New Trade Routes
- Population Growth
- Societal Aging
- Inequality
- Pollution
- Sectoral Shift
- Resource Scarcity
- Volatility
- Autocratization
- Populism

Demographic megatrends (8)

- Urbanization
- Global Power Shift
- Cyber Instability
- Health & Care
- Shift in Faith
- Middle Class
- Debt Challenge
- Globalization Reset

Economic megatrends (8)

- Natural Disasters
- Biodiversity loss
- Infectious Diseases
- Circular Economy
- Digital Economy
- Demonetize
- Economic Power Shift
- Redefine of Gross Domestic Product

Consumer megatrends (10)

- Radical Personalization
- Reality Merge
- Privacy & Security
- Convenience
- Ethical Living
- Sensory Stimulation
- Authenticity
- Empowered Individual
- Value Price Reality
- Wellness

Forces that shape business

The easiest way to comprehend trends and drivers is to categorize and break it down. Megatrends are the highest categorization of trends.

We have identified 6 main megatrends. Each megatrend has several macrotrends that are trends within its category. Then, finally, each macrotrend can be broken down into multiple microtrends.

There are 17 Technology megatrends that impact organizations as disruptive forces on current operations and emerging drivers that shape new business opportunities.

At this point there are 4 mega workforce megatrends, namely: Mobility, Diversity, Reskilling, and Connectedness.

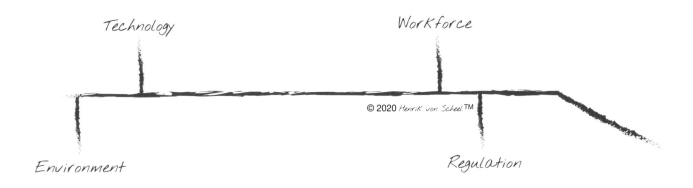

Technology

Workforce

© 2020 Henrik von Scheel ™

Environment

Regulation

There are 9 Environmental megatrends that companies have to consider in terms of how they source, produce, package, and ship, and how they brand themselves.

The megatrends are Climate Change, Water usage, Energy Efficiency, Sixth Mass Extinction, recycling renewables, footprint, waste management, CO_2 emission, and population.

Eight regulatory megatrends will affect the areas of Human Rights, National Security, Environment Protection, Technology & Science, Labor Market, Consumer Protection, Financial Market, and Trade & Investment

Drivers that change

The competitive driver is determined by the number of competitors and their threat level to your organization. The threat is increased by a larger number of competitors and the number of equivalent products and services that target similar customer segments.

The 11 Consumer megatrends that will drive our society and business are Radical Personalization, Reality Merge, Privacy & Security, Wellness, Ethical Living, Sensory Stimulation, Convenience, Authenticity, Value Price Reality, Empowered Individual, and Value Price Reality.

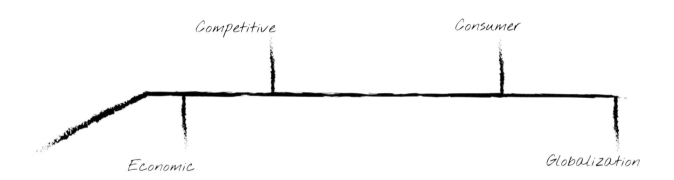

The 8 Economic megatrends that will reset our economic system are Infectious Diseases, Biodiversity Loss, Circular Economy, Digital Economy, Demonetize, Global Power Shift, Redefine of Gross Domestic Product, and Natural Disasters.

There are 11 colliding Global and 8 Demographic megatrends that will affect every aspect of our lives. These are Migration, New Trade Routes, Population Growth, Social Aging, Inequality, Pollution, Sectoral Shift, Resource Scarcity, Volatility, Autocratization, Populism, Urbanization, Global Power Shift, Cyber Instability, Health & Care, Shift in Faith, Middle Class, Debt Challenge, and Globalization Reset.

When Worlds Collide

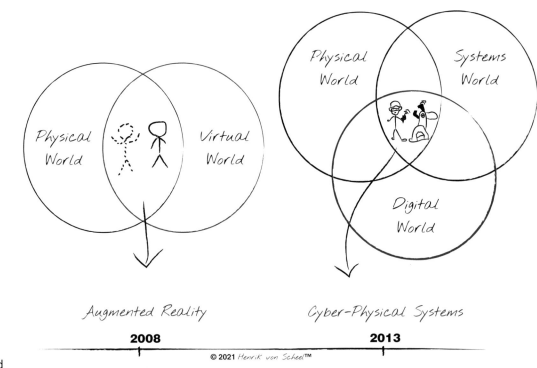

Augmented Reality — 2008

Cyber-Physical Systems — 2013

© 2021 Henrik von Scheel™

The collision of the digital, virtual, and physical worlds within Industry 4.0 or also called the "Pattern of Accurate Disruption."

The fusion of these worlds manifests as Augmented Reality, Cyber-Physical Systems, Metaverse, and Multiverse.

Augmented reality is the merging of our physical and virtual world to the enhanced version of the real physical world in a virtual representation such as a Zoom or Skype call. This is achieved through the use of digital visual elements, sounds, or other sensory stimuli delivered via technology.

A cyber-physical system is the merging of our physical, virtual, and digital systems into an intelligent system, thereby creating a tighter integration among humans, machines, and IT systems.

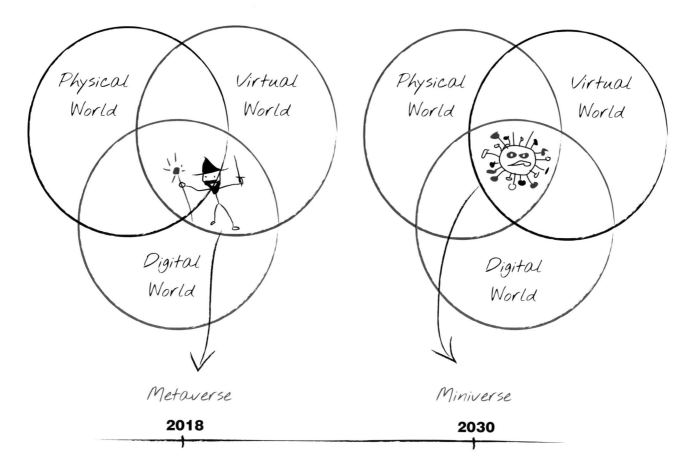

2018   **2030**

The Metaverse is the merging of our physical, virtual, and digital experiences of reality. A reality as an immersive and interactive shared virtual space that combines the physical and digital, all thanks to augmented reality and virtual reality technology.

The Metaverse is built on the Web 3 decentralized databases where data is stored. The user controls, owns, shares, and participates on his or her own terms.

The Miniverse is a nano dimensional layer of the physical, virtual, and digital experiences of reality.

The Miniverse connects our body, mind, and biology with a physical bioinformatic integration, making the experience of our health, feeling, and realities instantiable.

People are the centrepiece of the 4th Industrial Revolution.

Ever since the first caveman shaped a flint, humanity has defined itself by the capacity to equip itself with tools to manage its environment.

The Industry 4.0 era will be no different. Our ability for humanity as a group to *do remarkable things* hinges on how well we can *pull together as one*.

Ciprian Popa
"Paranormal Tour Guide"

the eight

(R)EVOLUTION

STAGES

A revolution emerges as an evolution

In essence, the 4IR is the fusion of the digital, virtual, and physical world.

Fueled by the collision of 77 megatrends that surface in eight metamorphosis stages of paradigm shift that changes everything, called the Industry 4.0.

When disruption happens, it happens fast

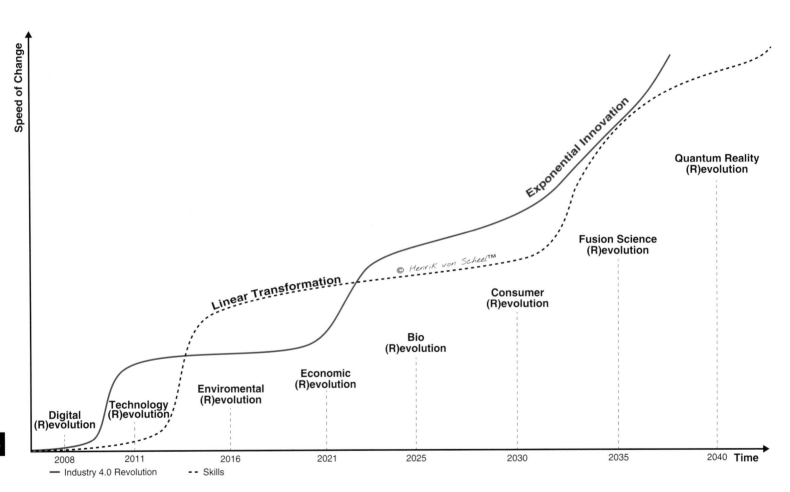

© Henrik von Scheel™

Speed of Change / Time

Digital (R)evolution · Technology (R)evolution · Enviromental (R)evolution · Economic (R)evolution · Bio (R)evolution · Consumer (R)evolution · Fusion Science (R)evolution · Quantum Reality (R)evolution

Linear Transformation · Exponential Innovation

2008 · 2011 · 2016 · 2021 · 2025 · 2030 · 2035 · 2040

— Industry 4.0 Revolution   - - Skills

Digital (R)evolution

Digitalization is about connecting the physical, digital, and virtual world.

Digitalization, also called the Internet of Things (IOT), is the first of the 77 megatrends, and one of the most fundamental dependency for all the other megatrends to evolve.

Consequently, digital technologies has changed our lives, society, business, service, and economy as we know it.

Widely misunderstood, digitalization is still in its infant stage!

The Nuts and Bolts of Digitalization with its Architect

In 2009, Prof. Henrik von Scheel and and Prof. August Wilhelm Scheer ignited the Global Digital theme of today. As part of the Advisory Council at the Federal Minister of Economy & Technology, they played a significant role to define Germany's future digital strategy in 2009. The "Digital Agenda" was adopted by the European Commission in 2010 as part of the Europe 2020 and evolved into the Global Digital theme of today.

Digitalization, also called Internet of Things (IOT), is the first of the 77 megatrends, and one of the most fundamental dependencies for all the other megatrends to evolve.

Digitalization is still an infant

Important to understand is that digitalization is about connecting the physical, digital, and virtual world. Widely misunderstood, digitalization today is still in its infant stage.

Its evolution is the backbone for the 3 technology waves described in the Technology (R)evolution. The digitalization of everything, from our body to our minds. Everything, everywhere, at the same time.

Digitalization purpose driven applied

As with everything in strategy, digitalization is always impact-driven applied. In my experience, there are three main digital phases to drive impact by using a value chain, namely:

- **Digital Connectivity and Sensors**: Focus on digital connectivity and sensory of main product and workflows (Machine to Human, Machine to Machine, and Machine to Systems) that support the service design and development, includes smart automation, sensors, hardware, embedded software guided by agile and workflow experts.

  Golden rule focuses on the high level of integration and automation of simple operation and aligns and optimizes performance toward complex operations.

- **Digital Engineering:** Prioritizes customer-centric data-driven (service and workflow driven) engineering and product lifecycle management (process driven) powered by digital twin technology.

- **Digital Operations:** End2End Shop floor-to-top floor integration with execution systems (MES), operations management (MOM) connected workers, robotics, 3D printing, & AI-powered production.

  Explore the latest operational practice to deliver maximal execution power with tangible impact that improves service, performance, quality, increases safety, lowers risk and cost.

Business impact based on a discrete manufacturing value chain

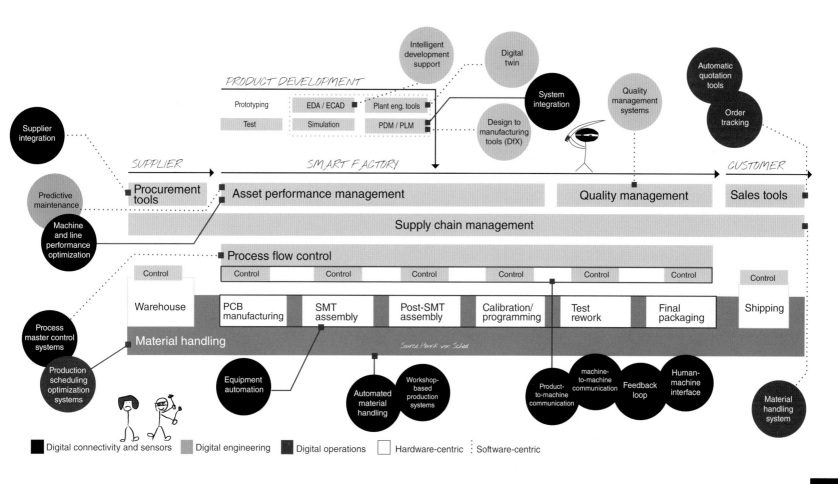

PRODUCT DEVELOPMENT

Intelligent development support

Digital twin

System integration

Quality management systems

Automatic quotation tools

Order tracking

| Prototyping | EDA / ECAD | Plant eng. tools |
| Test | Simulation | PDM / PLM |

Design to manufacturing tools (DfX)

Supplier integration

Predictive maintenance

Machine and line performance optimization

SUPPLIER SMART FACTORY CUSTOMER

Procurement tools

Asset performance management

Quality management

Sales tools

Supply chain management

Process flow control

| Control | Control | Control | Control | Control | Control | Control |

| Control | | | | | | | | Control |
| Warehouse | PCB manufacturing | SMT assembly | Post-SMT assembly | Calibration/ programming | Test rework | Final packaging | | Shipping |

Material handling

Source Henrik von Scheel

Process master control systems

Production scheduling optimization systems

Equipment automation

Automated material handling

Workshop-based production systems

Product-to-machine communication

machine-to-machine communication

Feedback loop

Human-machine interface

Material handling system

■ Digital connectivity and sensors   ■ Digital engineering   ■ Digital operations   ☐ Hardware-centric   ⋮ Software-centric

99

It's not because things are difficult that we do not dare. It's because we do not dare that they are difficult.

Seneca

Technology (R)evolution

The Technology (R)evolution arrives in three waves. Each wave has a compounding impact on the others that manifests itself as exponential, prosperous, and disruptive.

Consequently, each wave is exponentially more volatile and disruptive than its predecessor. Buckle up, brace yourself, and enjoy the ride!

The Technology (R)evolution arrives in three waves of disruption

The 19 exponentially accelerating emerging technology megatrends are the fuel for all the other 60 trends in the 4IR. They will define *the new boundaries of prosperity, and the future workplace, and will reset the policies landscape - the foundation for how companies compete and trade in the future.*

In fact, there are 19 distinct megatrends all working simultaneously to bring together the digital, physical, and virtual worlds.

Three Waves of Disruption

The technology trends evolve in 3 waves of maturity and adoption. *Each of these waves delivers unparalleled opportunities for growth and productivity, resetting the competitive landscape on a scale never seen before with smart products and new service models.*

The waves also create the next generation of operational excellence, smart automation, connectivity, and alignment across the entire value chain. In a world that is being disrupted faster than ever, the question is not whether you will join in, but how.

Accelerates globally economic growth

The overall importance of technology will increase within the next twenty years as new technologies are being adopted more widely, reaching significant diffusion milestones earlier as innovation cycles become shorter.

This development follows a long-term trend as product lifecycles become ever shorter with numerous new smart products penetrating multiple markets.

Fast technology diffusion is not restricted to advanced economies. The technology trends will enable new business models and the ease of doing business, ultimately fostering economic growth, especially in developing countries.

Also, transactions via cash-backed payment systems connected to mobile phones can be processed in real time, fostering financial inclusion. The influence of spatial distance between innovators and adopters, which in the past played a significant role in adoption speed, diminishes as accelerating digitalization reduces obstacles, e.g., in communication, and fosters an even stronger exchange of information worldwide.

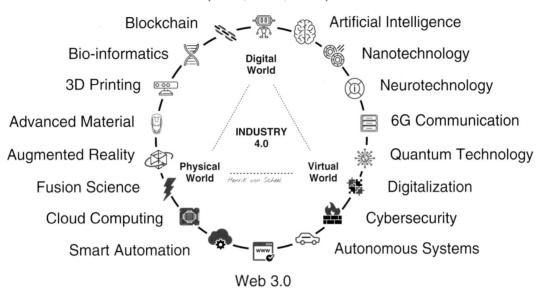

Robotics
(M2H, H2M, M2M)

Blockchain

Artificial Intelligence

Bio-informatics

Nanotechnology

3D Printing

Neurotechnology

Digital World

Advanced Material

6G Communication

INDUSTRY 4.0

Augmented Reality

Quantum Technology

Physical World

Virtual World

Fusion Science

Henrik von Scheel

Digitalization

Cloud Computing

Cybersecurity

Smart Automation

Autonomous Systems

Web 3.0

1st wave 2009–2016

- Advanced Analytics
- Augmented Reality
- Cloud Computing
- Digitalization (IOT)
- Robotics
- 3D Printing

2nd wave 2016–2025

- Artificial Intelligence
- Autonomous Systems
- Blockchain
- Smart Automation
- 6G Communications
- Web 3.0

3rd wave 2025...

- Advanced Material
- Bio-informatics
- Cybersecurity
- Fusion Science
- Nanotechnology
- Neurotechnology
- Quantum Technology

First wave = 2009-2016

The 1st wave of technology trends emerged in 2009 and brought forth the cyber-physical systems (CPS) and evolved into the 2nd wave in 2016.

The technology includes Advanced Analytics, Augmented Reality, Cloud Computing, Digitalization (Internet of Things), Robotics, and 3D Printing. The main driver in the 1st wave will digitalize propped by sensory, connectivity and automate all non-core activities in the organization. The most common mistake in digitalization projects today is that most of them are base processes and not the workflow.

The great re-make

The cyber-physical systems (CPS) are defined as the merging of our physical, virtual, and digital systems into one intelligent system, creating a tighter integration among humans, machines, and IT systems.

Once again, the epicenter of the industrial revolution is in manufacturing, and it will reshape it beyond recognition.

The cyber-physical systems hold the promise for growth and productivity within manufacturing. But as in any previous revolution, the evolution of manufacturing is always the most difficult as it was the last to adapt electricity over the combustion engine.

A CPS is an intelligent system that is sensory and digitally connected to boost productivity with automation, integration, and optimization.

Manufacturing is on the verge of a seismic, tech-driven shift in 3-D printing, human-machine interaction, such as touch interfaces and augmented-reality systems to name a few. The manufacturers in 2025 will look very different.

Today, the manufacturers have never been so disrupted. Digitalization has become a requirement and Smart Manufacturing an evolving to-do list.

The implementation of the cyber-physical systems will vary as Industry 4.0 is always an output-driven implementation. The impact is best illustrated in the "Industry 4.0 impact overview in one chart."

In my experience, digital transformation initiatives are notoriously difficult to scale up across factory networks; manufacturers may need to slow down to get ahead in the race to implement Industry 4.0.

Companies that get it right harvest the benefits across the entire manufacturing value chain such as increasing production capacity and reducing material losses, improving customer service and delivery lead times, achieving higher employee satisfaction, and reducing their environmental impact. Scaled across networks, these gains can fundamentally transform a company's competitive position.

The digitally enabled factory of today looks very different from the leading factory of ten years ago. Advances in data and analytics, Machine Learning, Artificial Intelligence, and the array of technology vendors in the market mean that manufacturers can choose from 100 potential solutions to improve their ways of working.

Implemented successfully, these solutions deliver irresistible returns. Across a wide range of sectors, it is not uncommon to see up to 45% reductions in machine downtime, up to 25% increases in throughput, up to 25% improvements in labor productivity, and 85% more accurate forecasting.

The chart below illustrates a holistic overview of the 4IR impact within the manufacturer.

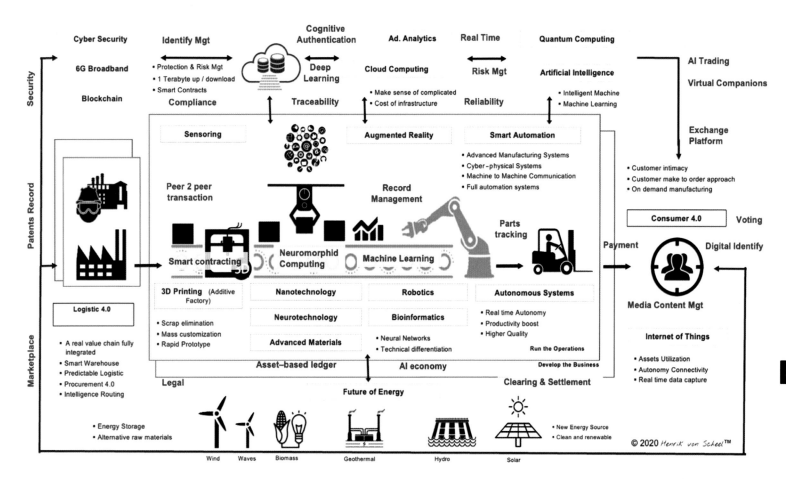

A wise man adapts himself to
circumstances, as water shapes
itself to the vessel that contains it.

Confucius

Environment (R)evolution

We live on a unstable planet. The Earth's climate and atmosphere have changed drastically over the last 4.5 billion years.

It is only the last 8,000 years, which have been relatively stable to enable agricultural development, that has seen permanent settlements and population growth.

The Environment (R)evolution is mainly about the changing of the water cycles that leads to climate changes with more melting ice, extreme weather such as increased rain, flooding, extreme drought, more heat waves, and stronger hurricanes. Basically, water is always on the move, and our water cycles are shifting.

Find the right balance

The Environment (R)evolution is propelled by a 2nd wave of the technology (R)evolution and a renewed society awareness that we are part of an ecosystem, resulting in key critical initiatives trying to find the right balance to be part of an ecosystem.

The Environment (R)evolution is mainly about the changing of the water cycles that leads to climate changes with more melting ice, extreme weather such as increased rain, flooding, extreme drought, more heat waves, and stronger hurricanes. Basically, water is always on the move and our water cycles are shifting.

It's a wake-up call to find the right balance to live in harmony with our environment.

Some of the key initiatives to focus on include:

Rethink consumption

Rethink the way what we eat, how we produce, package, and ship. The footprint thinking, zero waste with embracing re-use, repair, and recycling will be one of the main drivers of opportunity to change behavior.

It all starts with the production. Today, 14% of emission comes from livestock. Ninety percent of our protein needs to be cultured meat. Our aim should be to change our agriculture and the way we produce, package, and ship.

Redefine more with less

There is a need to *achieve more with less* by redefining the way we produce and consume energy and water with a need to rethink our transportation infrastructure, most importantly, our mode of transportation from airlines, cars, and ships to name a few.

It starts with *zero emissions in transportation.* Increase our efficiency by 50% by 2050 from light bulbs to cars, airlines, and ships.

Adaptive, efficient, *and scalable water, energy, and transformation infrastructure* with the least amount of waste. This includes ensuring a fair society distribution of energy, water, and food.

Rebuilding the Earth's lung capacity by an increase of 2mil. to 9.5 million sq. km. global forest area. Expand the boundaries of nature through the adoption of regenerative practices wherever feasible.

Refocus on new energy sources

With the rate of our energy consumption, it is of utmost importance that we find a new energy source. Today, there is a lot of new light on the horizon that we we need to test.

Meanwhile, our focus should remain on growing our renewables like wind and solar, which need to make up 97% by 2050. The aim should be to phase out natural gas and coal with a decline of 62% by 2050.

In essence, Environment (R)evolution is all about the changes of our water cycles such as melting, sublimation, evaporation, freezing, condensation, and deposition.

Water is necessary for every kind of life. Our Earth is truly unique in its abundance of 71% water. The water cycle is driven by energy from the sun that decides where life will flourish.

Homo sapiens have proven to be the most adaptive species. Once we recognize that we are part of the planet ecosystem rather than the consumers of it - we can find solutions and develop sustainable economies to live in harmony with it.

I rest my case.

2x

Planets are required by 2030 to maintain our consumption.

50%

of animal and plant species will be facing extinction by the end of 2030.

5B

People will be affected by water shortage by 2050.

A 30-year to do list

Rethink Energy

Phase out gas and coal

Natural gas and coal needs to decline 62% by 2050.

Grow renewables

Renewables like wind and solar need to make up 97% by 2050.

Redesign Infrastructure

Zero emissions transport

Increase our efficiency by 50% by 2050 from light bulbs to cars.

Increase lung capacity

Rebuilding the global forest area must increase from 2mil. to 9.5 million sq. km.

Remake Consumption

Change what we eat

We need to change 58% of the way we produce and consume by 2050.

Change our agriculture

14% of emissions come from livestock. Ninety percent of our protein needs to be cultured meat.

Repair Communication

Digitalize or die

We need to connect every aspect of our lives by 2050.

Zero marginal cost

IOT and renewable energy will bring on a zero marginal cost society, meaning nearly free of charge. The age of "money comes first" is over.

How we get there

Government

Need to set new rules that change behavior related to how we produce, consume, and pollute.

Corporate

Need to lead the innovation era of how we source, make, produce, ship, and consume.

Individual

We need to change our behavior and push companies and governments to change.

Financial Institutions

Need to take the lead to invest in the future of energy, transportation, and how we produce and consume.

Ever since the first caveman shaped a flint, humanity has defined itself by the capacity to equip itself with tools to manage its environment.

The 4th Industrial Revolution era will be no different.

Jack Ma
Founder, Alibaba Group

2nd wave of technology trends = Web 3.0 and Metaverse

2nd wave = 2016-2025

The 2nd wave of technology trends is 100 times more disruptive than the 1st wave. It emerged in 2016 with Artificial Intelligence, Autonomous Systems, Blockchain, Smart Automation, 6G Communications, and Web 3.0 technologies that brought forth the Metaverse and will evolve into the 2nd wave in 2025.

Artificial Intelligence

Artificial Intelligence (AI) is the automation of intelligence. The question is what do you define as intelligence. AI is going to change the world more than anything in the history of humankind, even more than electricity.

AI is not new. Founded as an academic discipline in 1955, it is practically as old as the first digital computer. As with most emerging technologies, a gradual convergence of cost reductions, performance improvements, and network effects has only recently conspired to make AI a boardroom-relevant agenda item.

AI is drastically important to our future because AI forms the very foundation of computer learning. Through AI, computers have the ability to harness massive amounts of data and use their learned intelligence to make optimal decisions and discoveries in fractions of the time that it would take humans.

The future of AI is around us, inside us, and upon us a bit like science fiction cyborgs. It is a slow, symbiotic coevolution of our own choosing, and it has already begun.

AI around us - The promise of "always on and connected" in a cyber-physical-system environment with ubiquitous computing access comes with the ability to reliably and regularly offload a meaningful share of our cognition and recollection to our mobile devices and AI assistants. This accelerates in the 2nd wave with nanotechnology, neurotechnology, and advanced material surges.

AI upon us - As hyperscale incumbents normalize smart devices like an exoskeleton, smart glasses, clothing, and shoes that merge physical body and mind to change our capabilities and reality, it alters the ways we experience and interact as humans to our surroundings.

The trendlines point toward a future where most of our everyday physical experiences will be mediated through a digital layer informed by machine intelligence. Just as we have gotten comfortable being seen with these devices, we are also getting increasingly comfortable with them seeing us at a level of detail once afforded only to medical professionals.

AI inside us - There is no getting around it, from chips in our brains, intelligent medicine, nascent neuromuscular implants to help people regain the use of their limbs, as well as with the blind and deaf to help them approximate sensations of sight and sound.

AI cyber-physical-system capabilities will evolve to how we monitor, control, and govern our body and mind. Fundamentally it will empower the medical, neuroscience and physiology, and psychology disciplines with more information and insight. This is just the beginning, and we can only speculate as to the increased nuance and intensity as we evolve from muscular augmentation to cognitive augmentation.

Artificial Intelligence is the automation of intelligence. The question is what do you define as intelligence.

AI is going to change the world more than anything in the history of humankind, even more than electricity.

Henrik von Scheel
Ignitor of the Global Digital Theme
"Chairman of Hair Is Overrated Movement"

Autonomous System

An autonomous system (AS) is a collection of connected internet protocol routing prefixes under the control of one or more network operators, architecture on behalf of a single administrative entity or domain, that presents a common and clearly defined routing policy to the internet.

Autonomous systems are more than autonomous vehicles; they will be all over our home, factories and package delivery, etc. The biggest fundamental change is the inevitable evolution of our architecture from IT driven to Services Oriented Architectures where complexity gives way to simplicity and flexibility that will solve workflow, safety, risk to a few.

Autonomous systems and blockchain (smart contract, distributed ledgers, and decentralization) have ignited a new evolution of trust, secure and service-oriented architectures that can operate in real-time in a cyber-physical system with digital smart automation approach. The business impact is the lowering of risk, reducing the cost of operational, complaints to security regulations, and enabling more cost-efficient transactions across a truly integrated value chain.

A inevitable architectural evolution driven by AS that meets the architectural demands of an integrated value chain is rated below on functional maturity versus potential impact by

Low					High

Strategic Choices
Virtual Scenarios
Finance Management
Service Management
Risk & Safety Mgt
Security (Defi)
Reliability
Scalability
Real-time Information

Workflow Management
Operational Excellence (performance vs cost)
Inventory Mgt (WMS)
Assets & Facility Mgt
Operational Mgt (MOM)
Monitoring & Reporting
Governance & Compliance
Capacity & Demand Mgt
Capability Mgt (HRM)

Virtual NW automation
Cyber Physical System (M2H, M2S, and S2H)
End-user tools
Incident & SLA Mgt
Access Management
Smart Automation
Quality Mgt (QMS)
Maintenance Mgt (MMS)
Operational Execution Mgt (MES)

Smart Automation

Around half of all existing work activities could be automated in the next few decades as next-level workflows automation and virtualization become more commonplace.

The key for digitization is not to use the traditional process thinking, but workflows to enable the link to the cyber-physical system. People rarely understand, but this is the difference of day and night if the requirement is to drive Operational Excellence by improving operations, increasing performance, and lowering cost though the focus of digital smart automation.

Smart Automation is the next digital frontier focusing on the level of integration and automation that supports the five key characteristics of operations, namely:

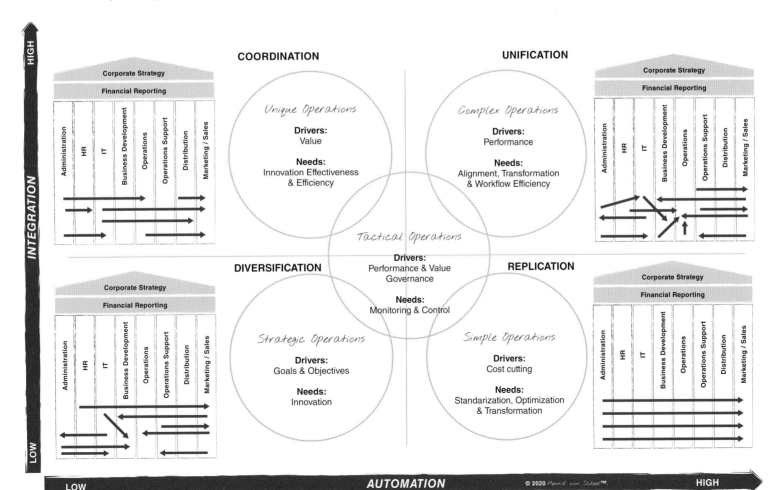

© 2020 Henrik von Scheel™

Blockchain

Blockchain is a distributed ledger, or database, shared across a public or private computing network. Each computer node in the network holds a copy of the ledger, so there is no single point of failure.

The blockchain technology foundation is rooted in cryptographic, decentralization, smart contact, trust and permission, connectivity, ubiquity, and token-based economics technology.

The blockchain, AI, and digitalization is the driving force in the Economic (R)evolution.

A new frontier for handling information and data, security, that holds the promise to reset our broken economic system (platform token, cryptocurrency coins, exchanges, lending, yield earning, investment), the global supply chain (product protocol, inventory management, financing) ownership of asset (NTFs, intellectual property, real estate, land and metaverse) to ownership of information (NFTS with intellectual property, codes, control rooms, . . .) like a person holds all information of himself in a wallet from birth certificate, tax, salary, etc.

The blockchain technology is growing with quantum leaps where no exact figures can predict the future of any particular technological instrument. This decentralized technology has already provided some mind-blowing solutions to the world, and a lot more is still to arrive. Now it is merely a question of our patience to witness how blockchain empowers communities worldwide to create a more open and free technological ecosystem worldwide.

It is one of my favorite topics and I could write a whole chapter, but this should do it.

6G Communications

The mobile data consumption has skyrocketed in recent years. In comparison to 4G, 5G on average sees 2-3 times the level of data consumption. The existing infrastructure can't sustain it. Hence, I intentionally mention 6G, as the promise of 5G was 1 terabyte upload and download. Now we got a new logo with 5G and a minimum improvement.

The future "Google" company will be a telecommunication provider that innovates a new blockchain and web 3.0 technologies that can distribute data for a low fee.

I am Superficially Intelligent.
Always available and connected.

Economic (R)evolution

All of our economic theories of growth and productivity today are based on Adam Smith from 1776.

The Father of Modern Economics uses Newton's metaphors in physics to resolve economic questions. There is only one problem with this: Newton's physics has absolutely nothing to do with economics. Nothing. Nothing.. . .

The Economic (R)evolution is the great remake of our economic machine from growth, productivity, and income inequality theories to digital assets-based monetary, currently, changing the fundamentals of trade, money, ownership, distribution, and trade. A reset of wealth distribution.

There have been at least seven major economic paradigm shifts in history, and they are very interesting anthropologically because they share a common denominator.

And that is, at a certain moment of time, three technologies emerge and converge to create what we call in engineering **"a general-purpose technology platform."** That is a fancy way of saying … "a new infrastructure." It fundamentally changes the way we manage power and move economic life.

What are those three technologies? First, **new communication technologies** allow us to more efficiently *manage* our economic activity. Second, **new sources of energy** allow us to more efficiently *power* our economic activity, and third, **new modes of mobility, transportations, and logistics** allow us to more efficiently *move* the economic activity.

So, when communication revolutions join with new energy regimes, and new modes of transportation, it changes the way we manage, power, and move economic life. It changes temporal-spatial orientation. It changes our habitats. It allows us to integrate into larger units. It actually even changes consciousness and governance.

Aggregate efficiency is the ratio of the potential work versus the actual useful work you embed in goods or services. Nature has the same economic conditions that we have in our human economy. Let me give you an example: If a lion chases down an antelope in the wild and kills it, about 10-20% of the total energy that is in that antelope gets embedded into the lion. The rest is energy lost in the conversion. That is the aggregate efficiency.

The 2nd Industrial Revolution in 1905 in the USA had 3% aggregate efficiency. At every conversion of nature's resources through the value chain, we lost about 97%; it did not get into the product or service. By 1990, the USA got up to about 14% aggregate efficiency. That was our ceiling; nothing has changed since then.

If your businesses are still plugged into a 3rd Industrial Revolution Infrastructure, you can't go above the ceiling of 20% aggregate efficiency anywhere in the world.

The productivity paradox

In the 1980s, Robert Solow wrote that the aggregate efficiency was growing at the slowest rate for decades - even slower than during the Great Depression. Technology seemed to be booming but productivity was almost stagnant. Economists called it the "productivity paradox."

To understand what was going on, we rewind 100 years. Another remarkable new technology was proving disappointing: electricity. Some corporations were investing in electric generators and motors, and installing them in the workplace. Yet the expected surge in productivity did not come.

The 4th Industrial Revolution currently has 20% aggregate efficiency and will probably end up at 25-30% by 2025. This is promising, but we still have a long way to go.

Why is this important? *Work is when people sacrifice the present for the future.*

A new generation of economists who happen to study physics have gone back and looked at the industrial record and they added a third factor to productivity: **Better machines, better workers, and aggregate efficiency.**

Yes, it is so obvious. The ratio of potential to work less and be more efficient accounts for much of the rest of productivity.

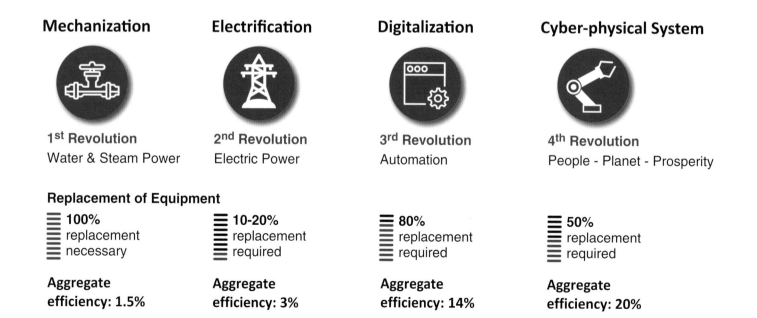

Mechanization	Electrification	Digitalization	Cyber-physical System
1st Revolution	**2nd Revolution**	**3rd Revolution**	**4th Revolution**
Water & Steam Power	Electric Power	Automation	People - Planet - Prosperity

Replacement of Equipment

100% replacement necessary	**10-20%** replacement required	**80%** replacement required	**50%** replacement required
Aggregate efficiency: 1.5%	**Aggregate efficiency: 3%**	**Aggregate efficiency: 14%**	**Aggregate efficiency: 20%**

Rethink the Economic Models

What do our economic models of productivity, Gross domestic product (GDP), measurement of growth, and the Monetary System have in common? They all do not reflect reality today and are based on wrong, outgrown economic models that do not mirror our economic reality and future need.

This is crucial to understand why our economic models do not work today. GDP is a monetary measure of the market value of all the final goods and services produced in a specific time period by countries. Our monetary system is not asset-based, but a wild card for a few to print and loan ad libitum.

The Great Economic Shifts

Our current economic model deserves a lot of credit. For it has brought humanity where we are today and has been a strong engine in the great shift over the centuries.

Meanwhile, the model is not built on principles that are adaptable to our changing environment. Today, the economic models of GDP, productivity, growth, and our monetary system have reached a breaking point where they have a negative effect that leads to inequality, poverty, unemployment, inflation, climate change, and the list goes on and on.

Work is when people sacrifice the present for the future.

The Economic (R)evolution Megatrends

1. Digital Economy

The digital economy is an economy that is based on digital computing technologies either web-based for FIAT currency or blockchain-based for cryptocurrency. Blockchain-based digital economies replace current monetary systems and change asset ownership with digital assets management. For example, a non-fungible token (NFT) is a digital asset on a blockchain that represents ownership of virtual or physical items and can be sold or traded.

The question is not *if* to join - but *when* you join as the benefits outweigh the current economic principles of increased trust, security, transparency, traceability, and delivers cost savings with new efficiencies.

2. Circular Economy

A circular economy entails markets that give incentives to reusing products rather than scrapping them and then extracting new resources. In such an economy, all forms of waste, such as clothing, scrap metal, and obsolete electronics are returned to the economy or used more efficiently.

At the center of the circular economy is humanity as part of an ecosystem. It is up to us to find solutions to climate change, biodiversity loss, waste management, and pollution. It calls into question how we manage resources: how we source, produce, and transport products, and what we do with the materials afterward.

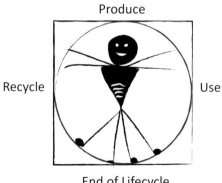

Produce

Recycle

Use

End of Lifecycle

3. Global Power Shift

The global economy is shifting its center of gravity. Sixty-four percent of the world's population lives in Asia, producing over 34% of the world's merchandise.

Since 2015, the economic power of the E7 (China, India, Indonesia, Brazil, Russia, Mexico, and Turkey) matched the G7 (USA, UK, France, Germany, Japan, Canada, and Italy), and by 2030 it is projected to double it.

Why you shouldn't date an economist:

If you get depressed, they lower their interest rate to zero.

The power shift is propelled by four infrastructures, namely,

1. *Trade Infrastructure* such as the Silk Road with ports and corridors within the routes. The engine is the exchange of human and natural resources, money, and products across borders.

2. *Economic infrastructure* that allows the free flow of assets.

3. *Technology advances infrastructure* on cross-disciplines and the application of technology from bio-informative to advance sustainable material from oil products.

4. *Information and communication infrastructure* that catapults our next era of Web 3 where the individual owns the information and not the product. It will unfold society's innovation to collaborate.

4. Infectious Diseases

The Covid-19 pandemic put our economy on hold for 2 years and crippled every aspect of our economy. This is not a new megatrend, but one that will reemerge in various forms.

Today, our society is so globally interconnected that this will not be the last of infectious diseases. Meanwhile, the pandemic has highlighted our weakness in the supply chain, vaccine distribution, science, and the decision of whom and what to trust. Remember, trust is the basis of our society and economy.

Economics Jokes?

There's just not enough demand.

5. Redefine Gross Domestic Product

Let me talk about productivity. This is crucial to understand why our economic model does not work today. Our economists are lamenting. They're asking: Why *has productivity been declining for 20 years? We have all these new killer products coming out of Silicon Valley, Germany, and China. Why is productivity declining?*

The Science of Productivity

I am going to share with you a dirty little secret in economics that economists don't like to talk about. We used to believe that there are two factors that drive productivity in standard economic theory: better machines and better-performing workers. But when Robert Solow won the Nobel Prize for economic growth theory in the mid-1980s, he actually revealed a little secret. He said, "We've got a problem here."

When we trace every single year of the Industrial Revolution, these two factors - better machines and better-performing workers - only account for about 14% of the productivity.

Robert Solow asked the big question: *Where does the other 86% of productivity come from? Don't know. . .?*

Now wouldn't you think economists would know where productivity comes from because that's the basis of the discipline? Here's what they don't say. When the classical economic theory was penned in the late 1700s, the "vogue" was Newton's physics. Newton was the big guy in town. Everybody wanted to use Newton's metaphor so they could be more scientific because he had discovered the laws that run the universe - supposedly.

Economists also fell in line. For example, you know Newton's Law: *For every action, there is an equal and opposite reaction*.

Newton's 3rd law:

For every parental action,
there is a teenage overreaction.

Adam Smith borrowed that metaphor for his invisible hand of supply and demand. *For every action on the supply side, there's an equal and opposite reaction on the demand side*. Newton's law: *A body in motion stays in motion unless disrupted*.

The French economist Jean-Baptiste Say borrowed that same metaphor when he suggested that: *Supply will stimulate demand, which will generate supply, which will stimulate demand - unless disrupted*.

If you go back and look, all our economic theories are based on Newton's metaphors in physics. There's only one problem with this: Newton's physics has absolutely nothing to do with economics. Economics cannot be governed by the same laws that govern the universe, the solar systems, and the biosphere on Earth.

It is time to rethink our economic models in order to fit society and environmental requirements and see humanity as being part of an eco-system instead of the consumer of it. The economic models must meet our social evolutionary stage for equality and accountability.

6. Demonetize

Demonetization is fueled by the uncontrolled issued debt, power shifts, distrust in authority, society age shift, and the breakup of the Petrodollar (Oil linked to USD). *The demonetization of our monetary system, or in other words, the act of stripping a currency unit of its status as legal tender is certain.*

The evolution of the concept of owner, money, privacy, and security changed the fundamental relationship to our economy. The demonetization will manifest itself in different phases, such as:

Disruptive

Change is a constant. Today, change is exponential - either disrupt or be disrupted.

The collision of trends is creating an exponential (Moore's Law) pressure of change and creating opportunities that move the tectonic plates of everything.

Digitalized

Anything can be digitized and everything containing the binary codes of 1s and 0s can be accessed, connected, and automated.

It changes every aspect of our lives - how we live, consume, work, and interact. This is driving the next era of the real end-to-end integration value chain, supply chain, and operational excellence.

Dematerialized

The colliding of the digital, virtual, and physical worlds has dematerialized physical products and ownership.

We live in a digital sharing economy where ownership becomes shared and less relevant. You use digital payment systems, share rights and music online, and meet up virtually.

Democratized

The trust in the key pillars of our society is disappearing. Trust in the government, financial, media, and religious systems are eroding in front of our eyes. More and more people have access to knowledge, equality, opportunities, and freedom, which is creating new borderless economic, social, and value systems.

Demonetized

We live in a society where millions of people create, share, and produce at "zero marginal cost" - Free!

As we connect, technology becomes cheaper and services are automated to the point of being free.

Deceptive

Our economic models of GDP, productivity and growth, and competitiveness are not working. We need a new economic vision for the world.

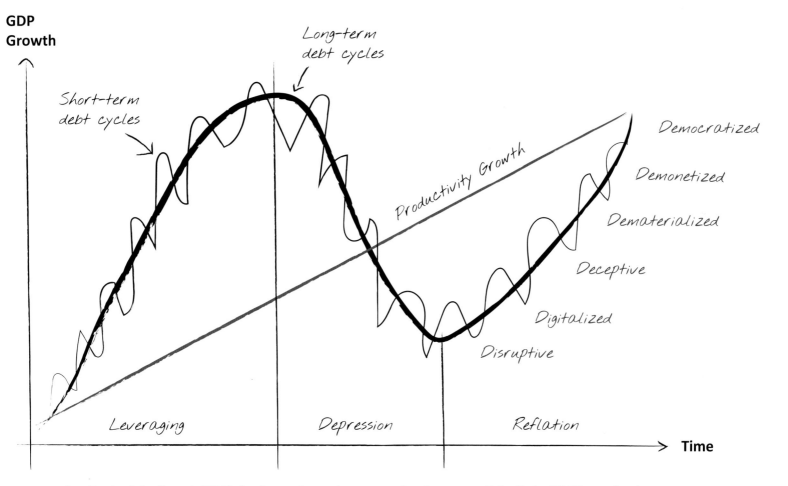

1. **Productivity Growth** (GDP). Our innovation and learning are normally around 1-2% a year.

2. **Short-term Debt Cycle** (5-10 years) such as expansions, recessions, and booms.

3. **Long-term Debt Cycle** (50-75 years), when you start a new type of monetary system and new world order.

4. **Politics.** how people deal with each other and wealth distribution.

127

The Economics of Love

To put it in laypeople's terms, let me compare our current economics system with the Economics of Love system of my wife.

Dead simple

The *Interest of Target* and the *Quantify of Love* fall in love when they meet at the Equilibrium, which is the sweet spot and perfect balance of demand and supply.

However, if the love is in high demand, but in a hard-to-get situation, then love will be withheld. If he or she loses interest, but the other party throws him at her, it will be too much.

It is obvious that our economy today is in a mismatch situation; it is not even a trade-off.

Especially when you consider the increasing debt, inflation rate, lack of interest, trust in authorities, and freedom for alternatives solutions.

It is even more evident once it is realized that the love story is built on wrong principles, so it is doomed to crumble. The demand only meets one part and the supply does not match demand.

We need to fall in love again with our economy, rebuild trust to support our future commitment for generations to come. To achieve this, the current setup must break to ignite a new love story with our economy.

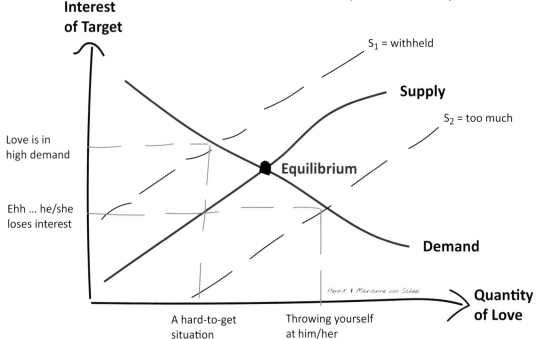

Bio
(R)evolution

Welcome to the Bio (R)evolution, also called the Miniverse, which will be 1,000 times more disruptive than the earlier stage.

The "Miniverse" is due the integration of our dimensional layer of our physical body, virtual reality, and digital experiences that alters every aspect of our human experience. It fundamentally changes the way we live, consume, work, and relate to another.

Reshaping our reality, sensory, dietary, and body - unlike anything humankind has experienced before.

A confluence of the 3rd wave of the technology (r)evolution, namely, Advanced material, Cybersecurity, Bioinformatics, Fusion Science, Nanotechnology, Neurotechnology, and Quantum Technology propel the advances and impact on society, including healthcare, agriculture, energy, and the environment.

It has been in the making for decades, but now it collides into an accelerating development of living software, biomachines, bio cyber-physical systems, promise of cure, future of food, bio fabrication, and how we experience our reality.

Bio (R)evolution is the science fiction of tomorrow's science

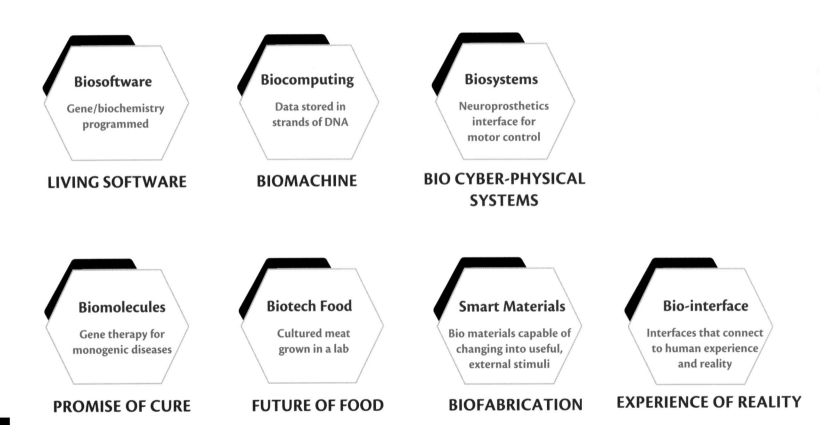

Biosoftware

Gene/biochemistry programmed

LIVING SOFTWARE

Biocomputing

Data stored in strands of DNA

BIOMACHINE

Biosystems

Neuroprosthetics interface for motor control

BIO CYBER-PHYSICAL SYSTEMS

Biomolecules

Gene therapy for monogenic diseases

PROMISE OF CURE

Biotech Food

Cultured meat grown in a lab

FUTURE OF FOOD

Smart Materials

Bio materials capable of changing into useful, external stimuli

BIOFABRICATION

Bio-interface

Interfaces that connect to human experience and reality

EXPERIENCE OF REALITY

Bio (R)evolution influential megatrends

Medical Affairs Megatrends (28)

Regulatory influencers
- Human Rights
- Environment Protection
- Technology and Science
- Labor Market
- Consumer Protection
- Financial Market
- Trade and Investment

Global influencers
- Migration
- New Trade Routes
- Population Growth
- Societal Aging
- Inequality
- Sectoral Shift

Demographical influencers
- Global Power Shift
- Middle Class
- Globalization Reset
- Cyber Instability
- Health and Care Systems

Economic influencers
- Natural Disasters
- Infectious Diseases
- Circular Economy
- Digital Economy
- Demonetization

Environmental influencers
- Water Usage
- Energy Efficiency
- Recycling renewables
- Footprint
- Waste management

Vaccine Megatrends (17)

R&D influencers
- Bio Cyber-physical Systems
- Bioinformatics (Biomolecules, Biosystems, Biomachine Interface, Biocomputing)
- Cybersecurity
- Nanotechnology
- Neurotechnology
- Quantum Technology

Operations influencers
- Metaverse (Augmented Reality)
- Digitalization (IOT)
- Robotics
- 3D Printing
- Artificial Intelligence
- Autonomous Systems
- Smart Automation
- Web 3.0

Workforce influencers
- Labor Market
- Reskilling (Peter Principles)
- Decentralize Organization

Patient Megatrends (11)

- Radical Personalization
- Reality Merge
- Privacy & Security
- Convenience
- Ethical Living
- Sensory Stimulation
- Authenticity
- Empowered Individual
- Value Price Reality
- Wellness
- Individual Immune System Protection

Examples of different manifestations of the emerging trends

Miniverse - Bio Cyber-physical Systems

- Gene therapy—skin aging
- Transplantable organs produced from stem cells
- 3D printed organs
- Embryo editing for medical purposes (e.g., via CRISPR)
- Gene drives to reduce vector-borne diseases
- CAR T-cell therapies for solid tumors
- Liquid biopsy
- DTC genetic testing - personal insights about health and lifestyle
- Health carrier screening
- Non-invasive prenatal testing
- DNA sequencing for forensics
- Synthetic organisms
- Commercial pet cloning
- Personalized meal services based on genetic and microbiome profile
- Biosensors for monitoring of personal health, nutrition, and fitness based on omics data
- Genetic testing for inherited diseases
- Body hacking for sensory augmentation
- Pre-emptive medical interventions based on genome
- "Pharming" humanized animals for medicine
- DNA dating agencies

Biofood Systems

- Marker-assisted breeding
- Genetically engineered crops - faster growth through enhanced photosynthesis
- Plant-based proteins
- Plastics from crops
- Cultured meat
- Biosolar cells and biobatteries
- Genetically engineered animals - faster growth
- Novel materials - biopolymers, e.g., PLA, PET
- Biosequestration of CO_2 Bioremediation for pollution
- Genetic tracing of food origin, safety, and authenticity
- Crop microbiome diagnostics and probiotic treatments
- Novel materials - biopesticides/ biofertilizers, e.g., RNAi pesticides
- Improved existing fermentation processes - food and feed ingredients, e.g., amino acids, organic acids
- Genetic tracing of food origin, safety, and authenticity

Consumer (R)evolution

A new era of consumerism is emerging, where you are not the product, but you are compensated to view products. You are not going on the internet, but your internet is designed by you and how you want to consume in a secure and safe manner.

If this sounds like utopia, you have seen nothing yet.

The 2nd wave of the decentralized web 3.0 technologies will drive an entirely new epoch of internet and consumerism.

The new epoch is propelled by megatrends of radical personalization, reality merge, privacy & security, convenience, ethical living, sensory stimulation, authenticity, empowered individuals, value price reality, and wellness focus.

Web 3.0 redefining privacy and the search of the future

In the 1990s, **Web 1** emerged as the first internet based on 3 main technologies: HTLM (Hypertext Markup Language (HTLM), Uniform Resource Locator (URL), and Hypertext Transfer Protocol (HTTP). The first internet was a one-way information highway and not very user friendly because it was static and users could not interact.

Web 1 was a read-only internet as there were no algorithms that could dynamically serve pages, so the adoption of the first internet was driven by emails and news.

Around 2005, **Web 2** was born, a new paradigm shift on how we used the internet emerged. Driven by technologies like JavaScript, Cascading Style Sheets (CSS), and HTLM 5, interactive content was enabled and allowed users to create and engage.

Web 2 was a read-write internet and evolved with the mobile phone and social media into the social web. Web 2 fundamentally changed the way we interact, discover, learn, consume, and buy.

BUT Web 2 is centralized with a few big companies, like Facebook, Google, and Amazon, owning and controlling the platform. They are the gatekeepers of any information on the internet. As a golden rule, if anything is free on the internet - then you are the product.

Web 3 is a next evolution of the internet that is decentralized and permission based. Web 3 is based on blockchain technologies in their full blossom. The main difference between Web 2 and Web 3 is that there are no centralized databases where you store application status. This is made possible by a back-end architecture that is decentralized, a cryptographic secure web, where you don't have to trust others with your data with an open-source code for everyone to see.

Web 3 is a read-write-own internet, where users create content, control the governance, and can own and earn.

Web 3 main technologies incorporate concepts of cryptographic, decentralization, smart contact, semantic web, trusted and permission-based, connectivity, and ubiquity with time-token and and token-based economics. There are four conceptual paradigms:

Decentralization

Semantic Web

Connectivity
& Ubiquity

Trusted &
Permission-based

The evolution of search drives the Consumer (R)evolution

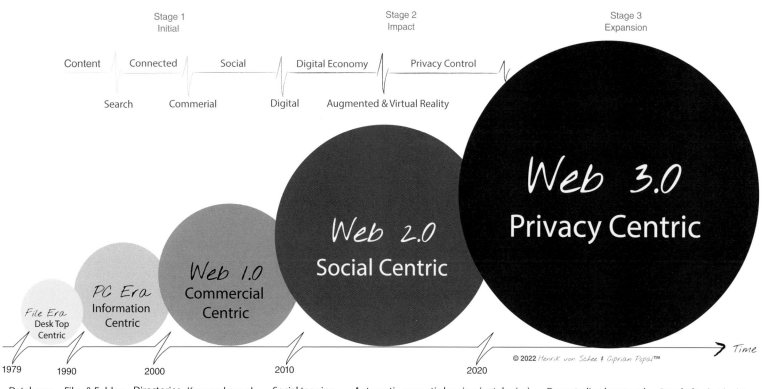

Stage 1 — Initial
Stage 2 — Impact
Stage 3 — Expansion

Content | Connected | Social | Digital Economy | Privacy Control

Search | Commerial | Digital | Augmented & Virtual Reality

File Era — Desk Top Centric
PC Era — Information Centric
Web 1.0 — Commercial Centric
Web 2.0 — Social Centric
Web 3.0 — Privacy Centric

1979 — 1990 — 2000 — 2010 — 2020 — Time

© 2022 Henrik von Schee & Ciprian Popal™

Databases | Files & Folders | Directories | Keyword search | Social tagging | Automatic semantic lagging (ontologies) | Decentralized protocol | Proof of Individuality

File Servers | IM | P2P File Sharing | Search Engines | Pub-Sub Push | Taxonomies | Ontologies | Natural language search | Semantics Weblogs | Pseudocode

Website | Content Portals | Usenet | Enterprise Portals | Marketplaces | Knowledge Mgt | Personal Assistants | Lifelogs | Time Tokens | Harmonic Geo-social Systems

E-mail | RSS | Weblogs | Wiki | Community Portals | Social networks | AI | Semantics Webs | Intelligent Agent | Information Entropy | Avatars

135

Another important characteristic of Web 3 is that it is permission-based. All you need is a Wallet. Web 3 is owned by the user who can participate and earn from it.

In Web 3, privacy will become commoditized based on blockchain technologies like time, token and decentralized finance protocols, which will put privacy, earning, and control back to the user.

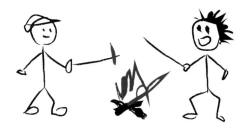

It's all fun, until some loses a wiener.

Web 3 is destined to succeed

Web 3 promises to transform the experience of being online as dramatically as PCs and smartphones did.

Decentralized technologies will trump centralized status quo, whether that be in the case of finance with crypto or the internet with Web 3.

When a community comes together to build something, all benefit from it, and it is destined to succeed. Look at the example of cryptocurrency from a cyberpunk pipe dream 13 years ago to a Wall Street wet dream this year.

While Web 2 has transformed the way we view the world, it has also made us slaves to a system that enriches a few. Web 3 is really our best chance to take back control and distribute it among the rest of us. It is our best shot for building a more inclusive internet that respects all who use it.

Yes, there are many challenges that still need to be overcome, and it won't be smooth sailing.

The further I explore the Web 3 ecosystem, the more I am convinced that this installment of the web will be the best one yet.

Web 3.0 enables a future where distributed users and machines are able to interact with data, value, and other counterparties via a substrate of peer-to-peer networks without the need for third parties.

The result is a composable, human-centric, and privacy-preserving computing fabric for the next wave of the web and search engines.

Evolution of the stickwoman

Metaverse depends on the evolution of Web 3.0

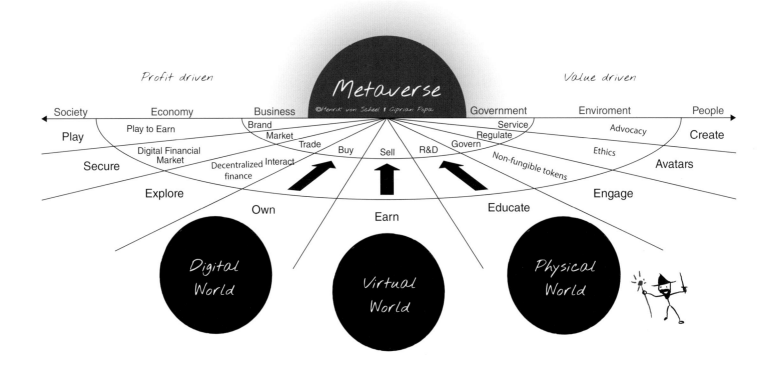

The Metaverse is defined as the merging of our physical, virtual, and digital experiences of reality.

As with most things, it is an evolution, and as I stated to Mark Zuckerberg in a Facebook meeting in 2011: "The Metaverse builds on the Web 3 privacy architecture with no centralized databases." Soon they realized that Web 3 will be the end of the Facebook Business Model, hence the desperate move to highjack the Metaverse storyline to develop metaverse experiences to sell services and hardware.

Let me say it again: The Metaverse will be built based on the Web 3 decentralized databases where data is stored. The users control, own, share, and participate on their own terms.

The truth of the matter is that some of the early games like Minecraft, Second Life, World of Warcraft, and the Sims kick-started the evolution of the Metaverse.

This leads to the happy marriage of online gaming and non-fungible tokens and gives us a clear glimpse of what the most authentic form of Metaverse will evolve toward.

The practical application of Metaverse goes beyond gaming and entertainment to corporate applications like product lifecycles and supply chain management, organizational structure of breaking down the silos, assessment management, to name a few.

For society, it represents new ways of how to earn, own, educate, experience, socialize, engage, create, play, share, and secure assets, to name a few.

For governments, the examples include educate, regulate, safety and new levels to engage, secure, research, and to collect and deliver services.

The Metaverse is inviable and we foresee this to grow at a rapid pace going forward over the next few years. As always, don't fall for the hype. Many will try and fail; few will succeed.

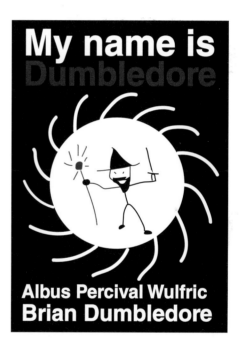

My name is Dumbledore

Albus Percival Wulfric Brian Dumbledore

7th Stage:

Fusion Science (R)evolution

A fusion of science disciplines that will open a epoch of how we see ourselves, reshape the way we make, produce, and consume energy, agriculture, architecture, medicine, and many other disciplines.

This is the most disruptive period as the science fiction becomes reality.

The Fusion (R)evolution is the fruit of the 3rd technology wave of interdisciplinary effort.

It is difficult to describe as nobody knows fully how it will manifest itself.

Today's science fiction is tomorrow's reality

Bioinformatics

Bioinformatics is super essential for the analysis of data in modern biology and medicine. And this global collaboration is going to grow by leaps and bounds in the next years.

Bioinformatics relates to genetics and genomics, and evolves how we monitor and interact with our biological, chemical rhythm that controls our life, emotions, and behavior.

The scientific discipline involves using Information technology to collect, store, analyze, interact, and disseminate biological data and information, such as DNA and amino acid sequences or annotations about those sequences.

The future of our life is a bioinformatics data-driven lifecycle. It goes beyond our comprehension. Some of the first that will unfold are

- *Biocomputing*, using cells and cellular components for computation.

- *Bio Cyber-Physical Systems*, the interconnection of Biomolecules, Biosystems, Biocomputing, and Biomachine.

Cybersecurity

Data has become the new currency on the web, with cyber-criminals targeting it in all its forms. The traditional security model that everything inside an organization's network should be trusted has been eroded.

In an ever-changing cyber landscape, the only certainty is that cybercrime will continue to grow.

So far, the history of cybersecurity has been one of evolution rather than revolution, but it is about to change and change the landscape of information security forever.

The true promise of cybersecurity will evolve once Web 3.0, AI, and blockchain merge with quantum science, putting the information into a unbreachable and unbreakable fortress across cyber-physical systems.

Fusion Science – the future of Energy

Energy is the pulse of our day-to-day life, and how we create and use it is changing rapidly. Going forward, the energy mix rapidly shifts toward power, synfuels, and hydrogen, representing 32% of the global energy mix by 2035 and 50% by 2050. Power consumption is projected to triple by 2050 as electrification and living standards grow.

What the future will look like is not certain, but what is clear is that we are well on our way to a new energy future, better energy storage, energy transmission, renewable energy like solar, wind, hydro, tidal, geothermal, biomass energy, and new sources of energy like seawater, salt, quantum material. Imagine the possibilities. . . .

a world where energy is sustainable and abundant. We need to find new renewable energy sources, and change the way we consume, produce, and distribute energy.

This will be one of the biggest challenges of our generation that we need to invest in. The research will push the frontiers on new and existing energy. It's an exciting time to be alive.

It is more than just a new source of energy; renewable energy, cleaner and greener transport, energy-efficient buildings, and sustainable water consumption are at the heart of clean tech trends. As the costs associated with clean-tech fall, their use becomes more widespread and their disruption is felt across a growing number of industries.

Nanotechnology

Nanotechnology has already done so much to improve products and the quality of life.

Nanotechnology is manufacturing with atoms. The future with nanotechnology is tiny and very small from nanomaterial like graphene, energy storage, electronic devices, 3D printing, nano medicine, nanorobotics, nanomaterial, and fertilizers as well as environmental implications.

Some examples include improved fertilizers to longer-lasting phone batteries and many smaller/smarter electronic devices, nanomaterials, improved packaging with nanomaterials with anti-microbial properties, nano-engineered sheeting

bullet-proofing that is better than Kevlar, or nanoelectronic-engineered transdermal patches. Nanotechnology is already being used everywhere.

In the future, nanotechnology could also enable objects to harvest energy from their environment. New nanomaterials and concepts are currently being developed that show potential for producing energy from movement, light, variations in temperature, glucose, and other sources with high conversion efficiency.

As nanotechnology merges with the evolution of the other 2nd and 3rd wave technology, it will take on an exponential expansion so radical that nanotechnology will be all around us, inside us, and upon us.

This includes but is not limited to inside our bodies; sensors that connect to anything, everywhere; self-healing structures; ultra-dense memories that make big data possible; tackling climate change.

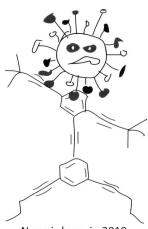

Nano is huge in 2019.
Quote by Covid-19

Neurotechnology

Neuroscience is by far the most exciting branch of science because the brain is the most fascinating object in the universe. Every human brain is different - the brain makes each human unique and defines who he or she is.

As augmented reality, AI, bioinformatics, blockchain, cyber-physical systems, and nanotechnology evolve, they will slingshot neurotechnology into new fields of sensory, smells, and sounds into the frontier of digital and virtual realities that change every human experience.

The power to move things with the mind. One of the most popular branches of neurotech is brain-computer interfaces, which allow control of electronic devices just by thinking. They can be used to control computers, robotic limbs, wheelchairs, drones, or games, to name a few.

The power to revolutionize psychiatry. Combining the power of state-of-the-art brain-recording technology with the promise of commercialization of psychedelic therapy.

The blind future of justice. Can neuroscience and technology shape the future of criminal and civil law to

- Detect lies and memories

- Distinguish levels of culpability

- Decide an appropriate punishment.

Neurotechnology will change our lives. It'll revolutionize healthcare and rehabilitation, psychiatry and psychology, human interaction, law, and education.

However, it'll also create possibilities for mental control of the masses, jeopardize cognitive privacy, or, as in the movie *Minority Report* create a dystopian future in which we are blindly trusting something we don't understand. Overall, the aim is to positively impact the quality of life and well-being of everyone.

Pull yourself together.

Quantum Technology

Quantum physics has taken a quantum leap that will shape our technologies and reality.

It is a game-changer in fields such as cryptography, security, chemistry, nanotechnology, material science, agriculture, and pharmaceuticals, and other technologies once it is more mature.

At the core, quantum technology has a dynamic nature, acting as a useful solution for complex mathematical models, such as encryption methods that have been designed to take centuries to solve even for supercomputers. However, these problems could possibly be solved within minutes with quantum computing.

Even though the modeling of a molecule does not seem likely to happen in the near future with classical computing, quantum computing can make it possible by solving equations that impede advances in extracting an exact model of molecules. This development has the potential to transform biology, chemistry, and material science.

Quantum technology can solve linear problems like simple and complicated patterns as it has nonlinear properties of nature such as complex and chaotic patterns.

Quantum information technologies are based on the properties of quantum physics - i.e. at the atomic and subatomic levels. Consequently, they will be capable of solving problems far beyond the reach of today's classical information technologies. They include:

Quantum computing: using quantum for computation, especially to solve specialized problems that would take traditional computers hundreds or thousands of years. Data is stored as quantum bits, or qubits, particles that can take on multiple combinations of 1 and 0 simultaneously and act as a group - exponentially increasing the information density. Quantum supremacy was achieved when it took a quantum processor just 200 seconds to solve a specific task that would have taken the world's best supercomputer 10,000 years to complete. That being said, quantum computers are not suitable for all kinds of computation.

Quantum communication and security: securing data using the laws of quantum physics is used for quantum key distribution, the exchange of secret symmetric keys used for encryption and authentication. These keys are secure, even against eavesdropping attempts powered by quantum computing.

Quantum cognition: *models* the human brain, language, decision-making, memory, and conceptual reasoning by using quantum computing. Quantum cognition is based on various cognitive phenomena defined by the quantum theory of information in order to describe the process of decision-making using quantum probabilities.

Quantum cryptography: *creates* secure encryption method by taking advantage of quantum mechanical properties. Quantum cryptography makes it impossible to decode a message using classical methods. This is the next development path of blockchain and AI. For example, if anyone tries to copy quantum encoded data, the quantum state is changed while trying to attempt. The beauty of quantum cryptography is that it's unhackable.

Quantum optics: is an area that examines the interaction of photons with particles and atoms, which provides a solution to problems encountered in semiconductor technology and communication. In this way, quantum computing can enable the further development of classical computers.

Quantum neural networks: combine classical artificial neural network models with the advantages of quantum computing in order to develop efficient algorithms. Quantum Neural Networks are algorithms that can be used in modeling networks, memory devices, and automated control systems.

Quantum sensors: technologies that can measure stimuli, such as the flow of electricity or magnetic fields or high-frequency signals. It can be used to detect early-stage multiple sclerosis, monitor and give advanced warning of volcanic activity, and help self-driving vehicles see around corners.

Quantum as a service: is on the horizon. One of the current drawbacks to quantum computing is cost. As adoption and innovation grow, no doubt the cost of equipment will also decline. Today, however, the hardware of quantum computers can be expensive and difficult to maintain for the average business. Enter quantum computing as a service. Accessing quantum capabilities in the cloud may put quantum security and speed within reach of present-day technology.

Quantum internet: Web 3.0 will catch up with the vision of a quantum internet. While small-scale quantum networks are being built, the idea of a widespread quantum internet is limited by how well the photons can maintain their viability as distances grow. We are beginning to see increased research into developing quantum memory and quantum repeaters, which will be necessary for the quantum internet. The memory will store the quantum state of a qubit and swap that state with another photon through teleportation.

Quantum repeaters amplify photons and propel them down the line before they can degrade. Both techniques will be crucial to building the physical infrastructure needed for a quantum internet.

Quantum infrastructure: critical infrastructure grids will be early adopters of quantum communication and security. The surge in cyberattacks is not abating, putting utilities in the potential cross-hairs for a debilitating assault. This would create a security goal of creating a smart grid, smart control centers (refinery or airlines), and smart city using secure two-way communication to protect the infrastructure and customers.

Quantum (R)evolution

Let's not fool ourselves into mistaking the world as we experience it for the world as it really is.

Reality is an evolved illusion of our consciousness, perception, evolution, and the nature of reality.

The impact of the Miniverse and Fusion Science era will enlarge our understanding and experience of reality beyond our wildest dreams.

The Quantum or Reality (R)evolution will impact every aspect of our reality - even more radical than the previous revolutions.

It will alter every aspect of our lives and what it means to be human, changing the way we feel, see, and communicate; reshaping our societal, political, business, and economic structures beyond recognition, creating a new dawn for humanity.

Reality is an evolved illusion

The science behind the quantum leap makes us question the nature of our reality in every aspect.

At its root of the Reality (R)evolution lies making practical sense of the key idea of quantum science that everything is relative. From atoms and molecules that obey rules that go against our everyday physical reality such as quantum logic.

Level of Abstraction

In the past century, we have evolved from simple pattern recognition such as software programming into complicated multiple cause-effect relationships based on binary logic. The binary logic is a set of rules for dealing with propositions that must be either true or false or as Shakespeare would say: "To be or not to be." Today, our software, global supply chain, and everything we have built on is based on a binary system.

Meanwhile, we know today, with the technologies like GPS, smartphones, and the advances in quantum science that the frontier is in quantum logic applying complex and chaotic systems in real-world use.

Quantum logic is a set of rules for reasoning about propositions that rely on the quantum principles that everything is relative, so true can be true, false, and neutral at the same time. Mind-blowing and in a quantum Shakespeare term: "To be **and** not to be."

This has paved the way for the 3rd wave of exponential technologies.

What did one Photon say to another?

I am sick and tired of your interference!

Level of Abstraction

Complex
- Retrospectively coherent
- Octonion complex patterns

Method
- Automata System (control in motion)
- Semantic Intelligence (pattern relationship)
- Quaternion (3-dimensional space) System
- Multi-level Experimentation Scenario planning
- Risk Intelligence
- Deep Machine Learning

Complicated
- Potential knowable
- Oscillating patterns

Method
- Multiple cause-effect relationships
- Automated System thinking (real-time response)
- Artificial Intelligence (autonomous systems)
- Ontology Sentiment Analysis
- Real-time Precious Decisions
- Computational Intelligence
- Machine Learning

Reality

Chaotic
- Incoherent
- Automata patterns

Method
- No perceivable cause-effect
- Automata Octonion Systems
- Swarm Intelligence
- Octonion Intelligence
- Sedenions (16 dimensional) Systems
- Real-time response scenario planning

Simple
- Known
- Rule-based cause-effect

Method
- Simple pattern recognition
- Perceivable, predictable & repeatable
- Resource intensive
- Based on historical data
- System Parameters Settings

Quantum logic ←——————→ Binary logic

Source: Henrik von Scheel

148

The
Gigantic Shifts
that every person should know

The 4IR can lead to a doomsday feeling. Personally, we believe in humanity. It has proven to somehow make the right choices over time.

Fundamentally, we should be optimistic about the future and here is why.

Our biases related to what we hear, what is real, and what are our experiences may be out of focus.

Let's myth bust those biases about what we have accomplished as a human race over the past 100 years. We have undergone some of the biggest economic, technological, environmental, and ideological shifts in history.

If we have made those changes, then we are capable of tackling the biggest problem of our times.

The Great Economic shift that everybody should Know

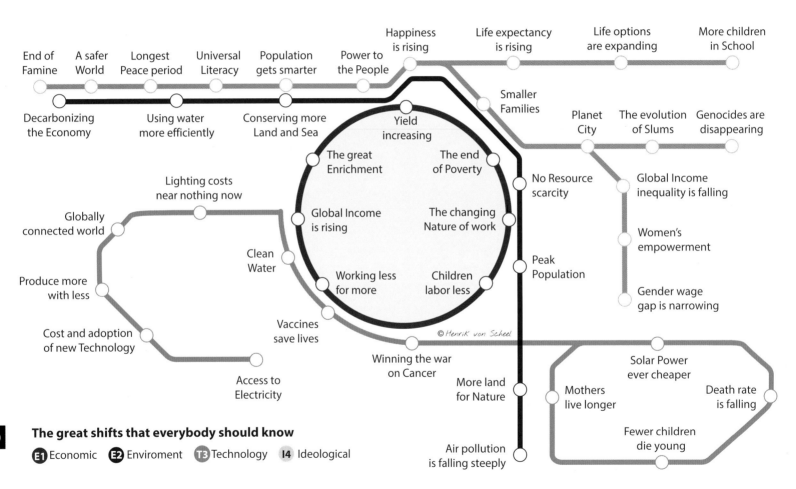

© Henrik von Scheel

The great shifts that everybody should know

- **E1** Economic
- **E2** Enviroment
- **T3** Technology
- **I4** Ideological

The great Enrichment

Since 1820, the size of the world's economy has grown more than 100 times. The world population grew less than 8 times.[7]

Global Income is rising

Humanity made over 2 times as much progress in 100 years as it did in the previous 1880 years. By 2016, income had risen to $14,574 per person per year. That amounts to 621% since 1900.[8]

Working less for more

The overall number of hours worked has declined in tandem with increasing prosperity. Plainly put, the richer the country, the fewer hours people work. In 1830, the workweek was 70 hours per week; in 2020, it is 37 hours per week.[9]

The changing Nature of work

In 1790, 90% worked in agriculture to less than 2% today. In 2016, over 80% were employed in the service sector.[10]

Yield increasing

Farming grain yield has increased from 1960 to 2020 by 2.5 tons per hectare due to improved hybridization, synthesis of nitrogen fertilizer, and genetic enhancement.[11]

The end of Poverty

The percentage of people living in extreme poverty globally fell to a new low of 10% in 2015.[12]

Children labor less

From 1851, the global child labor decreased from 98% to 9% in 2016.[13]

The great shifts

E1 Economic

Don´t be so negative

The massive Environment changes that mislead you

Conserving more land and sea

Humanity is well on the way toward achieving the goal of setting aside 59 mil. sq. km. of land (17%) and sea (10%) for nature by 2020.[14]

No resource scarcity

Humanity has not yet run out of a single supposedly nonrenewable resource. In fact, resources tend to become more abundant over time relative to the demand for them.[15]

Peak population

Today, global population stands at about 7.7 B. Population numbers are slowing and the peak will be reached at 10 B. and then decline.[16]

Using water more efficiently

Sixty-nine percent of the world's freshwater withdrawals are committed to agriculture; 19%, to the industrial sector; and 12%, to households. Today, 86% of the water that goes down the drains is recycled.[17]

More land for nature

Expanding woodlands suggest that humanity has begun the process of withdrawing from the natural world, which, in turn, will provide greater scope for other species to rebound and thrive. The tree canopy has increase 35% in Europe, 34% in the USA, 15% in China.[18]

Air pollution is falling steeply

Between 1970 and 2018, the OECD country's GDP increased by over 275% and population, transportation, and energy output all grew. During the same period, the total emission of the six air pollutants dropped by 74%.[19]

As a result of local municipal action, emissions of smoke, soot, ozone, and sulfur dioxide have been falling for decades.

Decarbonizing the economy

In the past two centuries, the size of the world's economy has increased more than a hundredfold. Since 1960, the world has decreased 64% of the CO_2 emitted per dollar.

This downward trend in emissions per dollar is largely the result of businesses, constant effort to reduce energy cost.[20]

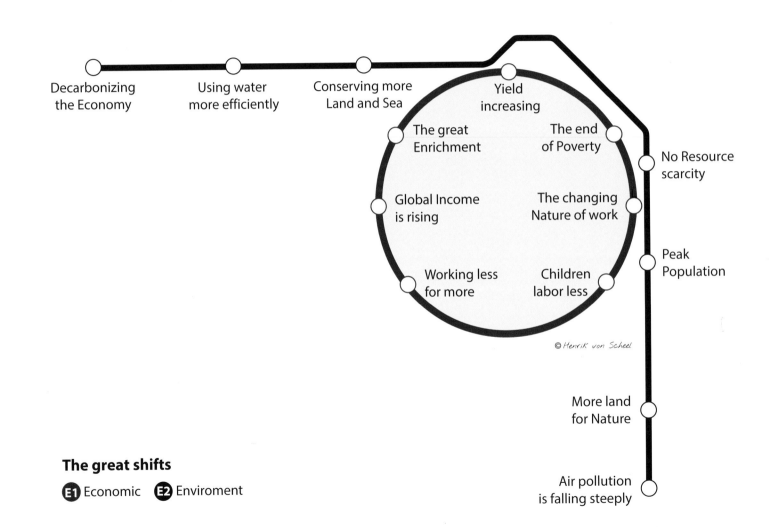

Decarbonizing
the Economy

Using water
more efficiently

Conserving more
Land and Sea

Yield
increasing

The great
Enrichment

The end
of Poverty

No Resource
scarcity

Global Income
is rising

The changing
Nature of work

Working less
for more

Children
labor less

Peak
Population

More land
for Nature

© Henrik von Scheel

Air pollution
is falling steeply

The great shifts

E1 Economic   E2 Enviroment

154

The mammoth Technology leaps that you should be aware of

The death rate is falling

In 1900, nearly 30% of deaths were due to infectious diseases, such as tuberculosis, typhoid, pneumonia, and diphtheria. By 2014, deaths from infectious diseases had fallen to 5%.[21]

Vaccines are saving lives

Vaccines prevented at least 10 million deaths between 2010 and 2015 alone. Many millions more lives were protected from illness.[22]

Globally connected world

Today, all of humanity's knowledge can be accessed via cellphone easily and instantaneously. Ninety percent of the global population has access to mobile internet today. The average global internet user spends almost 7 hours online each day.[23]

Fewer children die young

By 1900, out of 1,000 babies born, about 300 died before reaching their first birthday. By 2017, the mortality rate dropped to 64.8 per 1,000 births. Access to modern medicine is a major factor in falling infant mortality.[24]

Lighting costs near nothing

By 1800, it took 5.4 hours of work to produce 1,000 lumens hours of light. Today, it requires 12 seconds to produce with minimal cost.[25]

Winning the war on Cancer

Globally, about 1 in 6 deaths was caused by cancer. In 1990, 161 people globally died of cancer. In 2006, this had fallen to 134.[26]

Produce more with less

Dematerialization refers to the process of declining consumption of material (300-fold) and energy (100-fold) per unit of gross domestic product. That makes economic sense since spending less on inputs can swell profit margins and make outputs cheaper and therefore more competitive.[27]

Cost and adoption of new Technology

It took 50 years from the invention of the telephone to the time when 50% of US households owned one. In contrast, it only took 12 years for the smartphone.[28]

Clean drinking water

Between 1990 and 2015, access to improved water sources rose from 76% of the world's population to 91% in 2020. That's roughly 1 in 10 people on Earth.[29]

Solar Power ever cheaper

The cost of solar power cells fell from $76 per watt in 1977 to $2.7 per watt in 2020.

Mothers live Longer

After doctors started to disinfect their hands, maternal mortality began to fall from 100 per 1,000 lives per birth to 70 in 2022.

Access to Electricity

At a global level, the percentage of people with access to electricity has been steadily increasing over the last few decades. In 1990, around 71% of the world's population had access; this has increased to 87% in 2016.

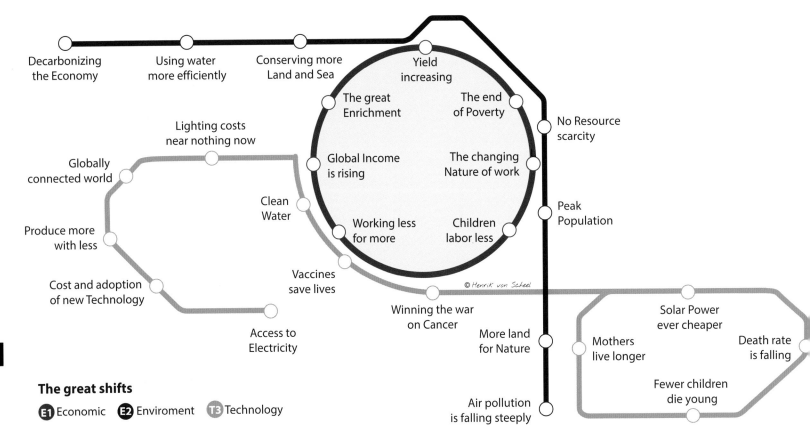

© Henrik von Scheel

The great shifts

E1 Economic   E2 Enviroment   T3 Technology

The grand Ideological advances that will reset your bias

The end of the Famine

Today, famines have disappeared. Agricultural productivity has greatly improved because of more scientific methods of farming, The global average food supply rose to 2,900 calories per day in 2017.[30]

Smaller Families

The world population grew from 1.6 B. in 1900 to 7.7 B. in 2019, not because people are multiplying, but because they are no longer dropping in numbers. Most women gave birth to an average of 8 children throughout human history. Today, the global fertility rate is 1.5 children and will continue to fall.[31]

Life options are expanding

Since the Human Development Index, the developing countries are growing more than 2 times faster than the OECD countries. The gap between the two is shrinking fast.

Power to the People

Forty-nine percent of countries qualified as full-fledged democracies in 2017. Thirty-nine percent are in a premature democracy with democratic and autocratic characteristics.[33]

Genocides are disappearing

The Genocide Convention outlawed genocide in 1948.[34] In 2017, genocide accounted for 7,098 death, a fraction of decades earlier.

The evolution of Slums

In 1990, 47% of world's population lived in slums. That figure fell to 30% by 2014.[35]

Longest period of Peace

Over the past half-century, wars between countries have become rarer, and those that do occur kill fewer people.[36]

Planet City

Historically, 90% of humanity lived in rural areas. Today, 80% live in cities. Cities are the center of innovation, growth, and home to the richest segment of the population.[37]

A Safer World

People today are much more likely to survive natural disasters because of increased wealth and technological progress. The chances of a person dying from a natural disaster have declined 99% since 1920.[38]

More children in School

Rising incomes across the globe have liberated increasing numbers of children from the obligation to work. Since 1970, 89% of children attend primary school. The World Bank calculated that another year of schooling raises an individual's earnings by 9% a year.[39]

Population is getting smarter

Global average IQ test scores have increased by 30% over the past century.[40]

Life expectancy is rising

During the past 200 years, life expectancy has more than doubled, now reaching more than 72 years.[41]

Achieve Universal Literacy
Nearly 90% of the world's population in 1820 was illiterate. Today, 90% can read.

Global Income Inequality is falling
Since 1950, the global income inequality has declined by 26%, primarily due to faster growth in non-Western countries in 2016.

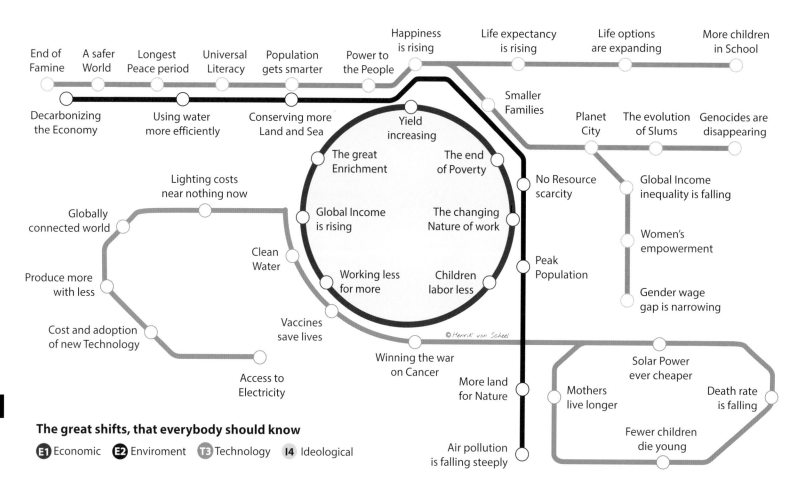

© Henrik von Scheel

The great shifts, that everybody should know

E1 Economic   **E2** Enviroment   **T3** Technology   **I4** Ideological

The best is yet to come

The changes of the 4IR are immersed in a scale and complexity unlike anything humankind has experienced before, and it will change every human experience.

Spoiler Alert

Not to spoil the ending for you, but everything is going to be OK. The authors are unshakable optimists who believe in a bright future and our ability to build it together.

The great shift should give us hope that our society somehow finds the balance and chooses wisely. It gives a glimmer of hope that the best is yet to come.

The pocket philosopher

As a preacher's son, let me bring my pocket philosophy on how to cope with change. When you see change as the only constant available, you start to recognize it as an expression of ongoing life that is a welcome clue to your own purpose and meaning.

All things come and go. There is a fixed lifecycle, and it materializes in a variety of forms - life begins, and then at some point it ends in what we call death. This is the ultimate constant because it never ceases.

The constancy of the cycles of life is an opportunity to return to our roots, where what is and what is to be are located.

The reality is when we change the way we look at things, the things we look at change!

Take time to be an impartial observer of life, particularly when an ending is causing despair, and say to yourself: "this too shall pass." Everything you realize is the cycle of change. In essence, everything works to our advantage. If we remain in an impartial observer state, we have the perfect viewpoint to glimpse the opportunities within change.

Shift Happens

In the words of our strategy hero, Sun Tzu: "In the midst of chaos, there is also opportunity."

In reality, when a shift happens, there are only two choices: adapt or be replaced.

The next chapter will focus on what strategy we can choose to adapt and evolve.

Shift **HAPPENS**

Now, here is a lesson from my 89-year-old mother when both of my sons went through a difficult time in their early 20s and asked her for guidance.

One son got the advice:
"Seek silence and you will find the answer in you."

The other son got the counsel:
"Shit happens, deal with it, and move on."

Same goes for when disruption happens.

Strategic *Choices*

Stop making plans - start making decisions

Chapter Five

In a nutshell, strategy is about making three choices:

What not to do, where to be different, and what to focus on. In that order.

Henrik von Scheel
Leading Authority on Strategy

Anticipate trends to avoid being blindsided

Disruption is not a new phenomenon. It is, more explicitly, the accelerating frequency of disruption that poses a new challenge for organizations.

To understand disruption, it is important to begin by understanding our own bias in seeing it. What we cannot see, we cannot respond to. Finding and understanding disruption is a core approach to defining an organization's strategic choices and demonstrating how capturing these opportunities enhances shareholder value. And because organizational strategy development is an inherently people-driven process, it is subject to bias and misinterpretation.[1] Recognizing the forces that drive disruptive change, including where, when, and how it might happen, combined with what forces drive industry change and organizational transformation, goes hand in hand with this new way of thinking.

To make the most of opportunities, organizational leaders and their teams must know how to transform at speed and make the right strategic choices along the journey.

Of particular interest in this book is how organizations can derive exponential value when an inflection point is reached.

An organization can deliver extraordinary value from finding and exploiting this nonlinear change and evolution in the market. Technology plays an important role in identifying these unique opportunities.

Anticipating trends is a rare, but much-needed, discipline. Get a solid understanding of your operation and anticipate trends on current and future business models. Lao Tzu highlighted that "those who have knowledge do not predict. Those who predict do not have knowledge."

However, the inflection point is often only reached when other factors combine to bring this to fruition - for example, the cost base of the technology, the application of this technology to new markets, regulatory change, and consumer behavior changes.

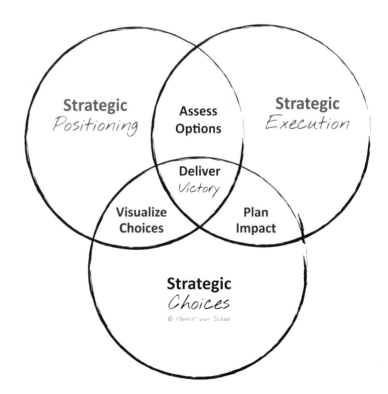

A business model is the most _powerful_ way to describe how an organization creates, delivers, and _captures_ value.

It is the _preeminent_ Executive's _design and decision toolbox_ for strategic choices to manage the present and create the future of an organization.

Whatever it is,
It was Aliens

Henrik von Scheel
Ancient Alien Expert

Why a Business Model Matters

Business models are the most critical design and decision tools that allow Executives to manage the present and shape the future of an organization within:

- *Understand the business to take design decisions*: Analyzes the business functions as a set of discrete specialist areas, groups, and tasks that can be organized and viewed in a value chain, accountability, or service flow view.

- Recognized disruptive forces to manage the present (operating, cost, and performance models) and act on emerging drivers to create the future (service, value, and revenue models) to define competitiveness, and rethink customer value and services.

- *Identify how the organization performs:* Analyzes and identifies how the functional areas and groups perform on their task.

- Functional areas, groups, and tasks are essential ways to analyze the organizational capabilities and resources of an organization.

- *Value Creation:* Analyzes and identifies how the functional areas, groups, and the tasks create value for the organization.

- *Service Model:* Analyzes and identifies the business workflow of how the functional areas, groups, and tasks service each. The reorganization and redeployment of services in different ways can optimize the whole flow in order to create a new service flow.

- *Organizational premise:* The potential to organize the business according to the functional areas, groups, and tasks to release the functional silo bottlenecks and thereby the duplicative work that is done in many places.

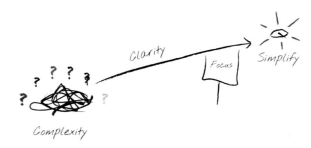

Simplicity is complexity resolved.
Constantin Brancusi
Romanian sculptor

Business Model 4.0 - the strategy choices decision board

166

BUSINESS VIEW	General Administration	Human Resource	Technology	Operations Support	Business Development	Operations	Channel	Customer Relationship
Strategic — Mission, Vision, Strategy, Business Planning, Forecast, Budget, Value & Performance Mgt.	Strategic Planning	Organizational Planning	IT Planning	Operations Support Planning	R&D Planning	Operations Planning	Distribution Planning	Segmentation Planning
	Legal & Regulatory Affairs	Recruitment	Deployment	Assets	Product Design	Component Manufacture	Scheduling	Selling
Tactical — Administration, Control & Monitoring, Evaluation & Reports, Operational Plan, Policies Rules & Guidelines, Measurements, Audits	Information Analysis	Administration	IT Business Management	Quality	Research	Operations Procurement	Order Fulfillment	Market Analysis
	Project Management	Benefits	Risk & Compliance	Environment & Health	Production Setup	Product Manufacture	Transportation	Channels
	Finance	Performance Evaluation	Information Management	Sourcing & Procurement	Intellectual Property	Inbound Inventory	Import & Export	Brand Management
Operational — Operational Administration, Operational Reporting, Operational Oversight, Executing, Delivery, Processing, Operational Measurements	Facility Management	Compensation	Service Delivery	Safety & Security	Product Deployment	Product Assembly	Distribution	Customer Account
	Accounting	Education	Development	Equipment & Plant	Content	Refining	Finished Goods Inventory	Servicing
	Travel Management	Payroll	Support & Relationship	Data Management	Product Maintenance	Packaging	Costing	Customer Acquisition

Tiers

Functional Areas — Clear categorization of **where** functional areas are located functional groups.

Functional Groups — Categorize functional groups' focus of subgroups and **where relate**.

Brand Management: Brand Strategy, Brand Development, Brand Tracking, Brand Awareness, Marketing & Advertisement, Sponsorship & Events

Functional Groups — Categorize **what** happens in subgroups and **who** is responsible for it.

1 Operating Model
★I = Integration Opportunity; ① = Maturity Level; # = People Distribution; ✔ = Governance, Policies & Guidelines; = = Standardization Opportunity

2 Performance Model
★P = Performance Opportunity; % = Measurements; ○ = Control & Monitoring; R = Reporting Flow; BPM = Effectiveness & Efficiency

3 Cost Model
★C = Cost Opportunity; TCO = TCO Opportunity; ☐ = Cost Flow; $ = Evaluation & Audits; ⊗ = Cockpits, Dashboards & Scorecards

4 Value Model
V = Value Opportunity; ▷ = Value Creation; ROI = ROI Opportunity; ▷ = Value Governance; ▷ = Value Identification

5 Service Model
S = Service Flow; ⊗ = Complex Service; ▯ = Simple Service; ✿ = Unique Service; ◉ = Main/Supporting Service

6 Revenue Model
★R = Revenue Opportunity; CD = Core Differentiating Competency; R = Revenue Flow; CC = Core Competitive Competency; Q = Channel

Decision Board — Used to determine opportunities, core differentiating competencies, core competitive competencies, maturity level, head counts, and other factors that make better informed decisions.

HEAT MAP: Projects — Example: ■ = Project 1, ■ = Project 2, ▨ = Project 3

Heat Map: Roles Involved — Example: 1 = Project Manager, 2 = Business Analyst, 3 = Solution Architect, 4 = Business Process

Heat Map: Flows — Example: A = Risk-assessed, B = Revenue flow, C = Cost flow

Heat Map: Critical Systems — Example: 1 = SAP, 2 = Siebel, 3 = Salesforce

Heat Map Legend — In order to represent a business in a business model, shapes, symbols, connections, flows, and other components are used to represent the business. It determines opportunities, core differentiating competencies, core competitive competencies, maturity level, head counts, and other factors that make better informed decisions.

Simplify complexity by connecting the dots

An organization's ability to differentiate, compete, and perform is rooted in its core differentiating, core competitive, and non-core competencies.

The strategist and philosopher Sun Tzu wrote in *The Art of War:* "Strategy without tactics is the slowest route to victory. Tactics without strategy are the noise before defeat." In order to work and use business models, we will introduce three levels of business models that represent how organizations operate with a different variety of detail and choices. These choices are found in the decision board.

A business model represents an accountability view with functional areas and groups classified into strategic, tactical, and operational tiers.

The power of classification and categorization that unfolds in it provides the nervous system in the organization to link strategy planning with strategy execution of the enterprise into strategic, tactical, and operational aspects, which becomes a tool to understand the enterprise as a whole.

Tiers of a Business Model

Used to assemble the competencies by order according to the three tiers.

The strategic tier deals with budgeting, strategy, and forecasting.

The tactical tier deals with control, management, and governance.

The operational tier deals with general administration and daily operations.

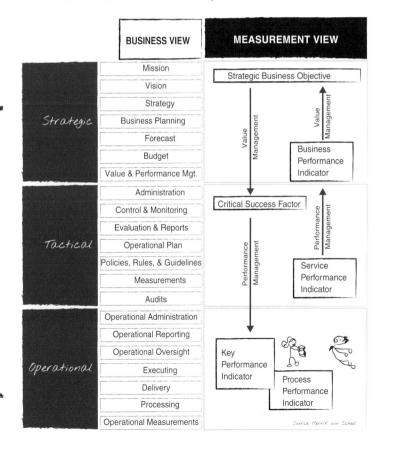

Source: Henrik von Scheel

Definition: The deliverable or output of a function and activity.

Why work with services:
Because you can optimize what is being delivered (between different parties).

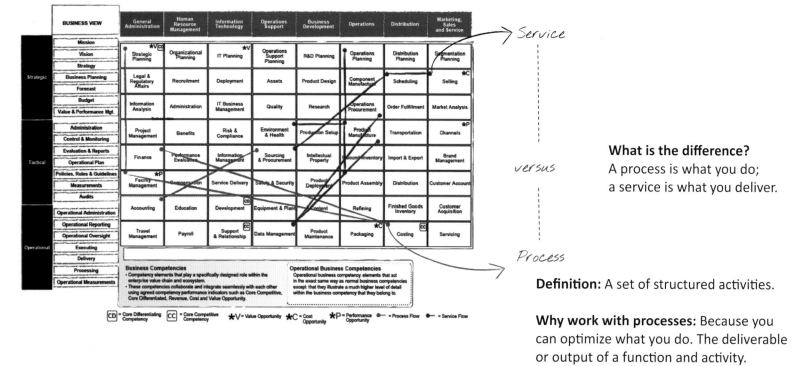

Service

versus

Process

What is the difference?
A process is what you do;
a service is what you deliver.

Definition: A set of structured activities.

Why work with processes: Because you can optimize what you do. The deliverable or output of a function and activity.

Business Model
decision cockpit

Strategy is about making choices.

Strategy is about
where to play, how to win.

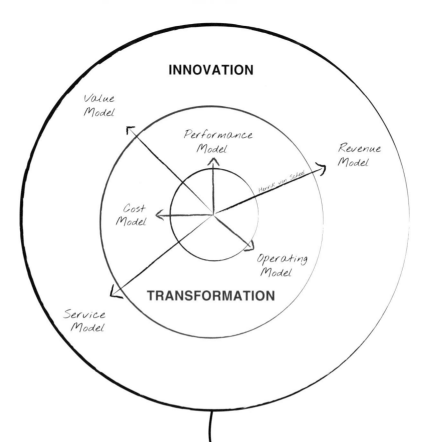

Transformation focus:

- Transformation happens across the operating model, cost model, and performance model.

- You apply transformation principles in the **problem chain** (Where and When), e.g., measurement, performance expectations, and performance drivers.

Innovation focus:

- Innovation occurs across the value model, service model, and revenue model.

- You apply innovation principles in the **goal chain** (Whither & Why), e.g., value driver, value expectations, and scorecards.

Don´t let the fear of falling
keep you from climbing up.

Operating Model

An organization's operating model describes how an organization operates across business competencies, functions, process, organization, and technology domains in order to deliver the performance and value defined by the organization.

The purpose of an operating model is to make better-informed business decisions and to improve organization performance and profitability.

Characteristics found in an operating model:

- Operating model strategy.

- Development and transformation of operating model to ensure continued consistency of core competitive and core-differentiating competencies.

- Process integration and standardization for a focused, responsive, flexible, and robust operating model.

- The owner's responsibilities for standardizing and integrating the operating model of his organization.

- Roles involved in the operating model concept and developments.

- Business flow that needs to be standardized, changed, or optimized to support the new operating model concept.

- Media that will be involved in operating model development and delivery.

- Channels that are needed in the wished operating model.

- Technology adoption, e.g., applications, data, platform, and infrastructure, for the level of enterprise operating model integration, standardization, optimization, and renewal.

- Operating Model measurements in terms of critical success factors and key performance indicators that are linked to the business strategy.

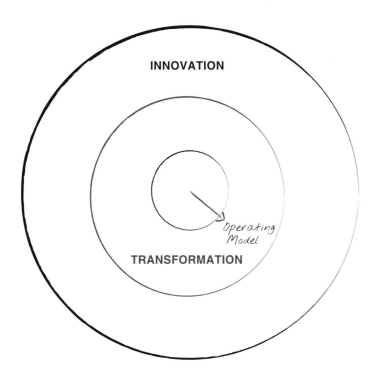

- Compliance with business regulations and laws.

- Services delivered internally as well as externally to partners, suppliers, and customers around the new or transformed operating model initiative.

- Objects in terms of products, application, or data that need to be standardized and/or integrated.

- Rules in terms of standards, guidelines, and policies to ensure the right monitoring, control, and optimization initiatives.

Examples: Levi Strauss set up its first retail store in India in 1995 while partnering with multiple local manufacturers, and even today the bulk of the company's denim products in India are manufactured by Arvind Mills, now the world's third-largest denim manufacturer and supplier to other marque apparel brands.

An organization's operating model describes how an organization operates across business competencies, functions, process, organization, and technology domains in order to deliver the performance and value defined by the organization.

The decision cockpit includes:

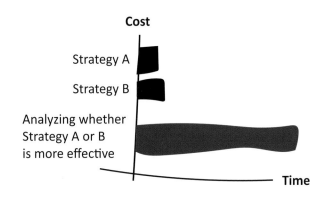

The reason I am so inefficient

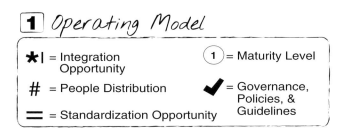

Performance Model

A performance model defines an organization's ability to perform effectively and efficiency to determine success or alignment with value objectives and goals.

As a part of any performance model is the definition of *performance goal*, *indicators*, and *measures*, e.g., Business Process Improvement (BPI), Key Performance Indicators (KPIs), and Process Performance Indicators (PPIs).

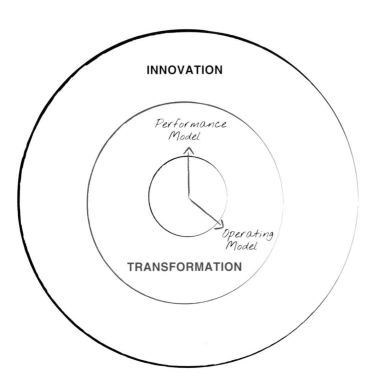

This includes personalized key performance indicators (KPIs) and benchmarks that drive the financial and operational success of the company as well.

The performance model is used with strategy development and execution to help the organization focus on key activities such as managing processes, employee workflows, and production. Some of the most important components are:

- Plan for transformation toward operational excellence.

- Identify the performance drivers.

- Optimize of operational efficiency.

- Invest in new and innovative ways of product development.

- Sett measures for production and process governance.

I had followers before Twitter.

Characteristics found in a performance model:

- Performance strategy.

- Business competencies that need to perform in order to create the right results.

- Process and activity optimization or innovation to create the needed performance.

- Performance owner's responsibilities for performance developments.

- Roles involved in the performance concept and developments.

- Business flow that needs to be changed or optimized to support the new performance model.

- Media that will be involved in the performance development and delivery.

- Channels that are needed in the wished performance model.

- Performance increased by technology adoption and thereby the level of performance automation through data, applications, platform, and infrastructure.

- Performance measurements in terms of business performance indicators, key performance indicators, and process performance indicators.

Examples: Toyota developed the Kaizen performance model. Kaizen's strategy calls for a never-ending effort of improvement involving everyone in the organization - managers and workers alike.

The decision cockpit includes:

2 Performance Model

★P = Performance Opportunity	% = Measurements
🔍 = Control & Monitoring	R = Reporting Flow
BPM = Effectiveness & Efficiency	

Abduct me, prove me, show me Uranus.
Just get me back before 8 for my performance review.

Cost Model

The cost model describes all costs incurred to operate in an organization supporting the service model and revenue model.

The cost model is used with strategy development and execution to manage costs, identify potential cost-cutting opportunities to lower production costs, and conserve or eliminate specific sets of resources around each strategy.

The key components are:

- Investigate opportunities for potentially lowering overall production costs.

- Identify and manage critical cost flows.

- Set up and conduct timely internal evaluation.

Characteristics found in a cost model:

- Cost-cutting strategy.

- Cost construct (main, supporting, and management cost).

- Identification of no non-core competencies for the potential of standardization, integration, and or outsourcing.

- Process and activity optimization or standardization to cut costs.

- Cost owner's responsibilities for cost-cutting.

- Capture cost drivers, not just cost elements.

- Cost reduction to impact the total cost of ownership.

- Cost-benefit analyses' supporting role.

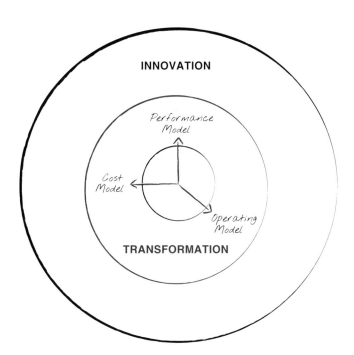

- Roles involved in the service concept and developments.

- Business flow that needs to be changed or optimized to reduce cost.

- Media that will be involved in the cost reduction.

- Channels that are impacted by the cost reduction potential.

- Technology adoption is the level of standardization and integration within the automation through applications, data, platform, and infrastructure.

- Cost measurements in terms of critical success factors and key performance indicators.

Money often costs too much.

Examples: Over the years, the McDonald's Corporation has worked with suppliers to develop a sophisticated model to optimize operating costs.

Nokia overcame high network infrastructure costs through innovative "village work" solutions that allowed it to offer affordable phone service to rural consumers in India.

The decision cockpit includes:

3 *Cost Model*

★C = Cost Opportunity   ⟁TC = TCO Opportunity

C = Cost Flow $ = Evaluation & Audits

X = Cockpits, Dashboards & Scorecards

Value Model

The value model describes the different value perspectives in an organization. A value model considers the aspects of external and internal value drivers, business strategy (SBO), business objectives (CSF, plan, forecast, budget), value expectation, value proposition, and value management.

It is the strategic tool to redefine what are core competitive competencies and what are non-core competencies, and thereby what can and cannot create value.

The value model is an important tool to be used with strategy development and execution. Some of the components are:

- Identifying and understanding potential value opportunities.

- Pinpointing the value drivers.

- Setting roles for identifying value concepts to enable profit gain, growth, production efficiency, etc.

- Mapping the value offerings scattered in the operating model.

- Adding measures and reporting for continuous value governance.

Characteristics found in a value model:

- Value management strategy.

- Core competitive and non-core competencies.

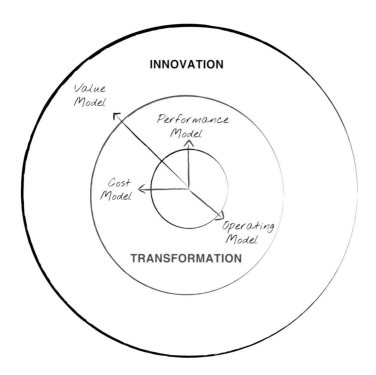

- Process and activity optimization or innovation to support service concepts and development.

- Value owner's responsibilities for value creation.

- Roles involved in the value identification, value concept, and developments.

- Business flow that needs to be changed, optimized, or developed to support a new value model.

- Media that will be involved in the value development and delivery.

- Channels that are needed in the desired value model.

- Value realization through technology adoption, and thereby the level of automation through applications, data, platform, and infrastructure.

- Value measurements in terms of critical success factors and key performance indicators to value planning, identification, creation, realization, and governance.

Examples: Over the past years, Apple has developed a sophisticated value model from R&D to development partners to retail stores to put the customer experience of value in the center by combining product, software, and service. Its revenue, profit, and stock price increases reflect the success of those transformation and innovation initiatives

The decision cockpit includes:

4 *Value Model*

V = Value Opportunity	▷c = Value Creation
ROI = ROI Opportunity	▷G = Value Governance
▷ = Value Identification	

RESPECT
MY AUTHORITY

Service Model

A service model defines an organization's core differentiating, main, and supporting services delivered.

Similar to the value model, the service model is an important component of strategy development and execution.

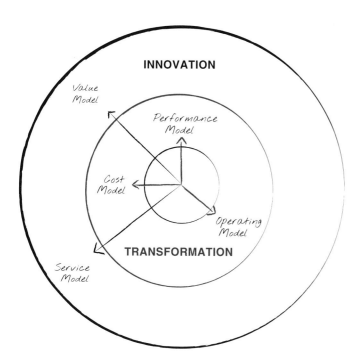

Some of the components that we focus on are:

- Identify and execute opportunities for service integration and standardization.

- Maintain continuous support of customer-centric services.

- Monitor and govern service platform channels.

- Identify and innovate the simple, complex, and unique services of your organization.

Characteristic found in a Service Model:

- Services strategy.

- Service objects (e.g., service product).

- Service construct (main, supporting, and management services).

- Development of core competencies and core differentiating services.

- Service owner's responsibilities for service developments.

- Roles involved in the service concept and developments.

- Business flow that needs to be changed or optimized to support the new service model (service provider and service consumer).

- Media that will be involved in the service development and delivery.

- Service channels that are needed in the wished service model.

- Service technology adoption is the level of service automation through applications, data, platforms, and infrastructure.

- Service Level Agreements with partners.

- Service measurements in terms of critical success factors and key performance indicators.

Examples: Apple Inc. transformed the music industry through a new way of connecting hardware with software to download music by using a combination of iPods/iTunes products and services.

Virgin transformed from one value chain to another, leveraging its brand across industries, including airline, media, and telecom.

The decision cockpit includes:

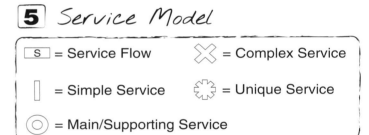

Roll Model

Revenue Model

A revenue model defines how an organization makes money by changing the value proposition (product/ service/value mix) - and what needs to be done to optimize the pricing model.

When it comes to growth or shareholder value (profit) strategy development and execution, a revenue model become the lever.

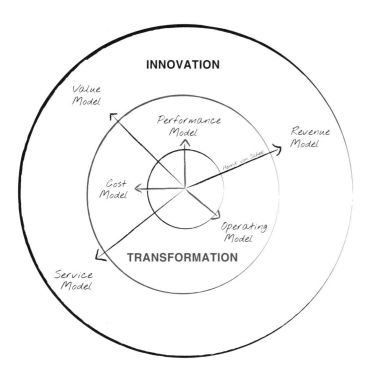

The revenue model is a useful instrument to use to document how and where the revenue flows are generated across organizational boundaries. Important components of the revenue model include, but are not limited to:

- Identify the core competencies that allow the organization to differentiate in the market.

- Identify the core competencies that allow the organization to compete in the market.

- Document revenue flows across the organization.

- Revise or evaluate the service channels of the organization.

Characteristics found in a revenue model:

- Revenue strategy.

- Development of core competencies and core differentiating competencies.

- Owners and responsibilities for optimization and development of the pricing model, value proposition, and cost-cutting.

- Pricing models and value trade-off.

- Process integration and standardization to support the wanted revenue model developments.

- Roles involved in the concept and developments.

- Business flow that needs to be changed or optimized to support the new revenue model concept.

- Media that will be involved in the revenue model development and delivery.

- Channels that are needed in the wished revenue model.

- Technology adoption for the level of automation development through applications, data, platform, and infrastructure to cut cost.

- Revenue model measurements, in terms of critical success factors and KPIs.

- Revenue model compliance with regulations and laws.

- Objects in terms of products and offerings that need to be developed for a new value trade-off.

- Rules in terms of standards, guidelines, and policies around the pricing model.

Examples: Gillette innovated the pricing model by giving away razors and making money on the blades. Netflix shifted its revenue model from product/rental-based to a subscription-based annuity model.

The decision cockpit includes:

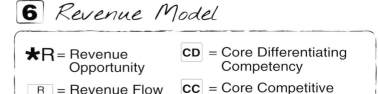

Nobody ever changed the world
by doing what everyone else was doing.

Key activities to achieve a Strategic Positioning

Prior to moving toward making strategic choices, the following essential activities are recommended. The more effort you put into it, the more design choices you have.

Most organizations end up with 2-5 value chains on how the business operates called "running the business" with cost, revenue, service flow with maturity, bottleneck, headcount distribution . . . and 10-15 value chains on how to "develop the business" with various scenarios to meet the internal and external opportunities and challenges.

The key activities to achieve _strategic positioning_ are

1. **Populate Value Chain 4.0**
   Map how you operate to deliver value.

2. **Chart cost structure, revenue steam**
   Understand performance and value requirements.

3. **Capture the forces and drivers**
   Detect external and internal forces and drivers that affect and influence the operation.

4. **Understand challenges**
   Understand gaps, issues, challenges, and maturity.

5. **Define opportunities**
   Spot revenue, service, value, operations, cost, and performance changes, needs, and opportunities.

You can't scare me,
I teach kindergarten.

Don't live by your own rules,
but in harmony with nature.

Epictetus

Strategic Choice:

What not to do?

A truth I was told by my Buddhist master that sums it up

There are 3 types of People

People who believe to see

People who believe when they see

People who see, but don't believe

Yige Dai

Simple strategies to manage uncertainty and the unexpected

Most problems arise because they are not properly thought through.

If you could look into a crystal ball and predict everything that would happen in the future with perfect detail, you'd be more than just a successful project manager. Unfortunately, none of us have that ability. Instead, we plan for and adapt to all the unknown circumstances life throws at us as best as we can.

Fortunately, it is possible to predict potential scenarios based on our experience as project managers and human beings. Nevertheless, **problems** can **arise** in simple contexts. First, **issues** may be incorrectly classified within this domain **because they** have been oversimplified.

Today, many are surprised when previously successful decisions or approaches fail in new situations, but different contexts call for different kinds of responses. Before addressing a situation, we need to recognize which context governs it - and tailor our actions accordingly.

Effective strategy that considers likely worst-case scenarios as a way to predict potential unknowns. One of the most effective methods for improving outcomes is performing a so-called premortem - imagining in advance that an initiative has failed and working to understand the reasons why.

This corrects against the natural bias we have to assume our project will be a raging success, and forces us to become the devil's advocate: If we have to assume it's a failure, what might account for that?" While not all unknowns will lead to project failure, it is important to consider how you will respond, adapt, and execute in the face of predictable and unpredictable worst-case scenarios to avoid failure.

Epiphanius of Salamis (310 AD) outlines in the limits of Heresiology of the Known Knowns and Known Unknowns, which helps us to sort our decision-making into four contexts:

Known knowns *(predictable):* *Simple* contexts are characterized by stability and cause-and-effect relationships that are clear to everyone. *Things you're aware of and understand (e.g., repeating the same tasks over-and-over at a slow paced corporate job).* Often, the right answer is self-evident. In this realm of "known knowns," you first assess the facts of a situation, that is, "sense" it - then categorize and respond to it.

Known unknowns *(blind spot that you did not see coming):* *Complicated* contexts may contain multiple right answers, and though there is a clear relationship between cause and effect, not everyone can see it. *Things you're aware of but don't understand (e.g., switching from doing business to making art, jumping from public corporation to fast-growing venture).* Here, one should sense, analyse, and respond.

***Unknown knowns** (Uncertainty):* In a *complex* context, right answers can't be ferreted out at all; rather, instructive patterns emerge if the leader conducts experiments that can safely fail. *Things you're not aware of but understand (e.g., encountering gender bias during the hiring process).* This is the realm of "unknown knowns." Here, one should need to probe first, then sense, and then respond.

***Unknown unknowns** (Unexpected):* In a *chaotic* context, searching for right answers is pointless. The relationships between cause and effect are impossible to determine because they shift constantly and no manageable patterns exist. This is the realm of "unknown unknowns," where much of contemporary business operates. These unknowables, like the events of September 11, 2001, fall into this category. In this domain, you must first act to establish order, sense where stability is present, and then work to transform the situation from chaos to complexity.

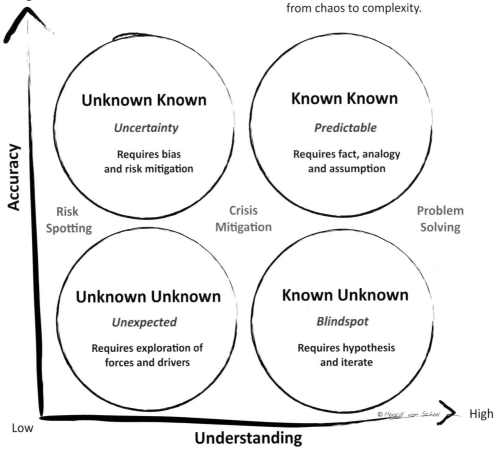

Outsmart your own biases

When making decisions, we all rely too heavily on intuition and use flawed reasoning sometimes. But it's possible to fight these pernicious sources of bias by learning to spot them and using the techniques

Most organizations operate from a distinct paradigm. This set of assumptions about how the world works prevents them from adapting, meanwhile the world around them changes.

Today, 80% of decisions are based on market research. It serves mainly to reinforce existing conclusions, not to test or develop new possibilities.

Organizations' competitive advantage will come from historically underdeveloped competencies or assets: the ability to capture and apply insights from diverse fields, not just from the business.

While working with Steve Jobs, I came up with the "can, want, should do" concept to outsmart one's own biases. *The idea was to solve the toughest problems by changing the way you look at them, and the problem you look at changes.*

The "can, want, should do" is a powerful diagnostic decision-making tool based on how an organization creates, delivers, and captures value.

The "can, want, should do" concept is a structured sequence to outmode your own biases to get clarity on what not to do, what to do less of, and what to focus on – in that order!

It is a powerful tool that aims to align the team to self-diagnose, what it can, want, and should do to improve the decision-making process.

A number of the iterative interrogative technique are used to explore the cause-and-effect relationships underlying a particular problem and opportunities.

190

The primary goal of the technique is to determine the root cause of a defective pain point and desired need.

It is a key secret to understand the current business state, what has been done from an internal view, and what are the options.

Creating a guided path helps capture what not to do; what to do less of; where, how, and with what to differentiate; what to do more of; where to innovate and when to transform. A simple way to broaden your thinking and make better decisions.

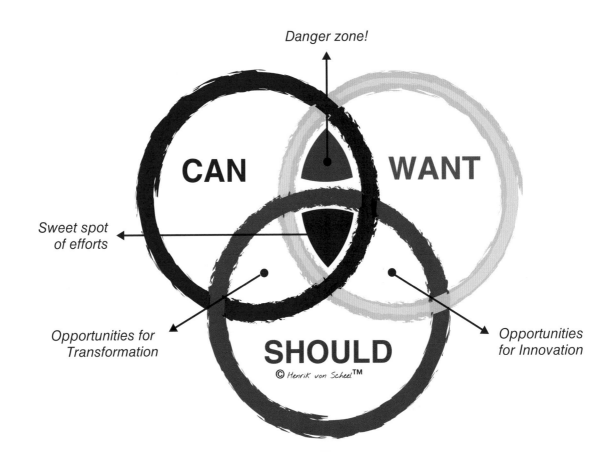

Danger zone!

CAN

WANT

Sweet spot of efforts

Opportunities for Transformation

SHOULD

© Henrik von Scheel™

Opportunities for Innovation

What you CAN DO

The **can do** is based on the organization's capabilities, strengths, and resources and defines its current operations, such as:

- Key resources

- Unique value proposition, i.e., product, service

- Core competencies

- Asset usage, i.e., machines, production, facility

- Customer impact

- Service or process, i.e., time-to-market

- Process, i.e., automation, measurements

- Partnerships

This puts the spotlight on the core the ability of what you can do, which provides a guiding principle of what you have to work from; what the current limits are. It sets a frame for what not to do and what to focus on.

What do you call a statistician with two butts?

Biased

CAN

What you WANT TO DO

What an organization **wants to do,** or the direction the leadership wants to move toward. Most executives take this path directly, which leads to the biggest danger zone or blind spot based on:

- Personal ideas and preferences

- Business concepts

- Relationships

- Ambitions and wants

- Value expectations

- Market research

They want to do identify your core ambition, preferences, and wants. But who is to say they are right? If you do what you want based on what you can, you are no different than a teenager who decides what's for dinner - it will probably be pizza every night. Hence the danger zone is between the CAN and WANT if you do not consider the SHOULD first.

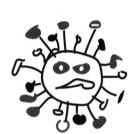

Danger zone!

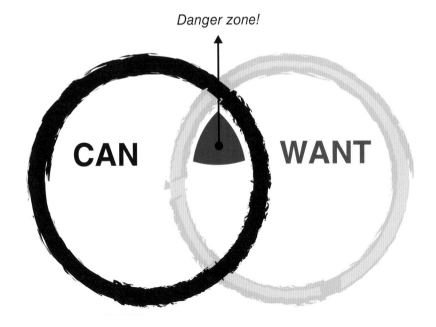

What you SHOULD DO

The **should do** area comprises internal and external forces where organizations need to take action. The space between the CAN and SHOULD indicates the transformation opportunities. What you need to adopt toward with existing capabilities.

Whereas the space between the SHOULD and WANT specifies the innovation opportunities, where to invest and align new capabilities. These should focus on:

- Market changes
- Competitive situation
- Rivals, complementary and potential new entrant
- Customer demands
- Supplier and distribution situation
- Regulation and compliance
- Partnership
- Internal leadership and operational issues

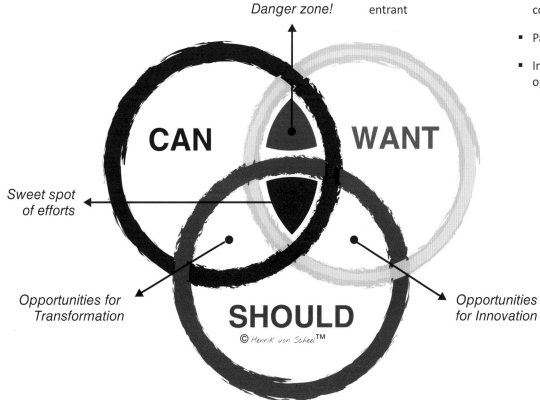

Danger zone!

CAN

WANT

Sweet spot of efforts

Opportunities for Transformation

SHOULD

© Henrik von Scheel™

Opportunities for Innovation

Example: Achieve Operational Excellence

The "can, want, should do" concept is often applied together with the six business models, for example, if you want to achieve operational excellence.

You would start by looking at what you *can do* in the operating model:

What you *should do* to achieve a better performance model, which specifies where to need to transform to get a more effective operation and innovate to be more efficient.

Resulting in a value-driven cost saving in cost model, which is what you *want to do*.

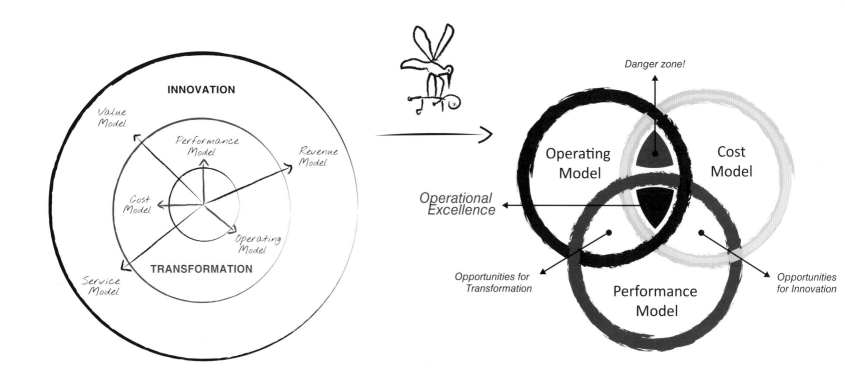

Rephrasing Dumbledore's conversation with Harry:

It is our choices that define who we are, not our abilities.

We are our choices.

Henrik von Scheel
Attenborough Impersonator Trainee

Strategic Choice:

Where to be different?

Make dust or eat dust.

The strategies choices in a competitive landscape

The essence of strategy is to make wise choices about where you are unique and how to compete.

Being unique is the ultimate competitive advantage. The secret to competing is the ability to strengthen core differentiating, core competitive, and non-core competencies.[2]

Competitiveness is not found; it is carefully crafted. It grows fundamentally out of the value a company is able to create for its buyers that exceeds the company's cost of creating it.

Finding the core to differentiate from the competition is not a matter of being better at what you do; it is a matter of being different at what you do. It means deliberately choosing a different set of activities to deliver a unique mix of value or cost leadership.[3]

A strategy for competitiveness requires making the ordinary extraordinary, defining actions that deliver real value and agility to adopt new realities to make an impact.

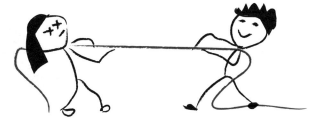

If you don't have a competitive advantage, don't compete.

Knowing where and when in the competitive lifecycle to innovate and what to transform to proactively define and redefine the advantages competitiveness consists of distinct traits that are designed based on the sequence of strategic choices, namely:

Competitive Advantage
- Core Differentiation
- Distinctive Competencies
- Hypergrowth >20% CAGR
- Sustained Competitive Advantage
- Unique Customer Value
- Market Leadership

Comparative Advantage
- Industry Differentiation
- Core Competencies
- Disciplined Growth >10% CAGR
- **Competitive Parity** anchored in Value / Price and E2EInformation
- **Competitive Dynamics** derived from Customer E2E Service Delivery

Hypercompetitive Advantage
- Temporary Competitive Advantage achieved with Capital & Reach
- Linear Growth >5% CAGR
- **Competitive Rivalry** obtained with Cost and Quality
- **Competitive Dynamics** secured with Timing and know-how

Grow from the core

Change is the only constant, especially for competitiveness. A master plan to achieve a competitive advantage has to be fine-tuned and redefined consistently. Competitiveness is a combination of a three-fold master plan across the organization business and operating model.

1. *Outthink* to create a competitive advantage that outperforms the market.
2. *Outwit* industry peers with comparative advantage.
3. *Outsmart* markets in hyper-competitive environments.

The ability to recognize and test the sources of your differentiation in this way is important for focusing on innovation. Most innovations affect only one part of a business model, leaving the rest intact. The more precise your understanding of your model and the sources of its success, the more precisely you can focus innovation resources on the areas where the threats and the need for change are greatest.

The best way to grow is usually by replicating your strongest strategic advantage in new contexts. Companies typically expand in one or more of four ways: They create or purchase new products and services, create or enter new customer segments, enter new geographic locations, or enter related lines of business.

A company can pursue each of these strategies in various ways—for example, by adding new price points or finding new uses for a product or service that will appeal to new customers.

The power of a repeatable model lies in the way it turns the sources of differentiation into routines, behaviors, and activity systems that everyone in the organization can follow so that when a company sets out on a particular growth path, it knows how to maintain the differentiation that led to its initial success.[4]

Supporting differentiation

Although differentiation is at the heart of a repeatable model, it needs the support of a rigorously focused yet flexible organization.

It's not a competition, but I'm winning.

BUSINESS RELEVANCE ← REPEATABLE PATTERNS → IT RELEVANCE

Core Differentiating	Leading Practices	Tailored Information Systems	VALUE
• Goal is competitive advantage • Focus on innovation • Design value experiences through services and products • Create new market demands and partnerships	Practices identified by outperformers focus on the: • Revenue model • Value model • Service model innovation	• Tailor the technology components to support the uniqueness • Requirement management to support business innovation • Diversify the technology components between business units	5%
Core Competitive	**Industry Practices**	**Industry Information Systems**	
• Goal is competitive parity • Focus on transformation and efficiency • Attention should be around the service and performance model	Practices identified by industry leaders focus on the: • Service model performance • Performance model • Operating model output	• Invest in industry-specific customizations • Requirement management to support business transformation • Replicate the technology components across business units	15%
Non-Core	**Best Practices**	**Standard Systems**	
• Goal is to meet market standard at lowest cost • Focus on transformation and effectiveness • Attention should be around standardization of the operating model	Practices identified focus on the: • Operating model • Cost model • Automation, standardization, and Integration	• Should be "Out-of-the-Box" technology functionality • No customization of the technology components • Full standardization across business units	80% COST

© Henrik von Scheel™

A company must be able to create a defendable position in order to cope successfully with competitive forces and generate superior profitability.

Superior performance can be achieved through cost leadership, differentiation, or focus.

Cost Advantage with cost leadership involves becoming the lowest-cost producer by pursuing strategies such as lower cost of resource and production, economies of scale, automation, know-how, quantity, supply chain efficiency, etc.

Differentiation Advantage means being unique based on your capabilities to deliver, which is widely value-based by buyers. Differentiation can be achieved on the basis of superior service, and products that give a better value experience.[5]

Focus means being the best in a carefully chosen product, market, customer, or partnership.

These are some of the basic introductions to designing competitive strategies. Companies should pursue one of these strategies and take care not to get stuck in the middle. But care must also be taken to maintain a proper balance between cost leadership and differentiation.

Thus, a cost leader should not be seen to be offering distinctly inferior products compared to rivals who are competing on the basis of differentiation. Similarly, a differentiator cannot afford to have a very high-cost structure. The costs should not exceed the price premium it receives from the buyers.

The sustainability of competitive strategies depends on three conditions.

The first is the particular source of the advantage. There is a hierarchy of sources of competitive advantage in terms of sustainability. Lower-order advantages, such as low labor costs or cheap raw materials, are relatively easy to imitate. Higher-order advantages, such as proprietary process technology, product differentiation, brand reputation, and customer relationships, are more durable. Higher-order advantages involve more advanced skills and capabilities such as specialized and highly trained personnel, internal technical capability, and often close relationships with leading customers. Such advantages also demand sustained and cumulative investment in physical facilities and specialized intangible assets.

The second determinant of sustainability is the number of distinct sources of advantages a firm possesses. If there is only one advantage, competitors can more easily nullify this advantage. Firms that sustain leadership over time tend to proliferate advantages throughout the value chain.

The third, and the most important, basis for sustainability is constant improvement and upgrading. A firm must keep creating new advantages at least as fast as competitors can replicate existing ones. The firm must improve its performance relentlessly against its existing advantages. This makes it more difficult for competitors to nullify them.

In the long run, competitive advantage can be sustained only by expanding and upgrading sources and by moving up the hierarchy to more sustainable types. To sustain a competitive advantage, a firm may have to deliberately destroy old advantages to create new, higher-order ones.

A company must learn to exploit industry trends and close off the avenues along which competitors may attack by making pre-emptive investments.

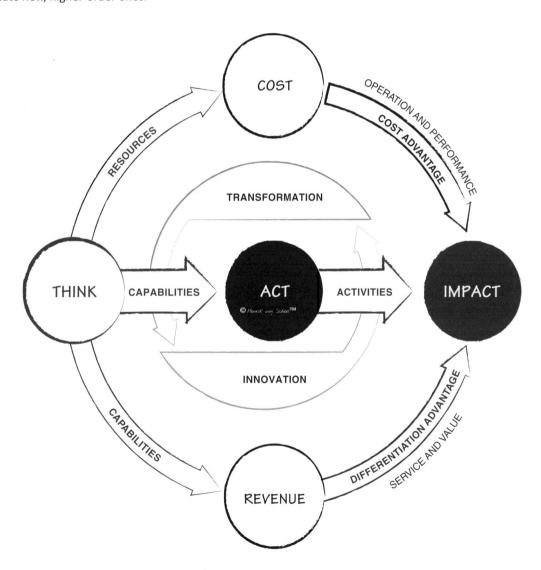

The strategic choices in a competitive landscape

Opportunities for differentiation are rich and varied in virtually every industry. As you deliberate about your key differentiators, you might consult these criteria:

Are they (1) truly distinctive? (2) measurable against competitors? (3) relevant to what you deliver to your core customers? (4) mutually reinforcing? (5) clear at all levels of the company?

Degree of preference \ Number of providers	1	2	One big and some small	Few big	Many	Commodity
Homogenous market	Monopoly	Duopoly	Partial monopoly	Oligopoly	Competition	Full competition
Heterogenous market		Differentiated duopoly	Differentiated, partial monopoly	Competition, but with differentiated oligopoly	Monopolistic competition	Head-2-head rivalry
Organization's market position	Unique	Strong	Robust	Secure	Fragile	Weakest
		Strongest	Most robust	Most secure	Delicate	Vulnerable
Industry exposure	Low				High	
Organization's ability to adopt to changes	Low		High		Low	High
Strategic situation	← Differentiation				Competitiveness →	

Chosen strategy

Competitive Differentiation

- Create uncontested market space
- Make the competition irrelevant
- Create and capturenew demand
- Break the value-cost trade-off
- Align E2E service delivery

Comparative Advantage

- Compete in exciting market + stand out via service and performance
- Differentiate from the competition
- Exploit customer base to reduce attrition + drive loyalty w. services
- Break the transactional market mindset to exceed expectations
- Align E2E information to differentiate

Hyper Competititon

- Compete in the same market space
- Beat the competition
- Exploit existing demand
- Align E2E system activities with strategic choice of low cost

Competitiveness is not found, it is carefully crafted

Differentiation is the essence of strategy, the prime source of competitive advantage. You earn money not just by performing a valuable task, but by being different from your competitors in a manner that lets you serve your core customers better and more profitably.

Gaining an edge over peers from competitive dynamics or comparative advantage requires relentlessly building on fundamental differentiation, going from strength to strength.

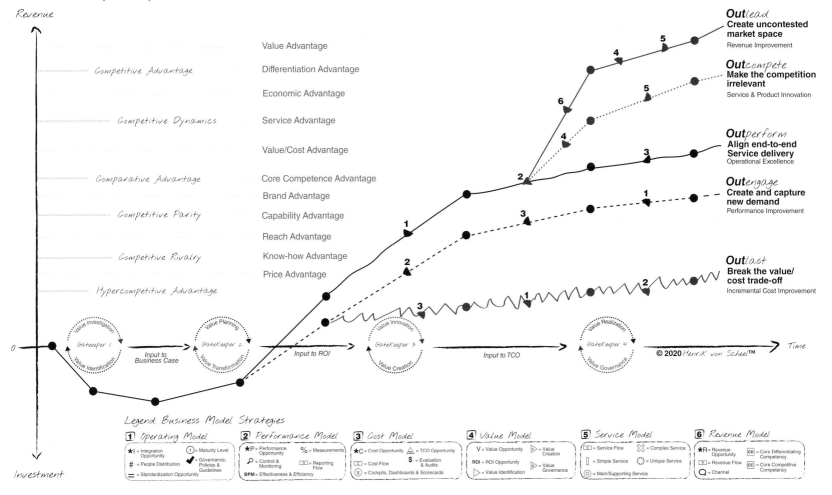

Strategic choices that produce different advantages

Learning how to make strategic choices to design different advantages calls for the ability to deliver differentiation for the front line, creating an organization that lives and breathes its strategic advantages day in and day out.[6]

Build capabilities on how to sustain it over time through constant adaptation to changes in the market. The result is a simple, repeatable business model that a company can apply to new products and markets over and over again to generate sustained growth.

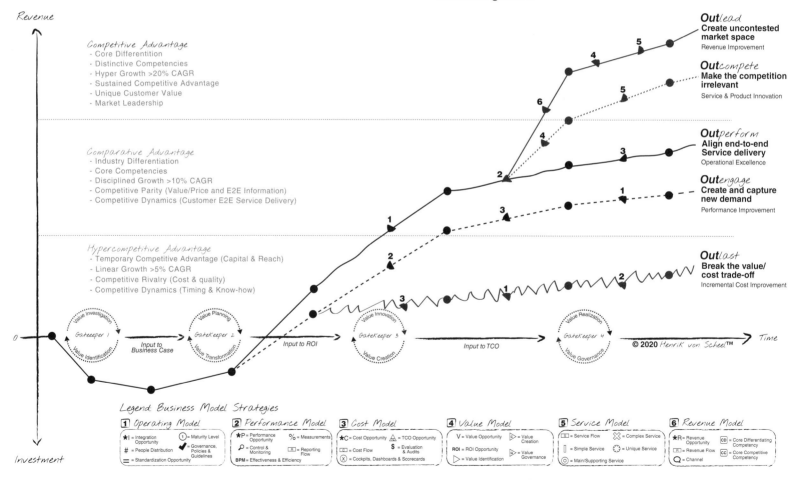

Example of strategic choices to craft a Cost Advantage

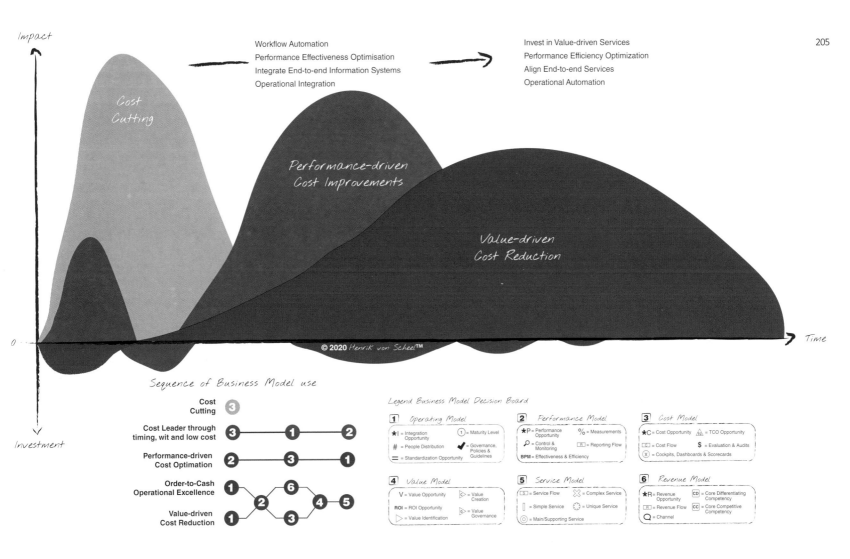

Impact

Cost Cutting

Performance-driven Cost Improvements

Value-driven Cost Reduction

Workflow Automation
Performance Effectiveness Optimisation
Integrate End-to-end Information Systems
Operational Integration

Invest in Value-driven Services
Performance Efficiency Optimization
Align End-to-end Services
Operational Automation

0

Time

Investment

© 2020 Henrik von Scheel™

Sequence of Business Model use

Cost Cutting	③
Cost Leader through timing, wit and low cost	③ ① ②
Performance-driven Cost Optimation	② ③ ①
Order-to-Cash Operational Excellence	① ⑥
	② ④ ⑤
Value-driven Cost Reduction	① ③

Legend Business Model Decision Board

1 Operating Model
- ★| = Integration Opportunity
- ① = Maturity Level
- # = People Distribution
- ✔ = Governance, Policies & Guidelines
- = Standardization Opportunity

2 Performance Model
- ★P = Performance Opportunity
- % = Measurements
- = Control & Monitoring
- R = Reporting Flow
- BPM = Effectiveness & Efficiency

3 Cost Model
- ★C = Cost Opportunity
- TCO = TCO Opportunity
- = Cost Flow
- $ = Evaluation & Audits
- X = Cockpits, Dashboards & Scorecards

4 Value Model
- V = Value Opportunity
- ▷ = Value Creation
- ROI = ROI Opportunity
- ▷ = Value Governance
- ▷ = Value Identification

5 Service Model
- S = Service Flow
- ✕ = Complex Service
- | = Simple Service
- = Unique Service
- ◎ = Main/Supporting Service

6 Revenue Model
- ★R = Revenue Opportunity
- CD = Core Differentiating Competency
- R = Revenue Flow
- CC = Core Competitive Competency
- Q = Channel

Example of strategic choices to craft a Cost Advantage

The strategic choices are often the sequence of why, when, where, and with what. Those who will win will know when to fight and when not to fight.

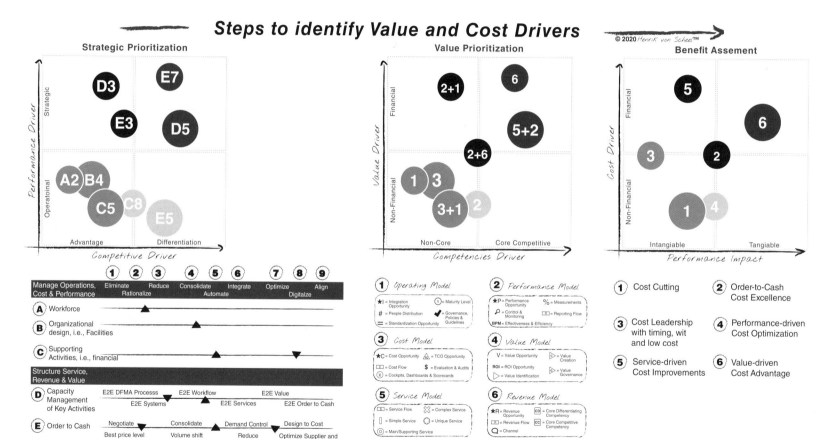

Steps to identify Value and Cost Drivers

© 2020 Henrik von Scheel™

Strategic Choice:

What to focus on?

Don't blame the distraction.
Improve your focus.

Rephrasing Socrates and my wife:

Where your attention goes, your energy flows. The secret of change is to focus all of your efforts on building the new, rather than the old.

Henrik von Scheel
Godfather of 4th Industrial Revoluation

The Art of Trend spotting

The Industry 4.0 is impact-driven applied

What to focus on is driven by the desired impact such as strengthening growth, improving operational excellence, lowering cost and risk, refining competitiveness, etc.

It requires the discipline to spot emerging trends and recognize how they will affect the business and where to adopt or take advantage of it. As Industry 4.0 is impact-driven, this is where the secret ingredients of the sauce are made.

The art of trend spotting

As trends emerge, they move through a hyper cycle of adoption and performance maturity. At first, trends manifest themselves as driver trends or opportunities and as they move though the performance maturity they reveal themselves as a force that disrupts the modus operandi.

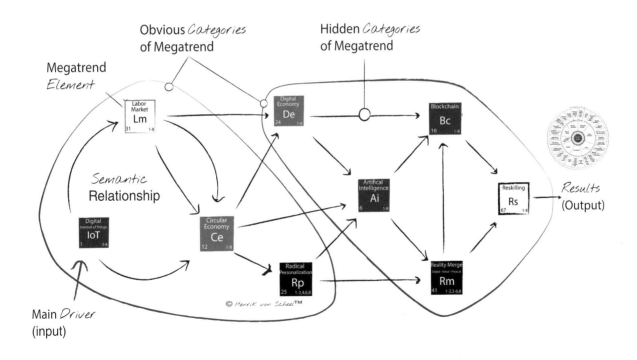

Early Adopters (5%) are the visionary innovators who pilot the first initiatives and are willing to take risks. The early adopters invest, take risks, and take the change to gain a competitive advantage that often exhibits hyper growth (>20% CAGR). This is the genesis of core differentiation that provides a unique customer value and market leadership. The early adopter develops the leading practices.

Industry Adopters (15%) are the first visionary leaders who spot an industry-specific application and harvest the fruits of comparative advantage and disciplined growth (>10% CAGR) with core competitive competencies. As industry adoption and performance increases, the practices evolve into industry standards.

Majority and Late Adopters (80%) embrace initiatives once a wide range of successful rollout demonstrates benefit, which leads to a wider range of adoption where you can't be successful without it. At this stage, the performance is a common best practice. The adopter of best practices can gain a hyper-competitive advantage with linear growth (>5% CAGR).

Knowing when and where to apply the leading practice, industry practice, and best practices is the core of what to focus on.

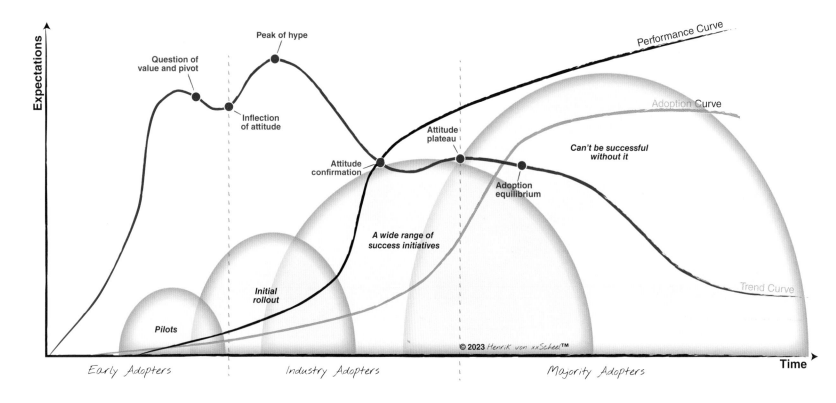

Knowing what to focus on, where and when

Competitive Differentition
5% of an organziation
is core differentiating

Comparative Advantage
15% of an organziation
is core compettitive

Hypercompetition
80% of an organziation
is non-core

Innovation*
Drivers
*Innovation dimensions for growth:
Invest in Services and Value

Transformation*
Forces
*Transformation dimensions to improve margin, and productivity:
Align, integrate, optimize and automate

Leading Practices
Industry Practices
Best Practices
Operating Model
Performance Curve
Cost Model
Adoption Curve
Performance Model
Service Model
Revenue Model
Trend Curve
Value Model

Expectations

Early Adopters
Industry Adopters
Majority Adopters
Time

© 2023 Henrik von Scheel™

Knowing when and where to apply leading practice, industry practice, and best practices is the core what to focus on.

Eighty percent of the organization is non-core where best practices are applied to support the cost, performance, and operating models. The main driver is transformation. Focusing on digitalization, automation, integration, and optimization to increase maturity and ensure low cost and smooth operation. Here, you constantly need to focus on what to do less of or stop doing.[7]

Fifteen percent of the organization is core competitive, where you compete. This is where industry practices are applied to support the service, value, and revenue models. The main driver is innovation and transformation, in that order.

The remaining 5% in the organization is the core differentiation, very few companies have them and they take years to develop. This is where leading practices are applied with the focus on innovation to support the revenue and value models. The innovation principles focus on investing in new capabilities, alignment of services, workflows, and E2E information.

BE STRONG
I whispered to my Wi-Fi signal.

80-15-5 rule – the secret of the outperformers

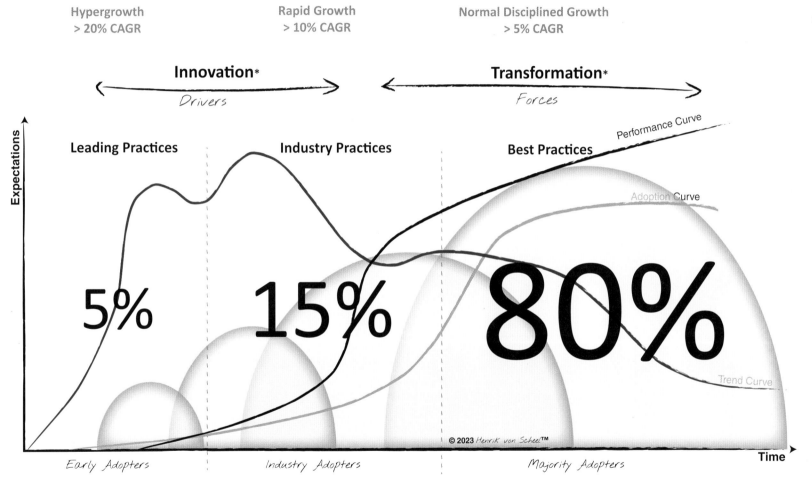

Hypergrowth
> 20% CAGR

Rapid Growth
> 10% CAGR

Normal Disciplined Growth
> 5% CAGR

Innovation*

Drivers

Transformation*

Forces

Expectations

Leading Practices

Industry Practices

Best Practices

Performance Curve

Adoption Curve

Trend Curve

5%

15%

80%

© 2023 *Henrik von Scheel*™

Early Adopters

Industry Adopters

Majority Adopters

Time

Example: What to focus on with digital strategies

It is no secret: Digital strategy is difficult for well-established companies. By and large, they are better executors than strategists and innovators, and most succeed less through game-changing creativity than by optimizing their existing businesses.

Since digital strategies are complex, company-wide endeavors, they require a set of crosscutting practices to structure, organize, operate, and encourage it.

As digital strategies are always impact-driven, there are nine essential strategies with organizational factors that are what separate a successful company from the rest of the field.

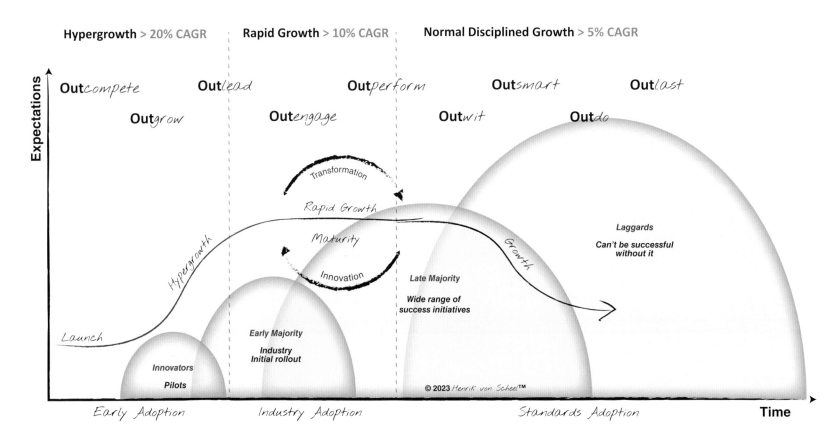

Hypergrowth > 20% CAGR   **Rapid Growth** > 10% CAGR   **Normal Disciplined Growth** > 5% CAGR

Expectations

Outcompete   **Out**lead   **Out**perform   **Out**smart   **Out**last

Outgrow   **Out**engage   **Out**wit   **Out**do

Transformation

Rapid Growth

Maturity

Hypergrowth

Innovation

Launch

Growth

Laggards

Can't be successful without it

Late Majority

Wide range of success initiatives

Early Majority

Industry Initial rollout

Innovators

Pilots

© 2023 Henrik von Scheel™

Early Adoption   Industry Adoption   Standards Adoption   **Time**

Outgrow

Regard innovation-led growth as absolutely critical and set cascaded targets to reflect this

- Innovation vision & model
- Required growth contribution from innovation
- Cascaded targets & accountabilities

Outperform

Invest in a coherent, time- and risk-balanced portfolio of initiatives with sufficient resources to win

- Clarity of innovation themes
- Portfolio balancing time & risk
- Resources sufficient for initiatives to win
- Portfolio governance

Outwit

Win by creating and capitalizing on external networks

- Strategic external networks
- Collaboration skills
- Partner of choice

Outcompete

Beat the competition by developing and launching innovations quickly and effectively

- Planning and execution rigor
- Cross-functional project culture
- Customer and market-based learning

Outengage

Launch innovations at the right scale in the relevant markets and segments

- Go-to-market planning
- Launch management
- Operations ramp-up

Outlead

Ensure your people are motivated, rewarded, & organized to innovate repeatedly

- People priorities
- Enabling structure
- Supportive culture
- Learning & adaptive organization

Outsmart

Have actionable and differentiated business, market, & technology insights that translate into winning value propositions

- Customer orientation
- Multiple-lens insight generation
- Differentiated value proposition

Outdo

Create new business models that provide defensible, robust, and scalable profit sources

- Exploration of new business models
- Changing value-chain economics
- Diversifying service streams
- Delivery-model changes & new customer groups

Outlast

Improve value chain productivity with real zero margin cost that brings lasting impact and performance

- Value chain zero marginal cost orientation
- Next generation of productivity
- Improve margin with zero marginal cost

Albert Einstein is often quoted (perhaps apocryphally) as saying, "If I had 20 days to solve a problem, I would take 19 days to define it." Innovation and transformation are particularly sticky problems because they so often remain undefined. We treat them as monoliths as if every innovation and transformation is the same, which is why so many expensive programs end up going nowhere.

So how should we go about it? Before you approach them or handle them, you need to identify the root cause that will define the source and the nature of it.

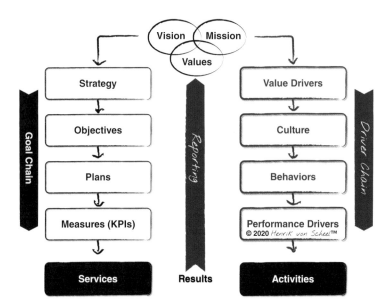

The golden rule is that when the origin derives from a challenge and performance driver, it often appears as a performance problem, cost issue, or operational pain point. This is often referred to as a problem chain and requires transformation. Transformation is always rooted in altering something that already exists.

When the origin derives from an opportunity and value driver, it often appears as a service opportunity, revenue potential, and desired client value This is often referred to as the goal chain and requires innovation. Innovation is always rooted in adding something new to something that already exists.

Defining an innovation and transformation approach starts with developing a better understanding of the problem and goals that need to be solved. What is the root cause? How does it appear?

A proven method to identify the source is to apply the classification form, namely

Transformation:
1. Where (location), 2. When (time), 3. Whence (source), 4. How (manner), 5. What (context), 6. Why (reason), 7. Who (personal - actor), and 8. Whether (options).

Guiding transformation principles on what to focus
Eighty percent of the organization is non-core where best practices are applied to support the cost, performance, and operating models. The main driver is transformation, focusing on digitalization, automation, integration, and optimization to increase maturity and ensure low cost and smooth operation. Here you constantly need to focus on what to do less off or stop doing.

Innovation:
1. Why (reason), 2. Whether (options), 3. What (context),
4. Where (location), 5. How (manner), 6. Whence (source),
7. When (time), and 8. Who (personal – actor)

Guiding innovation principles on what to focus
Fifteen percent of the organization is core competitive, where you compete. This is where industry practices are applied to support the service, value, and revenue models.

The main driver is innovation and transformation, in that order. The remaining 5% in the organization is the core differentiation; very few companies have them and they take years to develop. This is where leading practices are applied with a focus on innovation to support the revenue and value models. The innovation principles focus on investing in new capabilities, alignment of services, workflows, and E2E information.

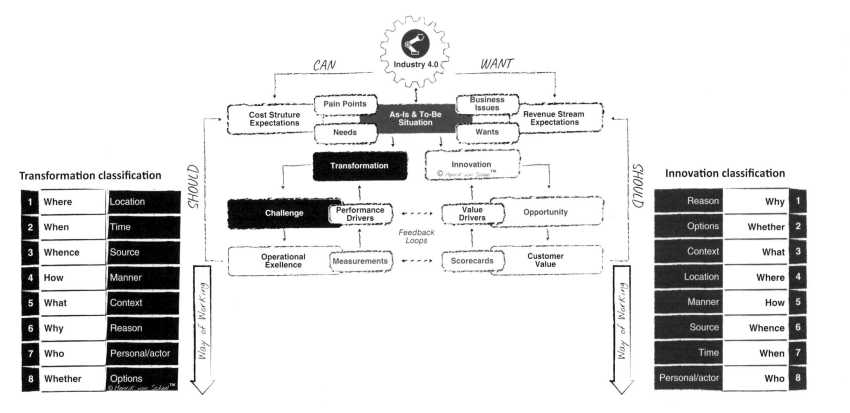

Key activities to make Strategic Choices

Outcome-driven focus

The problem is often not the lack of desire to make better decisions. It is that the bulk of the input does not apply to the kind of decision that is most challenging. Decisions must vary along two dimensions.

> 1st considers whether the decision-maker can influence the terms and the outcome.

> 2nd addresses whether the aim is to do well or to do better than others.

Before making any decision, the most important thing is to understand what kind it is. Decisions based on the value chain, business model, and operation model produces good insight and advice for routine choices and judgments, such as personal investment decisions, where people are choosing among the products before them, have no ability to change them, and are not competing with anyone.

For these decisions, it is important to avoid common biases. But strategic decisions, such as entering a new market or acquiring another company, are completely different. Executives can actively influence outcomes. Furthermore, success means doing better than rivals. For these decisions, executives need more than an ability to avoid common biases. They require a talent for clear-eyed analysis and the ability to take bold action.

Simultaneous, not sequential, decisions

A common pitfall in strategic positioning exercises is to make strategic choices independently of each other and without alignment. Strategic choices need to be made simultaneously, not sequentially. For example, key strategic decisions involve making choices about "where to play" and "how to win," but no "how to win" choice can be made outside of the particular context of a given "where to play" choice. Each decision must link together and reinforce the others.

Thus, the only productive and intelligent way to generate possibilities for strategy choice is to consider *matched sets* of choices. It does not matter whether the strategic question is whether to aim broadly or narrowly, or to pursue low costs or differentiation. What does matter is that the answers are in a perfectly matched pair.

Remain seated during
the entire performance.

Prior to advancing toward strategy execution, the following essential activities are critical.

The key activities to making _strategic choices_ are

1. **Assess the 80-15 and 5 rule** potential for innovation and transformation
2. **Determine the strategic choices**
   Outline strategic scenarios of what not to do, where to differentiate, and what to focus on, in this order.
3. **Define desired impact** with goals and critical success factors
4. **Take design decisions** with stakeholder. The quality of potential solution or prototype, impact scenarios.
   - Ratify solution, review capabilities, & define requirement
   - Ideate gains, execution capability, and budget potential
5. **Calculate performance and budget impact**
   - Define scope, business plan, and implementation roadmap
   - Map success factors, requirements, and deliverables with roles and budget

All men can see these tactics whereby I conquer, but what none can see is the strategy out of which victory is evolved.

Sun Tzu

* We have a Strategic Plan. *
It's called doing things.

Strategy *Execution*

The science of getting things done and making them stick

Chapter Six

"

An operating model describes how an organization is structured to execute.

It is the *ultimate* executive's decisions *toolbox* that monitors, measures, manages, and governs the strategy execution of an organization.

Henrik von Scheel
Paranormal Investigator

"

Operating Model 4.0 — Deliver maximum execution

Next-generation of Operations

How to profitably deliver services to customers has become a defining challenge for businesses today. There are several reasons for this. One is because customers don't just expect more; the expectations for themselves also change quickly, radically shifting profits.

The other is that executives face an increasingly complex landscape of technologies, methodologies, and both regulatory and compliance pressures to ensure that new processes are standardized and traceable.

These changes for both B2B and B2C businesses are fundamentally transforming what *services* means. Our research suggests that as much as 45% of employee activities can be automated by adopting current technologies. That is calling into question how businesses work, build skills, and deliver customer experiences. This reality is particularly important given the high-stakes nature of today's digital environment.

Operating Model 4.0

How to deliver the next-generation of digital operational excellence, smart automation, and how to put customer experience at the heart of operations is the pumping heart of an operating model.

The operating model is one layer deeper than a business model. An Operating Model 4.0 describes how an organization is structure to execute. It is the ultimate executive's decisions *toolbox* that monitors, measures, manages, and governs the strategy execution of an organization.

The next-generation Operating Model 4.0 alters every aspect of how an organization operates to deliver. Stepping back, looking at the bigger picture to visualize by modeling the current situation and potential future scenario. Visualization becomes more important than knowledge. Using visualization to explore the latest operational practice on how to run the current operation with programs, projects toward systems, and operation to deliver maximal execution with a tangible impact that improves service, performance, quality, increase safety, and lower risk and cost.

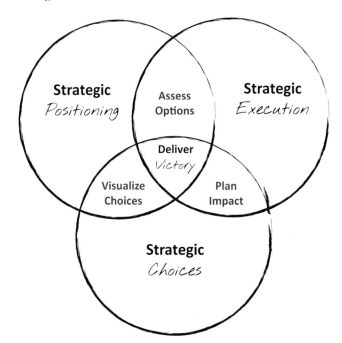

Operating Model 4.0 describes the detailed relationship and correlations of how an organization operates to deliver.

It would be a entire book in itself to cover the business model and operating model, but organizations that outperform apply them with rigorous discipline.

Operating Model 4.0 represents a comprehensive view of functional areas, groups, tasks, activities, people, processes, projects, systems, information, data, flows, and other types that are all classified into strategic, tactical, and operational tiers.

The purpose of an operating model is to make better-informed business decisions and to improve performance and profitability. Often it depends on where and how the organization operates, what kinds of products it sells, which customer segments it serves through its competencies, which processes will be outsourced or handled in-house, which relationships will be most critical, what results are expected, and how the decisions will be made and measured.

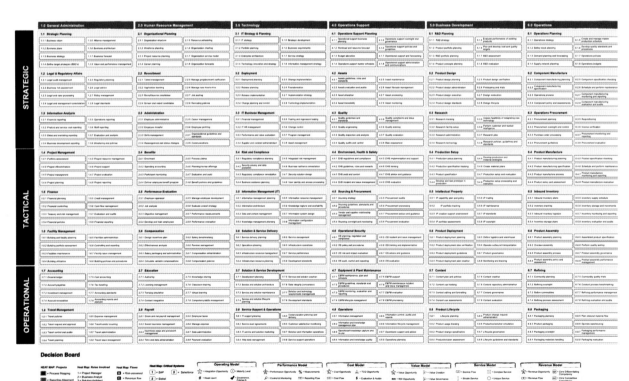

Why the Operating Model Matters

Run and develop the operations: It defines how to organize and structure the current projects, programs, services, processes, and systems with operating objectives, development and operating management, e.g., goals, requirements, business ownership, services, processes, rules, and compliance, applying the concepts.

Organizations that applied an operating model had typically a focus on the following main areas:

- Where to focus on transformation or innovation.

- Where to standardize, integrate, optimize, and automate, and achieve organizational effectiveness and efficiency.

- What is the right operating model being in consideration of the competitive market forces?

- How to run and develop the operations: structuring the current projects, programs, services, processes, and systems with operating objectives, development and operating management, e.g., goals, requirements, business ownership, services, processes, rules, and compliance, applying the concepts.

- Development and transformation of operational excellence, cost, and performance to ensure continuous consistency of core competitive and core-differentiating competencies.

- Transparent ownership and responsibilities for process integration and standardization for a focused, responsive, flexible, and robust operation.

- Which service, process, work, and information flow needs to be standardized, changed, or otherwise optimized to support new operational concepts.

- How and where digitization and technology adoption will be involved in the operational development and delivery.

- Which partners are needed to improve cost, performance, service, and delivery.

- How the operational measurements, in terms of critical success factors and key performance indicators, are linked to the business strategy.

- Governance & compliance with business regulations and laws.

- Produces semantic relations and correlations of the operational functional areas, groups, tasks, activities, people, processes, projects, systems, information, data, flows, requirement, lifecycles, and governance. This is critical to

  - Apply the right measurements, reporting, requirements, and governance for decision-making, e.g., information flow, critical systems, policy, and requirements.

  - To analyze and develop the operating maturity levels and to create an operating development path.

- Cater to the right interlink and guide on where to focus on transformation, i.e., performance, cost, and operating models, and when to invest in innovation to improve value, service, and revenue models.

- Unlocks the Next generation of operating model focus is on, e.g., standardizing, optimizing, and automating, as much of the organizational effectiveness and efficiency that could be achieved have already been achieved.

- Differentiate with operations: What should be the right operating model in view of competitive market forces? Outperformers use downturns to rethink their operating model innovation in areas where their competition does not act or to respond to a different set of customer behaviors and market requirements.

The science of delivery

Seventy-two percent of projects underestimate the importance of implementation and fail to deliver. Now more than ever, strategy implementations are under pressure to deliver results, while ensuring to deliver the impact on promises. All strategies set ambitious goals and develop strategic plans to achieve those goals.

The challenge often is to build the competencies with proven, reusable, and customizable standard ways to define and execute their highest-priority objectives so that they have the greatest possible impact.

The science of delivery embodies six phases that translate strategic objectives into operational performance, form a delivery unit, collect data to set targets and trajectories, and establish routines.

This enables teams to face the increased pressure to deliver, drive change, and track progress toward long-term objectives.

The result: Design to build competencies in an interactive classroom setting, practice and apply the learning to leave a longer-lasting impact on you and your organization. Each participant receives an individual performance mentoring on the selected project.

Be prepared for change

Create a winning strategy and implement it well, and you might cruise along for years without any problems. But no strategy is effective forever. Something in the external environment eventually changes - new technology appears, customer needs shift, and new competitors emerge - rendering it ineffective. Unfortunately, many management teams cannot recognize when their strategies have become obsolete.

The temporary nature of a successful strategy should caution you to continually scan the external environment for threats and new opportunities as described in Step 1. Does your company do this already? If it does not, who would be the people to conduct this duty?

Strategy formulation, then, is an ongoing requirement of good management. It is, to quote Michael Porter, "a process of perceiving new positions that woo customers from established positions or draw new customers into the market." This is a process you must permanently embed in your organization.

Deliver Strategy Execution on Promise

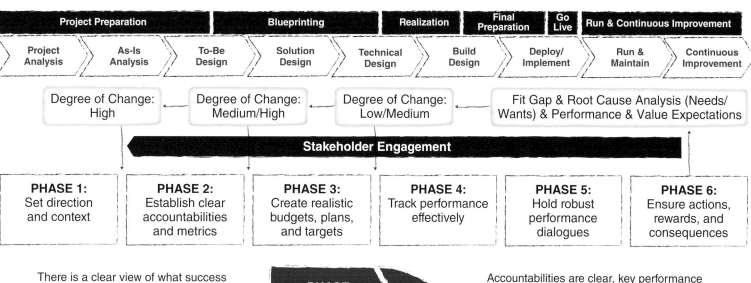

Project Preparation			Blueprinting		Realization	Final Preparation	Go Live	Run & Continuous Improvement
Project Analysis	As-Is Analysis	To-Be Design	Solution Design	Technical Design	Build Design	Deploy/ Implement	Run & Maintain	Continuous Improvement

Degree of Change: High ← Degree of Change: Medium/High ← Degree of Change: Low/Medium ← Fit Gap & Root Cause Analysis (Needs/Wants) & Performance & Value Expectations

Stakeholder Engagement

PHASE 1: Set direction and context

PHASE 2: Establish clear accountabilities and metrics

PHASE 3: Create realistic budgets, plans, and targets

PHASE 4: Track performance effectively

PHASE 5: Hold robust performance dialogues

PHASE 6: Ensure actions, rewards, and consequences

There is a clear view of what success looks like - across the organization and with relevant partners

Accountabilities are clear, key performance indicators and scorecards are balanced and cover both performance and health, and metrics cascade where appropriate

Actions are taken to improve performance, and there are visible consequences for good and bad performance

Targets stretch employees but are also fully owned by management, and they are supported by appropriate resources

Performance reviews are both challenging and supportive, and are focused, fact based, and action oriented

Reporting gives a timely view of performance with appropriate detail, and it does not burden the organization

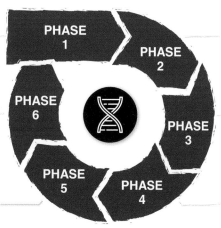

Step-by-step activities to deliver on promise

Phase 1: Set direction and context
Develop a foundation for delivery and establish a clear view of what success looks like - across the organization and with relevant partners.

- **Identify desired outcomes**

  - Capture purpose and goal (strategic intent)

  - Detect desire outcomes

  - Map stakeholders involved

- **Determine priorities**

  - Identify performance and value expectations

  - Understand implications and requirements

  - Evaluate risk involved

  - Determine priorities with stakeholders

- **Set targets/define success**

  - Determine measurements of success

  - Define executive accountabilities

- **Understand the challenge**

  - Evaluate past and present performance

  - Review the current state of delivery

- **Set direction and context**

Phase 2: Establish clear accountabilities and metrics
Define clear accountabilities, key performance indicators, and scorecards are balanced and cover both performance and health, and metrics cascade where appropriate.

- **Establish metrics and trajectories**

  - Capture performance and value expectations

  - Priorities are critical to outcome with time-bound goals and trajectories

  - Define key performance indicators and data source

  - Outline scorecards

  - Agree on routine scorecard review

- **Define clear accountabilities**

  - Establish clear accountabilities and metrics

  - Cascade performance metrics to roles involved

Phase 3:   Create realistic budgets, plans, and targets
Plan to deliver milestones, data, and trajectories. Understand the delivery chain. Build capacity at every level, including the center. Targets stretch employees but are also fully owned by management, and they are supported by appropriate resources.

- **Plan for delivery**

  - Specify the scope of delivery

  - Capture performance and value expectations

  - Gather high-level requirements

  - Develop a delivery plan with high-level activities, milestones, phases, and timelines

  - Chart methods used and systems impacted

  - Determine workload efforts, skills required, and roles involved

  - Define budget, performance measurements, and dependencies

Phase 4: Track performance effectively

Create routines. Reporting gives a timely view of performance with appropriate detail, and it does not burden the organization.

- **Build the delivery unit**

  - Establish a guide coalition and delivery unit

  - Understand the delivery unit challenges

  - Agree on delivery outcomes and metrics

  - Review delivery unit dependencies and risk

- **Delivery and track performance**

  - Put implementation plan into action

  - Set up performance effectively

  - Establish routines to drive and monitor

Phase 5: Hold robust performance dialogues

Solve problems as they arise. Performance reviews are both challenging and supportive, and are focused, fact-based, and action oriented.

- **Robust performance management**

  - Put implementation plan into action

  - Review scorecard performance effectively

  - Establish routines to drive and monitor

  - Solve problems early and rigorously

  - Sustain and continually build momentum

  - Create an irreversible delivery culture

  - Build systems capacity all the time

Phase 6: Ensure actions, rewards, and consequences

Establish the right relationships. Persist and take action to improve performance, and there are visible consequences for good and bad performance.

- **Continuous delivery improvement**

  - Routinely track delivery challenges

  - Identify performance gaps

  - Understand root cause

  - Define action required to improve performance.

  - Stakeholder communication of delivery

  - Communicate delivery status to a delivery unit

Key activities to deliver on promise

Align for execution

Build a good "fit" among strategy-supporting activities. Strategy is more than just a blueprint for winning customers; it is also about combining strategic positioning and strategic choices into a strategy execution of the company activities into a chain whose links are mutually supporting and effective in locking out imitators.

Define impact

A strategy must be impact- and output-driven focused. Thus, each activity supports the other and the strategic objective or higher goal. That strategic objective is supported by another critical success factor of activities, which includes highly motivated and effective gate personnel and groups that deliver the key performance indicators. Those activities make rapid impact possible.

This is where the business model and operating model link project management, where strategy and execution meets.

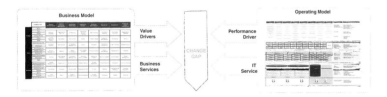

The superpower received by the mentor to achieve <u>strategic</u> execution is

1. **Set direction and context**
   - Review document and stakeholder deliverables sign-off
   - There is a clear view of what success looks like across the organization with relevant partners

2. **Establish accountability and performance metric**
   - Accountabilities are clear, key performance indicators and scorecards are balanced and cover both performance and health, and metrics cascade where appropriate
   - Targets stretch employees but are also fully owned by management, and they are supported by appropriate resources

3. **Design realistic budgets, plans, and targets**
   - Reporting gives a timely view of performance with appropriate detail, and it does not burden the organization

4. **Track performance management**

5. **Continuous delivery improvements**

Align activities

Once you've developed a satisfactory strategy from strategic positioning and choices, your job is only half done. Now you have to create alignment between people and the activities of the organization and its strategy.

Alignment activities are best visualized in a business model, operating model, and projects. The requirement gathering is a condition in which every employee at every level understands the strategy, and understands his or her role in making the strategy work.

As a manager, your role in creating alignment is twofold:

1. Communicate the strategy, activities, and roles. You must help people understand the strategy and how their jobs contribute to it. You want to create a situation in which even the lowest-ranking employees can articulate the goals of the organization and explain how what they do every day furthers them.

2. Coordinating work processes. You must align people's activities with the business's strategic intentions.

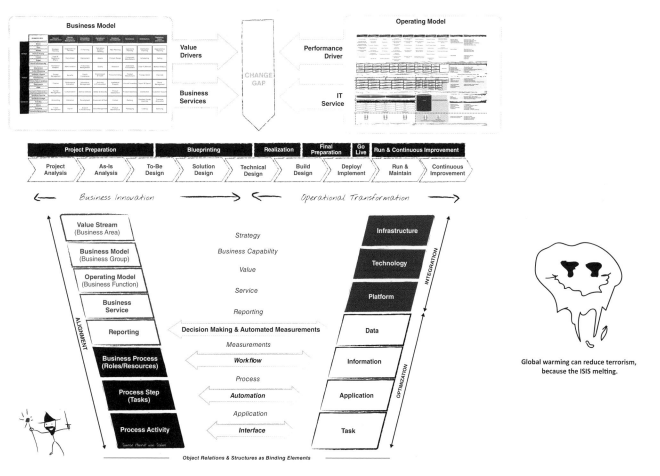

Global warming can reduce terrorism, because the ISIS melting.

PLAN

(YOUR EXECUTION)

EXECUTE

(YOUR PLAN)

Johan Troels Benthin

Master the *Art* of
Strategy Execution

A complete step-by-step guide to becoming a hero who kicks ass

Chapter Seven

The Calling

Refusal

Restore
Order

6

The Quest

Agent of
Change

5

New Era

The Mentor
Receive Power

Return with
the Elixir

Rebirth

Present World
(Known)

Crossing the
Threshold

Future World
(Unknown)

Reward

The Hero's Journey

based on the pattern of Perseus in
Greek mythology by ©Henrik von Scheel™

Temptation
& Failures

The Road of Trials

2

Meet the
Challenge

The Transformation

Allies &
Enemies

4

3

Accept
the new Role

Abyss

Growth &
Gain new skills

Death & Rebirth

The hero maker

As everybody goes though the strategy, my personal favorite way to apply the lifecycle of a strategy with Executive teams is called the *"Hero's Journey."*

This is a guided step-by-step path to make strategy + execution stick. The Hero's journey is a common narrative archetype based on Carl Jung's pattern of the Greek mythology of Perseus integrated with the key activities required across the six strategy execution lifecycle.

The Hero's Journey in which you as the character ventures into unknown territory of strategy to become a strategy execution hero.

The story involves a hero who goes on an adventure, explores new worlds, learns a lesson, wins a victory with that newfound knowledge, and then returns home transformed.

Facing challenges, conflict, and adversity, the hero ultimately triumphs before returning home, transformed. There are the three stages of the hero's journey:

THE DEPARTURE of the familiar ordinary present world.

THE INITIATION ventures into an unknown world, representing the future, and is birthed into a true champion through various trials and challenges.

THE RETURN in triumph to become a change of change and restore the order of a new era.

The hero journey is inside of you, open the mystery of yourself to undergo inner and outer transformation at each stage of the 12 steps to make you a strategy hero.

This journey will confront the dragons of fear and failure, and will reward you with the treasures of the true self - a hero. The hero takes the journey to confront dragons, and discover the:

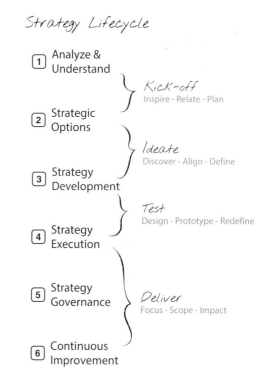

Strategy Lifecycle

1. Analyze & Understand
   Kick-off
   Inspire - Relate - Plan
2. Strategic Options
   Ideate
   Discover - Align - Define
3. Strategy Development
   Test
   Design - Prototype - Redefine
4. Strategy Execution
5. Strategy Governance
   Deliver
   Focus - Scope - Impact
6. Continuous Improvement

The art of simplicity is
a puzzle of complexity.

Douglas Horton

Five Steps to Strategy Execution

Manage the present and create the future

Step 1. Map the key and support activities as the blueprint for the value chain skeleton. Chart how the organization creates and delivers value by mapping the direct and indirect tasks and service flows.

Step 2. Outline the financial anatomy with its revenue stream and cost structure. Understand the performance and value requirements.

Step 3. Detect the external and internal, and identify trends of disruptive forces and emerging drivers that affect (where) and influence the organization. Map out the change needs in the current operation and opportunities for improvement and future business.

Step 4. Determine the strategic choices and scenarios of what not to do, where to be different, and what to focus on, in this order.

Step 5. Align to prepare for strategy execution and start to deliver on the promise.

Strategic Positioning   Strategic Choices   Strategic Execution

Twelve Steps of an Anonymous Failed Strategist

Welcome to the Hero's Journey Twelve-step Program, a recovery program for an addiction to failed projects. The program is a proven guided step-by-step rehabilitation journey to get the strategy right and stop the behavioral addictions to mind masturbating that are not real, and a compulsion to make things up.

Step 1. Ordinary World

In which we meet our hero. The journey has yet to start. Before our hero discovers a strange new world, he first must understand the the basics of strategy, the ordinary challenges, and the mundane reality of why so many strategies fail.

Step 2. Call to Adventure

In which an adventure starts. The quest for the adventure is all about booting the hero out of her comfort zone. In this stage, the hero is generally confronted with a problem or challenge she cannot ignore. This catalyst can take many forms. The stakes of the adventure and the hero's goals become clear. The only question: will she rise to the challenge?

Step 3. Refusal of the Call

In which the hero digs in his feet. Great, so the hero received his summons, and has self-doubt, previous or lack of experience. The hero might first refuse the call to action.

Step 4. Meeting the Mentor

In which the hero receives her superpowers. The heroes decided to go on the adventure - but they are not ready to spread their wings yet. Enter the mentor; the author of this book: someone who helps the hero, so that she does not make a total fool of herself. The mentor provides practical guidance and profound wisdom to instill new capabilities like grit and self-confidence.

The *superpower* received by the mentor to achieve strategic positioning is

1. **Populate Value Chain 4.0**
   Map how you operate to deliver value

2. **Chart cost structure, revenue steam**
   Understand performance and value requirements

3. **Capture the forces and drivers**
   Detect external and internal forces, and drivers that affect and influence the operation

4. **Understand challenges**
   Understand gaps, issue, challenges, and maturity

5. **Define opportunities**
   Spot revenue, service, value, operations, cost and performance changes, needs and opportunities.

Step 5. Crossing the Threshold

In which the hero enters the other world in earnest. Now the hero is ready to commit to the journey. This marks the end of the departure stage and is when the adventure really kicks into the next gear. From this point on, there is no turning back. Like our hero, you should think of this stage as a checkpoint for your story. Pause and re-assess your bearings before you continue into the unfamiliar territory of unknowns.

Step 6. The Temptation and Failures

In which the hero faces new challenges and gets a squad. Here we notice a definite shift. The hero might be discombobulated by this unfamiliar reality of the unknown and new rules. There are a series of tests to pass to apply the content. In this stage, often the protagonists of resistance will meet allies and enemies. This is often the most difficult part of trial and error, rejection, and naysayer. He will learn a new set of rules from them.

The Hero's Journey for Strategic Positioning

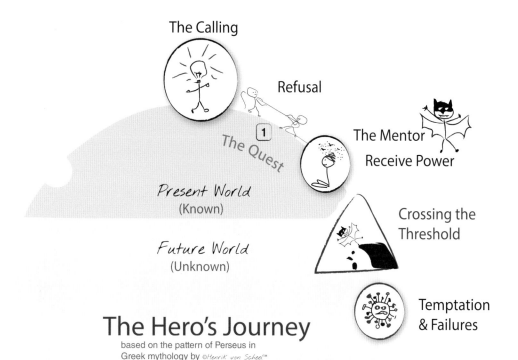

The Calling

Refusal

The Mentor
Receive Power

The Quest

Present World
(Known)

Future World
(Unknown)

Crossing the
Threshold

Temptation
& Failures

The Hero's Journey
based on the pattern of Perseus in
Greek mythology by ©Henrik von Scheel™

Manage the *present* and create the *future*

STEP 1

Populate
the Value Chain

Map the key and support activities as the blueprint.

Chart how the organization creates and delivers value.

Map the direct and indirect tasks and service flows.

Step 1: Map the Key & support activities as the blueprint

Human Resources

Human Resources manages the capabilities, skills, and competencies of an organization.

Technology

The technology consists of Information technology systems, applications software, digitalization infrastructure, and devices.

Finance

Finance manages the profit and loss of an organization and reflects the revenue income and expenses.

General Administration

Deals with the general-purpose administration that support the key activities.

Operations

Operations manage the activities, resources, and partners to produce the goods and services to deliver the value proposition.

Resources

Key resources describes all activities involved in Human Resources Management.

Partners

Key partners describes an ecosystem of partnerships, complementors, alliances, joint ventures, and suppliers, which improves the overall value proposition to the customer.

Value Proposition

Value Proposition describes the service, solution, or product that initiates the value for the customer.

The value proposition is one of the defining factors of why a customer would pick the product over a competitor.

Customer Relationship

Customer relationship expresses the type of relationship an organization establishes a different customer segmentations.

Customer

The customer is the one who consumes your value proposition.

The customer segments differ depending on the different groups of needs, wants, and buying behavior.

Service

The Service describes the overall value experience that the customer has throughout the entire lifecycle - i.e. brand association, order, delivery, product, quality, performance, and support.

Channel

The way the value proposition is delivered to the customer segmentation, such as distribution channel or digital channel.

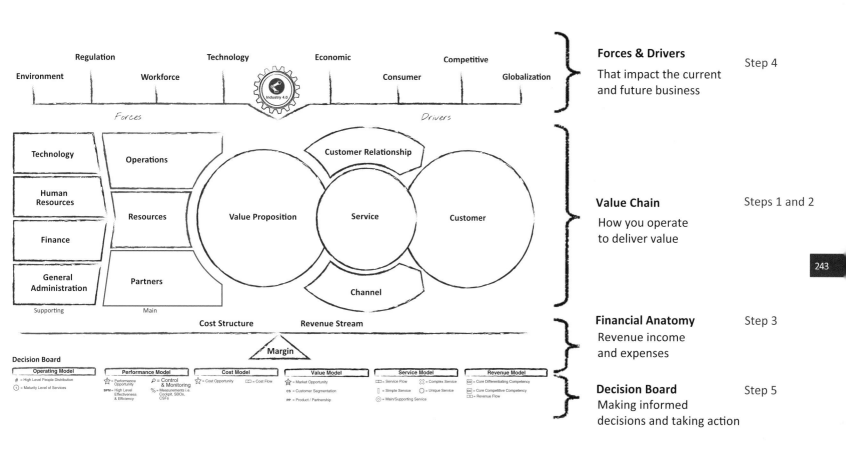

Forces & Drivers — Step 4
That impact the current and future business

Value Chain — Steps 1 and 2
How you operate to deliver value

Financial Anatomy — Step 3
Revenue income and expenses

Decision Board — Step 5
Making informed decisions and taking action

243

1 *Map value chain*

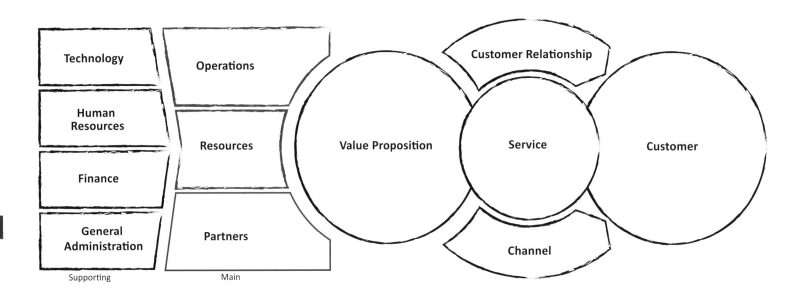

Be aware, not all crocodiles are vegetarians.

Detect the *opportunity* and *challenges*

STEP 2

Outline the
Financial Anatomy

Determine the cost structure and how it is being allocated.

Detail revenue stream and profitability.

Step 2: Outline the financial anatomy with the revenue stream

Cost Structure

determines how the costs are allocated. This includes the cost of key assets, direct costs, indirect costs, and economies of scale.

Revenue Stream

determines how much money can be made. Price multiplied by volume. Volume can be thought of in terms of market size, purchase frequency, ancillary sales, etc.

Cost Structure   **Revenue Stream**

Margin   © 2020 Henrik von Scheel™

Profit Margin

is how much each transaction should net in order to achieve the wanted profit.

Follow the money,
you'll have anything

Follow your passion,
you'll need nothing

Service Model

= Main and Supporting Service

= Unique, Complex, & Simple Service

= Service Flow

Operating Model

= High-level People Distribution

= Maturity Level of Services

= Where and How the Trend Effects the Operations

Value Model

= Customer Segmentation Opportunity

= Market Opportunity

= Product/Partnership

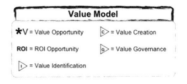

Performance Model

= Hight level Effectiveness & Efficiency

= Cockpit Control & Monitoring

= Cockpits Measurements

= Performance Opportunity

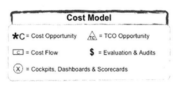

Revenue Model

= Core Competitive Competency

= Core Differentiating Competency

= Revenue Flow

Cost Model

= Direct Money Flow (cost)

= indirect Money Flow (value)

= Cost Opportunity

= Alliance, Partners, & Complementors

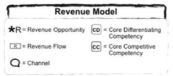

Cost Structure   **Revenue Stream**

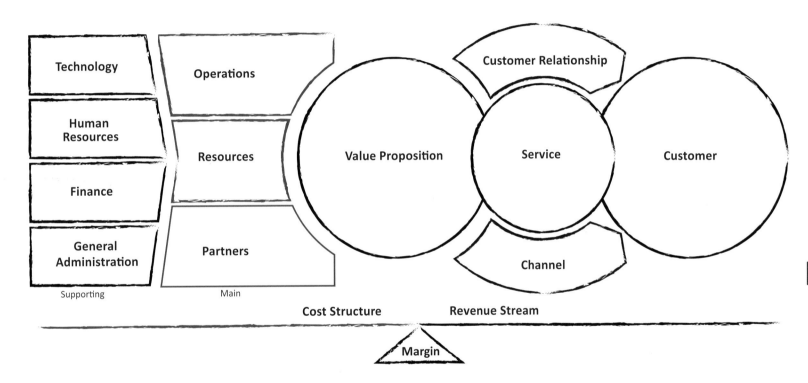

Technology

Human Resources

Finance

General Administration

Supporting

Operations

Resources

Partners

Main

Value Proposition

Customer Relationship

Service

Channel

Customer

Cost Structure   Revenue Stream

Margin

If you fart in space, you move forward.

Detect the *opportunity* and *challenges*

STEP 3

Detect the

Force and Drivers

Identify the external and internal trends that affect and influence the organization.

Detect the disruptive forces and emerging drivers.

Map the change needs in the current operation and opportunities for improvement and future business.

Step 3: Identify the external and internal trends that affect (where) and influence the organization.

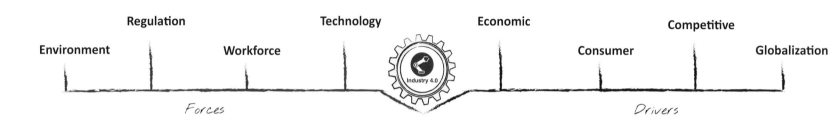

Environment   Regulation   Workforce   Technology   Economic   Consumer   Competitive   Globalization

Forces   *Drivers*

A force is an external or internal circumstance that shapes different aspects of an industry in a specific direction.

If acted upon, a force represents an opportunity to create future business.

If ignored, it will become a threat that manifests itself as an internal risk to current operations.

A business driver is an internal way to structure the current value stream (resources, operations, services, etc.) to exploit the opportunity of an external force.

If acted upon, the driver represents the opportunity to grow, strengthen competitiveness, capture new markets, and improve the operating margin.

The first step in reading trends requires that we first identify them. Trends can be classified into three levels: mega-, macro-, and microtrends.

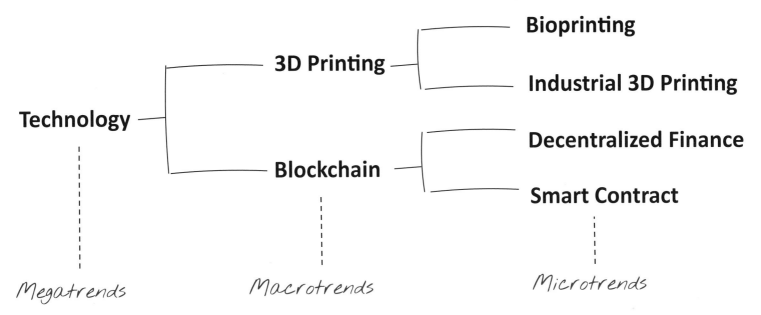

Megatrends

Mega is the highest level of trends. They are global forces that shape and impact our future in an ever-increasing speed. They affect our society, culture, finance, technology, and all facets of life.

The megatrends include globalization, economy, consumer demands, workforce, regulation, technology, and environment.

A megatrend typically lasts 10 to 15 years.

Macrotrends

Macro is a type of megatrend. There are many macrotrends to a megatrend. They are global and local large-scale sustained forces that have a significant future impact on the industry and regions.

Macrotrends always belong to a broader megatrend. An example of macrotrends is smart cloud, digital marketing, and 3D printing. These macrotrend examples belong to a technology megatrend.

A macrotrend typically lasts 5 to 10 years.

Microtrends

Micro is a type of macrotrend. They are local, smaller-scale forces that have an influential impact on smaller groups and areas.

They are the first concrete signs of an emerging movement and have a serious indication of future macrotrends.

A microtrend typically lasts 3 to 5 years.

Forces that shape business

There are 17 technology megatrends that impact organizations as disruptive forces on current operations and emerging drivers that shape new business opportunities.

There are 4 mega workforce megatrends, namely: Mobility, Diversity, Reskilling, and Connectedness.

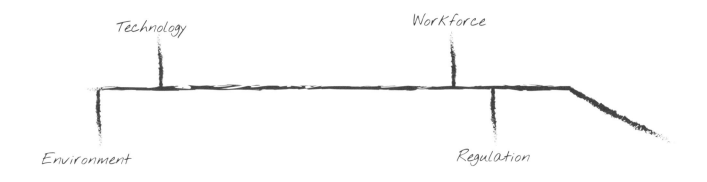

Technology

Workforce

Environment

Regulation

There are 9 environmental megatrends that companies must consider in terms of how they source, produce, package, and ship, and how they brand themselves.

The megatrends are climate change, water usage, energy efficiency, sixth mass extinction, recycling renewables, footprint, waste management, CO_2 emission, and population.

There are 7 regulatory megatrends that will affect the areas of human rights, national security, environment protection, technology and science, labor market, consumer protection, financial market, and trade and investment.

Drivers that change

The competitive driver is determined by the number of competitors and their threat level to your organization. The threat is increased by a larger number of competitors and the number of equivalent products and services that target similar customer segments.

The 11 Consume megatrends that will drive our society and business are Radical Personalization, Reality Merge, Privacy & Security, Wellness, Ethical Living, Sensory Stimulation, Convenience, Authenticity, Value Price Reality, Empowered Individual, and Value Price Reality.

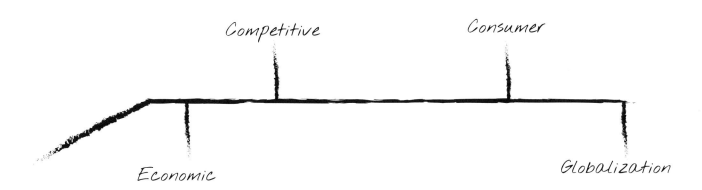

Competitive

Consumer

Economic

Globalization

The 8 Economic megatrends that will reset our economic system are Infectious Diseases, Biodiversity loss, Circular Economy, Digital Economy, Demonetize, Global Power Shift, and Redefine of Gross domestic product, Natural Disasters.

There are 11 colliding Global and 8 Demographic megatrends that will affect every aspect of our lives. These are Migration, New Trade Routes, Population Growth, Societal Aging, inequality, Pollution, Sectoral Shift, Resource Scarcity, Volatility, Autocratization, Populism, Urbanization, Global Power Shift, Cyber Instability, Health & Care, Shift in Faith, Middle Class, Debt Challenge, and Globalization Reset.

The forces and drivers of the Industry 4.0 Periodic Table are comprised of 77 Megatrends categorized into 6 Groups according to their characteristics.

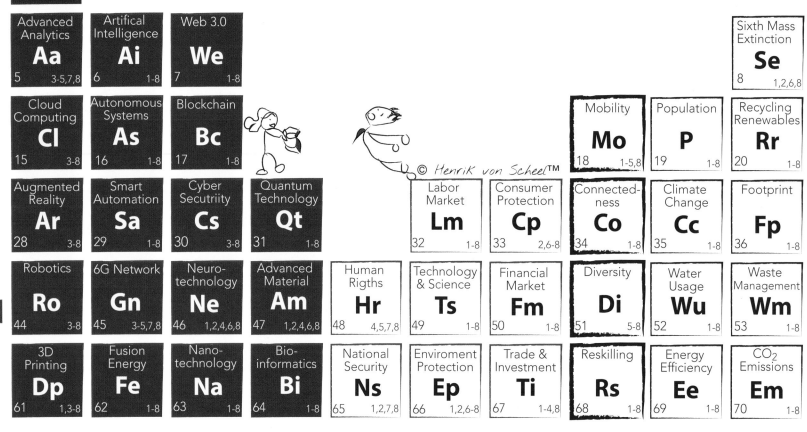

© Henrik von Scheel™

Element	Name	No.	Inclination
IoT	Digital Internet of Things	1	3-8
Aa	Advanced Analytics	5	3-5,7,8
Ai	Artifical Intelligence	6	1-8
We	Web 3.0	7	1-8
Se	Sixth Mass Extinction	8	1,2,6,8
Cl	Cloud Computing	15	3-8
As	Autonomous Systems	16	1-8
Bc	Blockchain	17	1-8
Mo	Mobility	18	1-5,8
P	Population	19	1-8
Rr	Recycling Renewables	20	1-8
Ar	Augmented Reality	28	3-8
Sa	Smart Automation	29	1-8
Cs	Cyber Secutriity	30	3-8
Qt	Quantum Technology	31	1-8
Lm	Labor Market	32	1-8
Cp	Consumer Protection	33	2,6-8
Co	Connected-ness	34	1-8
Cc	Climate Change	35	1-8
Fp	Footprint	36	1-8
Ro	Robotics	44	3-8
Gn	6G Network	45	3-5,7,8
Ne	Neuro-technology	46	1,2,4,6,8
Am	Advanced Material	47	1,2,4,6,8
Hr	Human Rigths	48	4,5,7,8
Ts	Technology & Science	49	1-8
Fm	Financial Market	50	1-8
Di	Diversity	51	5-8
Wu	Water Usage	52	1-8
Wm	Waste Management	53	1-8
Dp	3D Printing	61	1,3-8
Fe	Fusion Energy	62	1-8
Na	Nano-technology	63	1-8
Bi	Bio-informatics	64	1-8
Ns	National Security	65	1,2,7,8
Ep	Enviroment Protection	66	1,2,6-8
Ti	Trade & Investment	67	1-4,8
Rs	Reskilling	68	1-8
Ee	Energy Efficiency	69	1-8
Em	CO_2 Emissions	70	1-8

Group

● Technology   ○ Regulatory

● Globalization   ● Demographic

Strategic Archetype Inclination

1. Growth
2. Competitiveness
3. Cost Efficiency
4. Performance
5. Operational Excellence
6. Service or Product
7. Lower Risk
8. Sustainable Dev. Goals

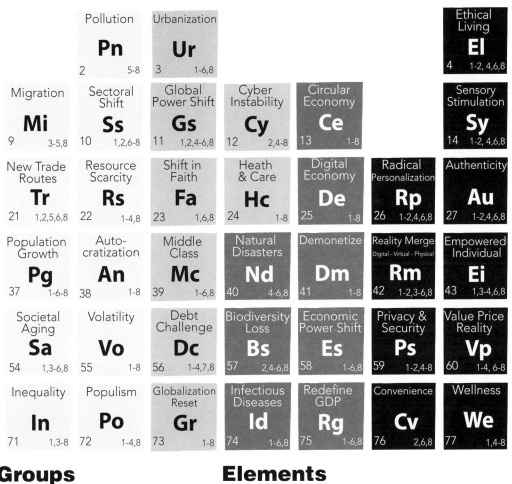

Name	Symbol	Number	Inclination
Pollution	Pn	2	5-8
Urbanization	Ur	3	1-6,8
Ethical Living	El	4	1-2, 4,6,8
Migration	Mi	9	3-5,8
Sectoral Shift	Ss	10	1,2,6-8
Global Power Shift	Gs	11	1,2,4-6,8
Cyber Instability	Cy	12	2,4-8
Circular Economy	Ce	13	1-8
Sensory Stimulation	Sy	14	1-2, 4,6,8
New Trade Routes	Tr	21	1,2,5,6,8
Resource Scarcity	Rs	22	1-4,8
Shift in Faith	Fa	23	1,6,8
Heath & Care	Hc	24	1-8
Digital Economy	De	25	1-8
Radical Personalization	Rp	26	1-2,4,6,8
Authenticity	Au	27	1-2,4,6,8
Population Growth	Pg	37	1-6,8
Auto-cratization	An	38	1-8
Middle Class	Mc	39	1-6,8
Natural Disasters	Nd	40	4-6,8
Demonetize	Dm	41	1-8
Reality Merge (Digital - Virtual - Physical)	Rm	42	1-2,3-6,8
Empowered Individual	Ei	43	1,3-4,6,8
Societal Aging	Sa	54	1,3-6,8
Volatility	Vo	55	1-8
Debt Challenge	Dc	56	1-4,7,8
Biodiversity Loss	Bs	57	2,4-6,8
Economic Power Shift	Es	58	1-6,8
Privacy & Security	Ps	59	1-2,4-8
Value Price Reality	Vp	60	1-4, 6-8
Inequality	In	71	1,3-8
Populism	Po	72	1-4,8
Globalization Reset	Gr	73	1-8
Infectious Diseases	Id	74	1-6,8
Redefine GDP	Rg	75	1-6,8
Convenience	Cv	76	2,6,8
Wellness	We	77	1,4-8

Each Megatrends Element is classified in line with the Strategic inclination of the potential impact delivered.

Groups

Elements

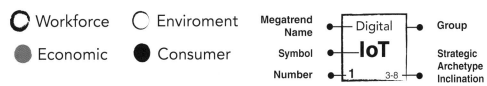

○ Workforce ○ Enviroment

● Economic ● Consumer

Megatrend Name
Symbol
Number

| Digital |
| **IoT** |
| 1   3-8 |

Group

Strategic Archetype Inclination

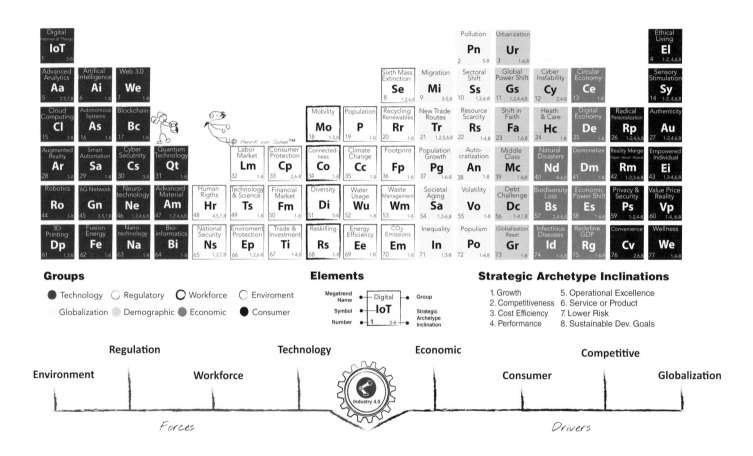

Groups

- ● Technology
- ○ Regulatory
- ○ Workforce
- ○ Enviroment
- ● Globalization
- ● Demographic
- ● Economic
- ● Consumer

Elements

Megatrend Name → | Digital | ← Group
Symbol → | **IoT** |
Number → | 1   3-8 | ← Strategic Archetype Inclination

Strategic Archetype Inclinations

1. Growth
2. Competitiveness
3. Cost Efficiency
4. Performance
5. Operational Excellence
6. Service or Product
7. Lower Risk
8. Sustainable Dev. Goals

258

Map the change needs in the current operation

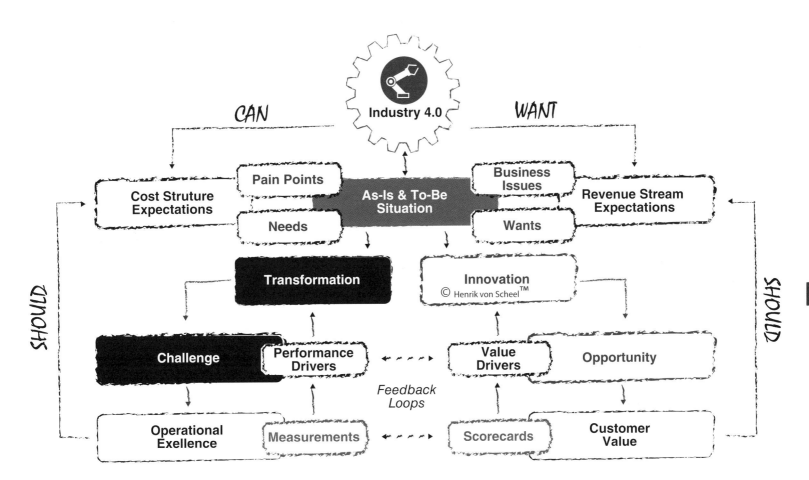

Industry 4.0

CAN

WANT

SHOULD

SHOULD

Cost Struture Expectations

Pain Points

As-Is & To-Be Situation

Business Issues

Revenue Stream Expectations

Needs

Wants

Transformation

Innovation

© Henrik von Scheel™

Challenge

Performance Drivers

Value Drivers

Opportunity

Feedback Loops

Operational Exellence

Measurements

Scorecards

Customer Value

Expectation

Pain point versus need...

Challenges...

Performance driver...

Transformation...

CAN DO...

SHOULD DO...

Transformation classification

1	Where	Location
2	When	Time
3	Whence	Source
4	How	Manner
5	What	Context
6	Why	Reason
7	Who	Personal/actor
8	Whether	Options

© Henrik von Scheel™

5 Define Opportunities

Expectation

Issues versus wants...

Opportunity...

Value driver...

Innovation...

WANT TO DO...

SHOULD DO...

Innovcation classification

Reason	**Why**	1
Options	**Whether**	2
Context	**What**	3
Location	**Where**	4
Manner	**How**	5
Source	**Whence**	6
Time	**When**	7
Personal/actor	**Who**	8

Take *design decisions*

STEP 4

Determine the

Strategic Choices

Analyze the scenarios and strategic choices of what not to do, where to be different, and what to focus on.

Step 7. Approach to Abyss

In which the hero gets closer to his goal of strategic positioning and strategic choices and moving toward strategy execution. This is not a physical cave, but a mental one. Instead, the "abyss" of outer darkness refers to the most dangerous spot in the other realm - whether that is the resistance, budget, or resource constraints in form of villains and fearsome dragons. Almost always, it is where the ultimate goal of the quest is located.

The *superpower* received by the mentor to achieve *strategic choices* are

1. **Assess the 80-15 and 5 rule** potential for innovation and transformation.

2. **Determine the strategic choices**
   Outline strategic scenarios of what not to do, where to be different, and what to focus on, in this order.

3. **Define desired impact** with goals and critical success factors.

4. **Take design decisions** with stakeholders. The quality potential of a solution, prototype, impact scenarios.

   - Ratify solution, review capabilities, and define the requirement

   - Ideate gains, execution capability, and budget potential

5. **Calculate performance and budget impact**

   - Define scope, business plan, and implementation roadmap

   - Map success factors, requirement, and deliverables with roles and budget

Step 8. Death and Rebirth

In which the hero faces her biggest test of all thus far. Of all the tests the hero has faced, none have made her hit rock bottom - until now. This is the "lack of moment and outer darkness." Both indicate some grim news for the hero.

The protagonist must now confront her greatest fear of failure. If she survives it, she will emerge transformed. This is a critical moment that will "inform every decision that the hero makes from this point forward and is reborn." The pieces of strategic positioning, choices, and strategy execution align.

In this ordeal, the hero actually earns the title of "Hero."

Teamwork is the secret that makes common people achieve uncommon results.

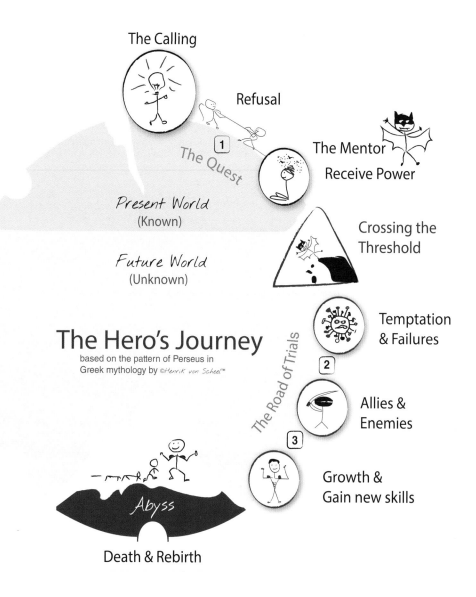

The Calling

Refusal

The Mentor
Receive Power

The Quest

Present World
(Known)

Future World
(Unknown)

Crossing the
Threshold

The Hero's Journey
based on the pattern of Perseus in
Greek mythology by ©Henrik von Scheel™

The Road of Trials

Temptation
& Failures

Allies &
Enemies

Growth &
Gain new skills

Abyss

Death & Rebirth

Where and when to be different

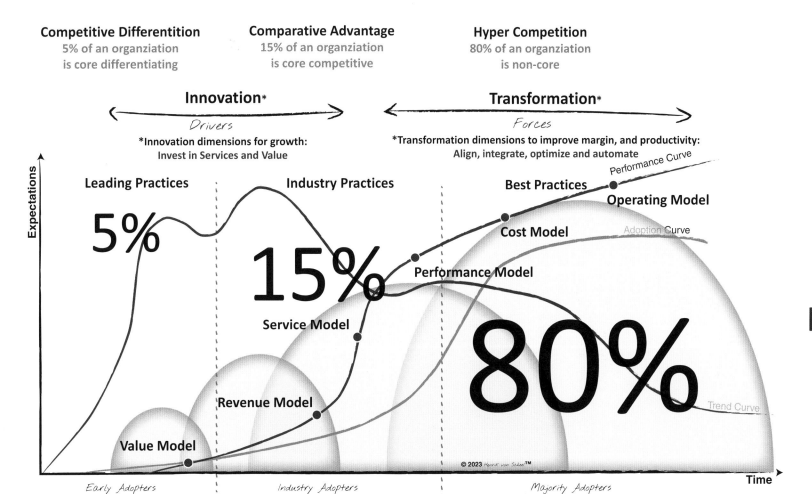

Competitive Differentition
5% of an organziation is core differentiating

Comparative Advantage
15% of an organziation is core competitive

Hyper Competition
80% of an organziation is non-core

Innovation*
Drivers
*Innovation dimensions for growth:
Invest in Services and Value

Transformation*
Forces
*Transformation dimensions to improve margin, and productivity:
Align, integrate, optimize and automate

Expectations

Performance Curve

Leading Practices

Industry Practices

Best Practices

5%

Operating Model

Cost Model

Adoption Curve

15%

Performance Model

Service Model

80%

Revenue Model

Trend Curve

Value Model

© 2023 Henrik von Scheel™

Early Adopters

Industry Adopters

Majority Adopters

Time

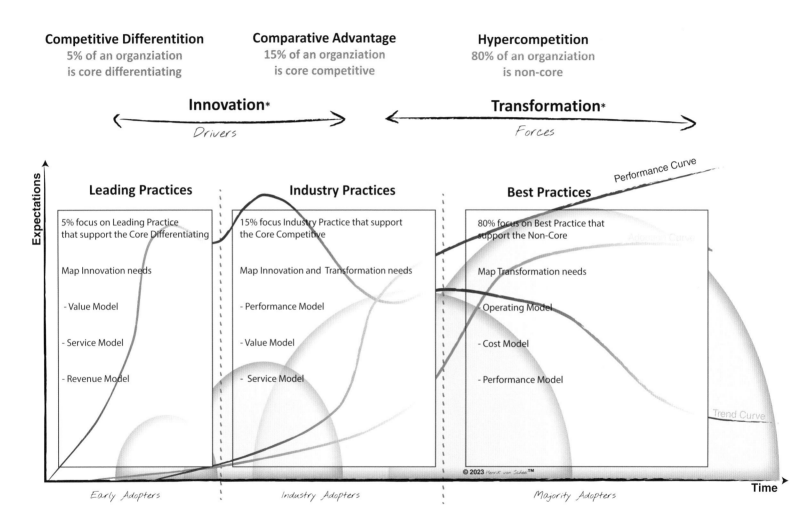

① Pinpoint the 5-15-80

Competitive Differentition
5% of an organziation
is core differentiating

Comparative Advantage
15% of an organziation
is core competitive

Hypercompetition
80% of an organziation
is non-core

Innovation*
Drivers

Transformation*
Forces

Expectations

Leading Practices

5% focus on Leading Practice
that support the Core Differentiating

Map Innovation needs

- Value Model

- Service Model

- Revenue Model

Industry Practices

15% focus Industry Practice that support
the Core Competitive

Map Innovation and Transformation needs

- Performance Model

- Value Model

- Service Model

Best Practices

Performance Curve

80% focus on Best Practice that
support the Non-Core

Map Transformation needs

- Operating Model

- Cost Model

- Performance Model

Advanced Curve

Trend Curve

© 2023 *Henrik von Scheel*™

Early Adopters   *Industry Adopters*   *Majority Adopters*

Time

266

② Determine Strategic Choices:

1. What not to do
2. Where to be different
3. What to focus on

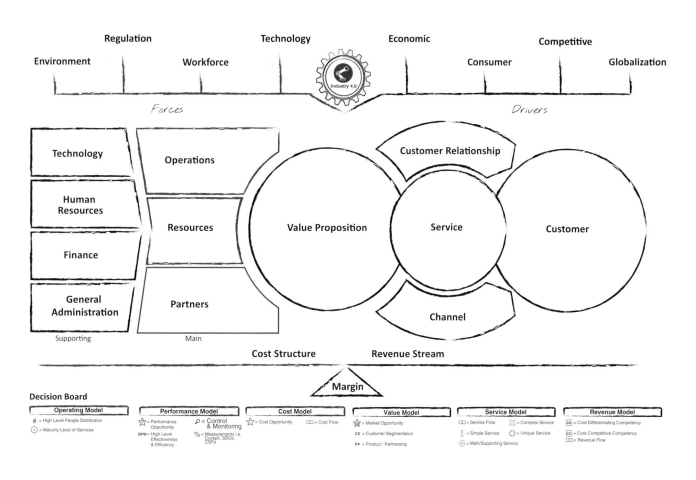

Environment Regulation Workforce Technology Economic Consumer Competitive Globalization

Industry 4.0

Forces   Drivers

Supporting
- Technology
- Human Resources
- Finance
- General Administration

Main
- Operations
- Resources
- Partners

Value Proposition

Customer Relationship

Service

Channel

Customer

Cost Structure   Revenue Stream

Margin

Decision Board

Operating Model	Performance Model	Cost Model	Value Model	Service Model	Revenue Model
# = High Level People Distribution	☆ = Performance Opportunity ρ = Control & Monitoring	☆ = Cost Opportunity ⬛ = Cost Flow	☆ = Market Opportunity	⬛ = Service Flow ✳ = Complex Service	CD = Core Differentiating Competency
① = Maturity Level of Services	BPM = High Level Effectiveness & Efficiency % = Measurements i.e. Cockpit, SBOs, CSFs		CS = Customer Segmentation	▯ = Simple Service ⬡ = Unique Service	CC = Core Competitive Competency
			PP = Product / Partnership	◎ = Main/Supporting Service	⬛ = Revenue Flow

What not to do

The primary goal of the technique is to determine the root cause of a defective pain point and desired need.

It is a key secret to understand the current business state, what has been done from an internal view, and what the options are.

Creating a guided path to capture what not to do; what to do less of; where, how, and with what to differentiate; what do more of; where to innovate; and when to transform. A simple way to broaden your thinking and make better decisions.

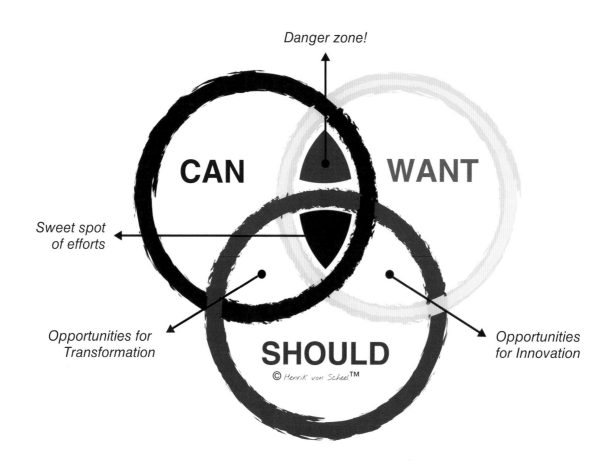

Danger zone!

CAN   WANT

Sweet spot of efforts

Opportunities for Transformation

SHOULD

© Henrik von Scheel™

Opportunities for Innovation

What not to do

Why to differentiate

Differentiation is the essence of strategy, the prime source of competitive advantage. You earn money not just by performing a valuable task, but by being different from your competitors in a manner that lets you serve your core customers better and more profitably.

Gaining an edge over peers from competitive dynamics or comparative advantage requires you to relentlessly build on fundamental differentiation, going from strength to strength.

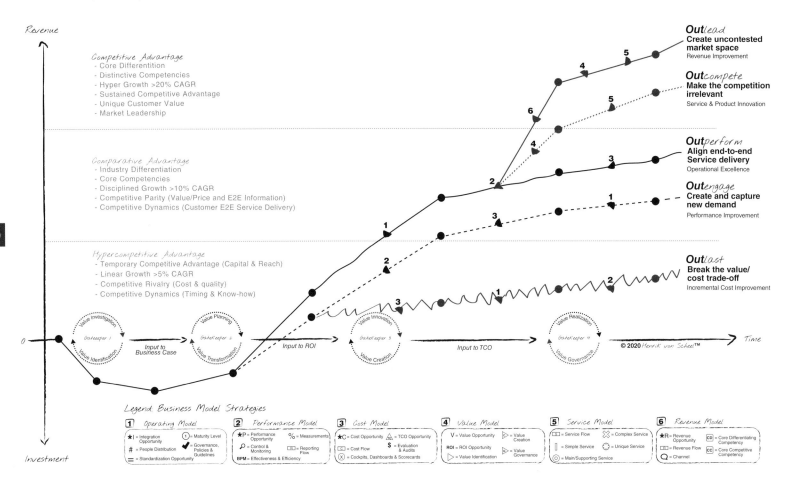

Competitive Advantage
- Core Differentition
- Distinctive Competencies
- Hyper Growth >20% CAGR
- Sustained Competitive Advantage
- Unique Customer Value
- Market Leadership

Comparative Advantage
- Industry Differentiation
- Core Competencies
- Disciplined Growth >10% CAGR
- Competitive Parity (Value/Price and E2E Information)
- Competitive Dynamics (Customer E2E Service Delivery)

Hypercompetitive Advantage
- Temporary Competitive Advantage (Capital & Reach)
- Linear Growth >5% CAGR
- Competitive Rivalry (Cost & quality)
- Competitive Dynamics (Timing & Know-how)

Outlead
Create uncontested market space
Revenue Improvement

Outcompete
Make the competition irrelevant
Service & Product Innovation

Outperform
Align end-to-end Service delivery
Operational Excellence

Outengage
Create and capture new demand
Performance Improvement

Outlast
Break the value/ cost trade-off
Incremental Cost Improvement

© 2020 Henrik von Scheel™

Revenue · Investment · Time

Value Investigation · Gatekeeper 1 · Value Identification · Input to Business Case · Value Planning · Gatekeeper 2 · Value Transformation · Input to ROI · Value Innovation · GateKeeper 3 · Value Creation · Input to TCO · Value Realization · GateKeeper 4 · Value Governance

Legend Business Model Strategies

1 Operating Model
- ★I = Integration Opportunity
- ① = Maturity Level
- # = People Distribution
- ✔ = Governance, Policies & Guidelines
- = = Standardization Opportunity

2 Performance Model
- ★P = Performance Opportunity
- % = Measurements
- ρ = Control & Monitoring
- ▭ = Reporting Flow
- BPM = Effectiveness & Efficiency

3 Cost Model
- ★C = Cost Opportunity
- ⚠ = TCO Opportunity
- ρ = Cost Flow
- $ = Evaluation & Audits
- ⊗ = Cockpits, Dashboards & Scorecards

4 Value Model
- V = Value Opportunity
- ▷ = Value Creation
- ROI = ROI Opportunity
- ▷ = Value Identification
- ▷ = Value Governance

5 Service Model
- ▭ = Service Flow
- ⊗ = Complex Service
- I = Simple Service
- ⊙ = Unique Service
- ◎ = Main/Supporting Service

6 Revenue Model
- ★R = Revenue Opportunity
- CD = Core Differentiating Competency
- ▭ = Revenue Flow
- CC = Core Competitive Competency
- Ω = Channel

How and where to differentiate

It's no secret that digital strategy is difficult for well-established companies. By and large, they are better executors than strategists and innovators, and most succeed less through game-changing creativity than by optimizing their existing businesses.

Since digital strategies are complex, company-wide endeavors, they require a set of crosscutting practices to structure, organize, operate, and encourage it.

As digital strategies always are impact-driven, there are nine essential strategies with organizational factors that separate a successful company from the rest of the field.

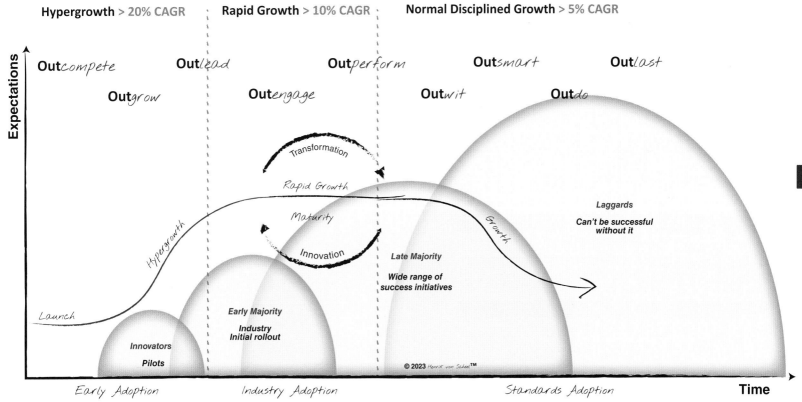

Hypergrowth > 20% CAGR   **Rapid Growth** > 10% CAGR   **Normal Disciplined Growth** > 5% CAGR

Expectations

Outcompete   **Out**lead   **Out**perform   **Out**smart   **Out**last

Outgrow   **Out**engage   **Out**wit   **Out**do

Transformation

Rapid Growth

Maturity

Innovation

Hypergrowth

Growth

Launch

Laggards

Can't be successful without it

Late Majority

Wide range of success initiatives

Early Majority

Industry Initial rollout

Innovators

Pilots

© 2023 Henrik von Scheel™

Early Adoption   Industry Adoption   Standards Adoption   **Time**

Where and when to differentiate

The strategic choices are often the sequence of why, when, where, and with what. He who will win, knows when to fight and when not to fight.

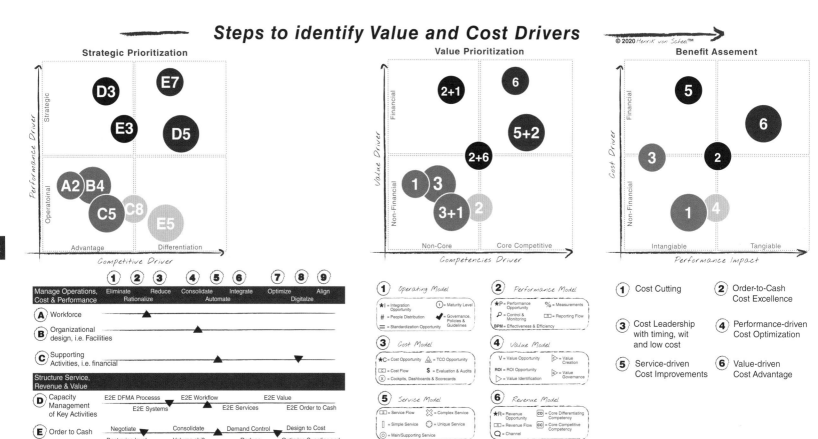

Steps to identify Value and Cost Drivers

© 2020 Henrik von Scheel™

Strategic Prioritization

Value Prioritization

Benefit Assement

Where, when, and how to differentiate

Competitive *Advantage*   Comperative *Advantage*   Competitive *Parity*

Competitive *Dynamics*   Competitive *Rivalry*   Hypercompetitive *Advantage*

Innovation*
Drivers

Transformation*
Forces

Hypergrowth
> 20% CAGR

Rapid Growth
> 10% CAGR

Normal Disciplined Growth
> 5% CAGR

Performance Curve

Adoption Curve

Expectations

5%

15%

80%

Trend Curve

© 2023 *Henrik von Scheel*™

Time

Early Adopters   *Industry Adopters*   *Majority Adopters*

Steps to identify Strategic Priority

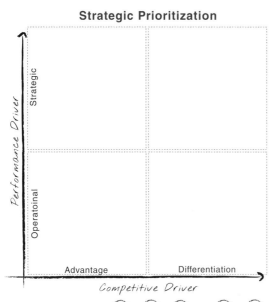

Strategic Prioritization

Performance Driver (vertical axis): Strategic / Operatoinal

Competitive Driver (horizontal axis): Advantage / Differentiation

	①	②	③	④	⑤	⑥	⑦	⑧	⑨
Manage Operations, Cost & Performance	Eliminate	Rationalize	Reduce	Consolidate	Automate	Integrate	Optimize	Digitalze	Align

Ⓐ Workforce

Ⓑ Organizational design, i.e. Facilities

Ⓒ Supporting Activities, i.e. financial

Structure Service, Revenue & Value

Ⓓ Capacity Management of Key Activities

Ⓔ Order to Cash

Steps to identify Value Priority

Value Prioritization

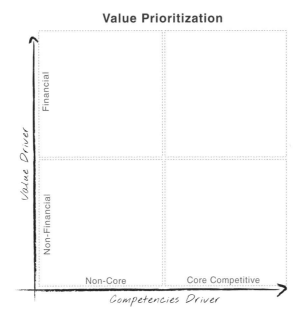

- Value Driver
  - Financial
  - Non-Financial
- Competencies Driver
  - Non-Core
  - Core Competitive

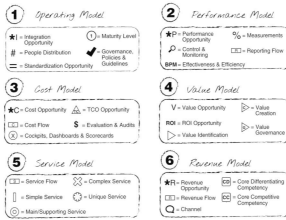

1 Operating Model

- ★I = Integration Opportunity
- ① = Maturity Level
- # = People Distribution
- ✔ = Governance, Policies & Guidelines
- ══ = Standardization Opportunity

2 Performance Model

- ★P = Performance Opportunity
- % = Measurements
- 🔍 = Control & Monitoring
- [R] = Reporting Flow
- **BPM** = Effectiveness & Efficiency

3 Cost Model

- ★C = Cost Opportunity
- 🔺TC = TCO Opportunity
- [C] = Cost Flow
- $ = Evaluation & Audits
- (X) = Cockpits, Dashboards & Scorecards

4 Value Model

- V = Value Opportunity
- ▷C = Value Creation
- **ROI** = ROI Opportunity
- ▷G = Value Governance
- ▷ = Value Identification

5 Service Model

- [S] = Service Flow
- ✕ = Complex Service
- | = Simple Service
- 🔅 = Unique Service
- ⊚ = Main/Supporting Service

6 Revenue Model

- ★R = Revenue Opportunity
- [CD] = Core Differentiating Competency
- [R] = Revenue Flow
- [CC] = Core Competitive Competency
- Q = Channel

Steps for Benefit Assessment

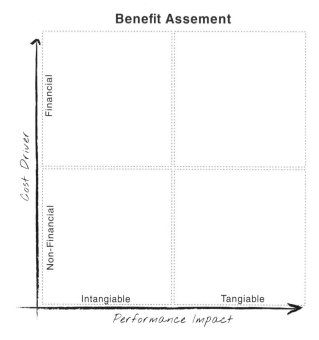

Benefit Assement

1. Cost Cutting
2. Order-to-Cash Cost Excellence
3. Cost Leadership with timing, wit and low cost
4. Performance-driven Cost Optimization
5. Service-driven Cost Improvements
6. Value-driven Cost Advantage

Example of define desired Impact

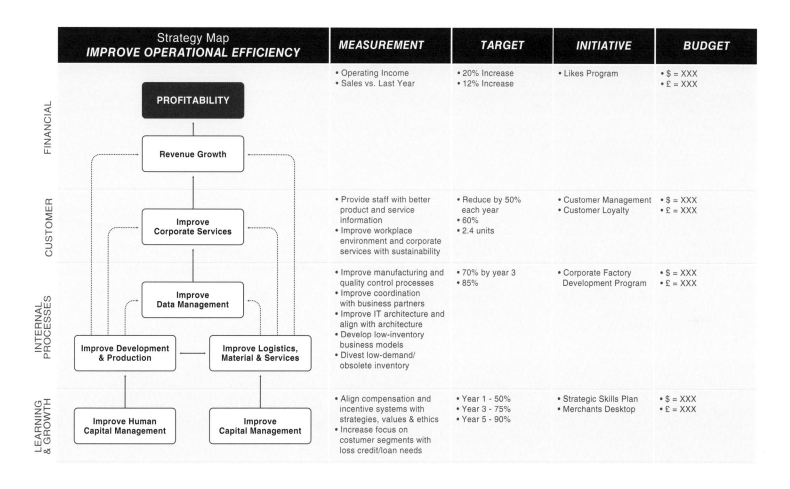

Strategy Map **IMPROVE OPERATIONAL EFFICIENCY**	MEASUREMENT	TARGET	INITIATIVE	BUDGET
PROFITABILITY (FINANCIAL)	• Operating Income • Sales vs. Last Year	• 20% Increase • 12% Increase	• Likes Program	• $ = XXX • £ = XXX
Revenue Growth				
Improve Corporate Services (CUSTOMER)	• Provide staff with better product and service information • Improve workplace environment and corporate services with sustainability	• Reduce by 50% each year • 60% • 2.4 units	• Customer Management • Customer Loyalty	• $ = XXX • £ = XXX
Improve Data Management (INTERNAL PROCESSES)	• Improve manufacturing and quality control processes • Improve coordination with business partners • Improve IT architecture and align with architecture • Develop low-inventory business models • Divest low-demand/ obsolete inventory	• 70% by year 3 • 85%	• Corporate Factory Development Program	• $ = XXX • £ = XXX
Improve Development & Production / Improve Logistics, Material & Services				
Improve Human Capital Management / **Improve Capital Management** (LEARNING & GROWTH)	• Align compensation and incentive systems with strategies, values & ethics • Increase focus on costumer segments with loss credit/loan needs	• Year 1 - 50% • Year 3 - 75% • Year 5 - 90%	• Strategic Skills Plan • Merchants Desktop	• $ = XXX • £ = XXX

Holistic view to link strategy with operations

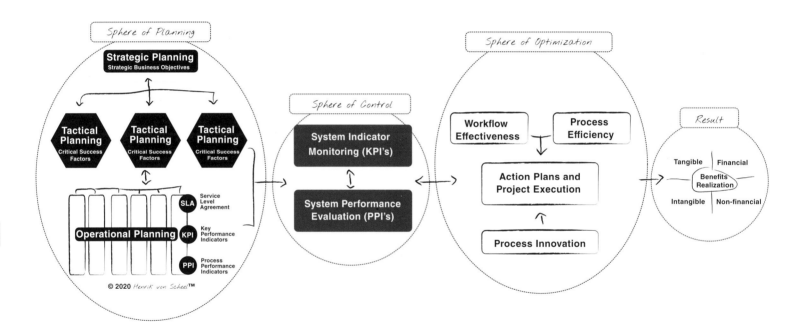

278

It takes more than systems and technology

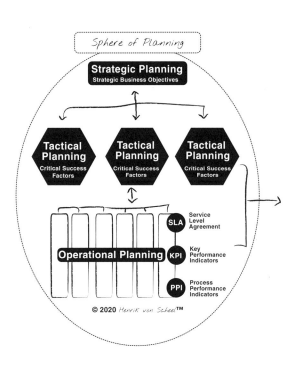

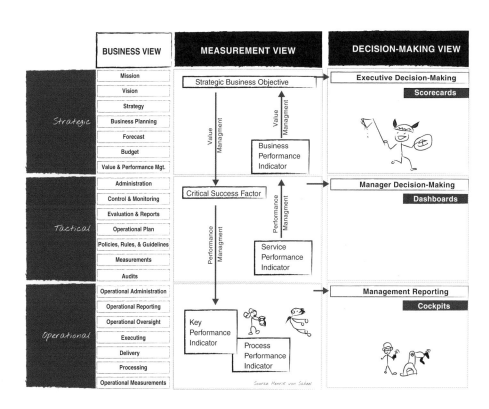

Example of how to link strategy with Operations

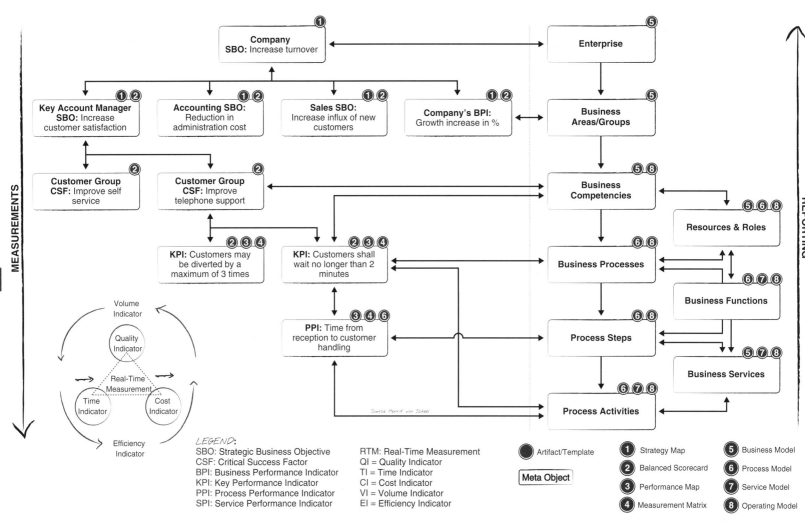

MEASUREMENTS

REPORTING

280

Company
SBO: Increase turnover ①

Enterprise ⑤

Key Account Manager
SBO: Increase customer satisfaction ①②

Accounting SBO:
Reduction in administration cost ①②

Sales SBO:
Increase influx of new customers ①②

Company's BPI:
Growth increase in % ①②

Business Areas/Groups ⑤

Customer Group
CSF: Improve self service ②

Customer Group
CSF: Improve telephone support ②

Business Competencies ⑤⑧

Resources & Roles ⑤⑥⑧

KPI: Customers may be diverted by a maximum of 3 times ②③④

KPI: Customers shall wait no longer than 2 minutes ②③④

Business Processes ⑥⑧

Business Functions ⑥⑦⑧

PPI: Time from reception to customer handling ③④⑥

Process Steps ⑥⑧

Business Services ⑤⑦⑧

Process Activities ⑥⑦⑧

Source: Henrik von Scheel

Volume Indicator
Quality Indicator
Real-Time Measurement
Time Indicator
Cost Indicator
Efficiency Indicator

LEGEND:
SBO: Strategic Business Objective
CSF: Critical Success Factor
BPI: Business Performance Indicator
KPI: Key Performance Indicator
PPI: Process Performance Indicator
SPI: Service Performance Indicator

RTM: Real-Time Measurement
QI = Quality Indicator
TI = Time Indicator
CI = Cost Indicator
VI = Volume Indicator
EI = Efficiency Indicator

⬤ Artifact/Template

Meta Object

① Strategy Map
② Balanced Scorecard
③ Performance Map
④ Measurement Matrix

⑤ Business Model
⑥ Process Model
⑦ Service Model
⑧ Operating Model

③ Define desired Impact

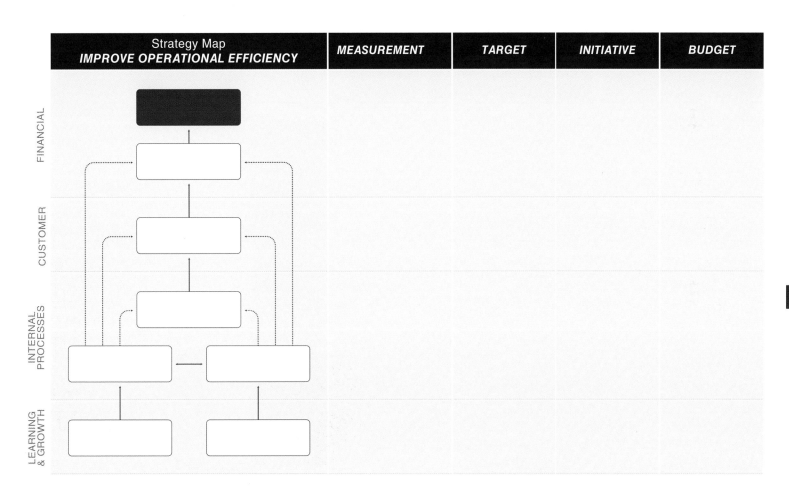

Strategy Map **IMPROVE OPERATIONAL EFFICIENCY**	MEASUREMENT	TARGET	INITIATIVE	BUDGET
FINANCIAL				
CUSTOMER				
INTERNAL PROCESSES				
LEARNING & GROWTH				

Strategic Business Objectives	Critical Success Factors	Ownership

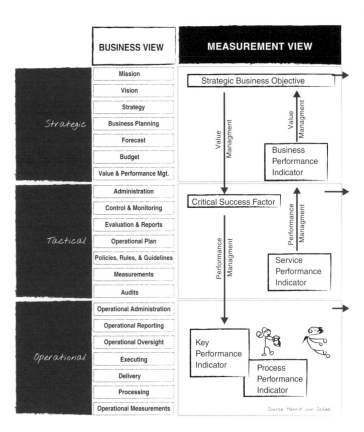

BUSINESS VIEW	MEASUREMENT VIEW

Strategic

- Mission
- Vision
- Strategy
- Business Planning
- Forecast
- Budget
- Value & Performance Mgt.

Strategic Business Objective

Value Managment

Value Managment

Business Performance Indicator

Tactical

- Administration
- Control & Monitoring
- Evaluation & Reports
- Operational Plan
- Policies, Rules, & Guidelines
- Measurements
- Audits

Critical Success Factor

Performance Managment

Performance Managment

Service Performance Indicator

Operational

- Operational Administration
- Operational Reporting
- Operational Oversight
- Executing
- Delivery
- Processing
- Operational Measurements

Key Performance Indicator

Process Performance Indicator

Source: Henrik von Scheel

Example of goals, critical success factors to KPI

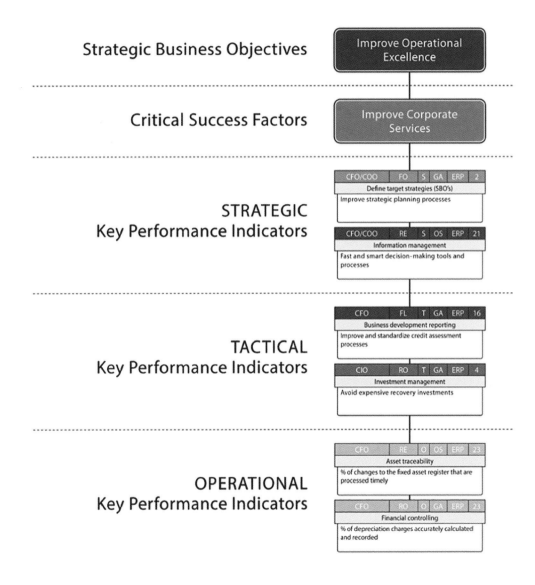

Strategic Business Objectives — Improve Operational Excellence

Critical Success Factors — Improve Corporate Services

STRATEGIC Key Performance Indicators

CFO/COO	FO	S	GA	ERP	2
Define target strategies (SBO's)					
Improve strategic planning processes					

CFO/COO	RE	S	OS	ERP	21
Information management					
Fast and smart decision-making tools and processes					

TACTICAL Key Performance Indicators

CFO	FL	T	GA	ERP	16
Business development reporting					
Improve and standardize credit assessment processes					

CIO	RO	T	GA	ERP	4
Investment management					
Avoid expensive recovery investments					

OPERATIONAL Key Performance Indicators

CFO	RE	O	OS	ERP	23
Asset traceability					
% of changes to the fixed asset register that are processed timely					

CFO	RO	O	GA	ERP	23
Financial controlling					
% of depreciation charges accurately calculated and recorded					

Example of goals and critical success factors

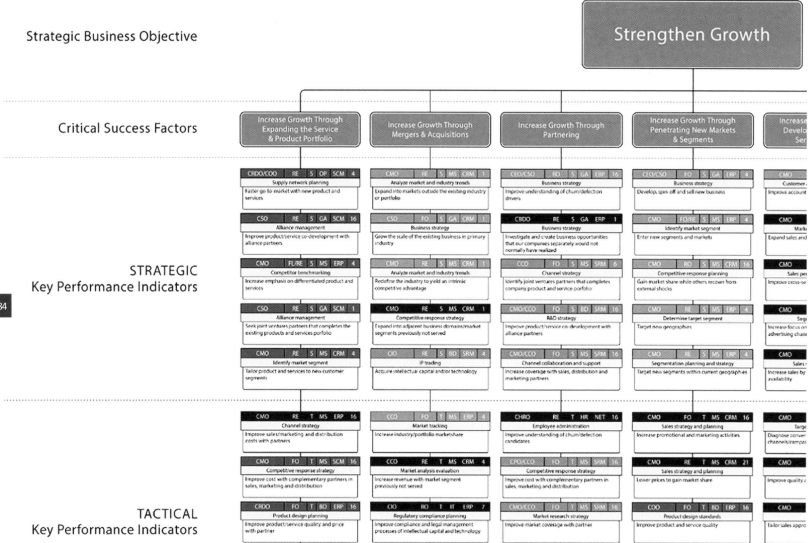

(4) Define value and performance goals

Strategic Business Objectives	Critical Success Factors	Ownership

④ Define value and performance goals

Key Performance Indicators	Major Business Process and Performance Measures	Ownership	Activity and Performance Measures
	Process:		Process:
	M1.		M1.
	M2.		M2.
	Process:		Process:
	M1.		M1.
	M2.		M2.
	Process:		Process:
	M1.		M1.
	M2.		M2.
	Process:		Process:
	M1.		M1.
	M2.		M2.

4 Take design decisions

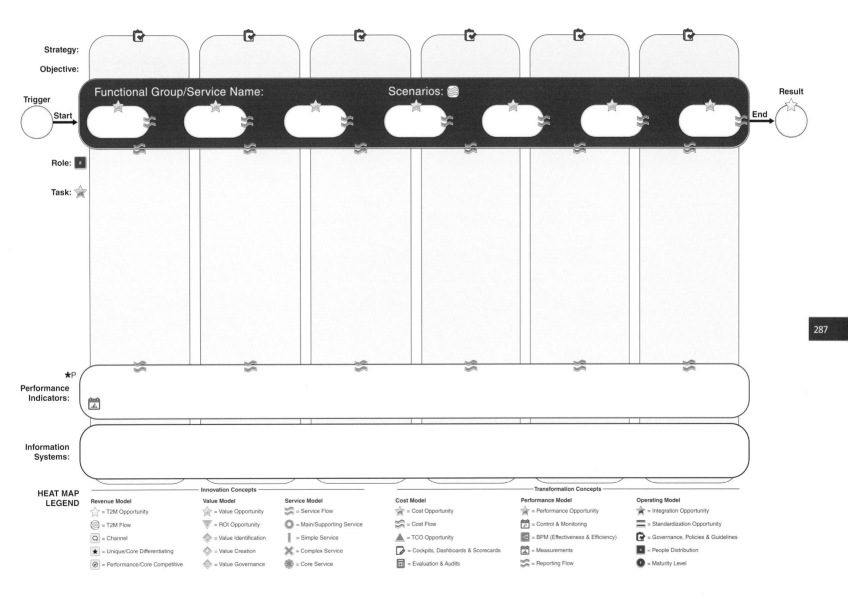

Strategy:

Objective:

Trigger

Start

Functional Group/Service Name:

Scenarios:

Result

End

Role: #

Task: ☆

★P

Performance Indicators:

Information Systems:

287

HEAT MAP LEGEND

─── Innovation Concepts ───

─── Transformation Concepts ───

Revenue Model
- ☆ = T2M Opportunity
- ≋ = T2M Flow
- Q = Channel
- ★ = Unique/Core Differentiating
- ⊘ = Performance/Core Competitive

Value Model
- ☆ = Value Opportunity
- ▽ = ROI Opportunity
- ◈ = Value Identification
- ◇ = Value Creation
- ◈ = Value Governance

Service Model
- ≋ = Service Flow
- ◎ = Main/Supporting Service
- | = Simple Service
- ✕ = Complex Service
- ✳ = Core Service

Cost Model
- ★ = Cost Opportunity
- ≋ = Cost Flow
- ▲ = TCO Opportunity
- ▱ = Cockpits, Dashboards & Scorecards
- ▦ = Evaluation & Audits

Performance Model
- ★ = Performance Opportunity
- ▱ = Control & Monitoring
- ▦ = BPM (Effectiveness & Efficiency)
- ▦ = Measurements
- ≋ = Reporting Flow

Operating Model
- ★ = Integration Opportunity
- = = Standardization Opportunity
- ✓ = Governance, Policies & Guidelines
- # = People Distribution
- ① = Maturity Level

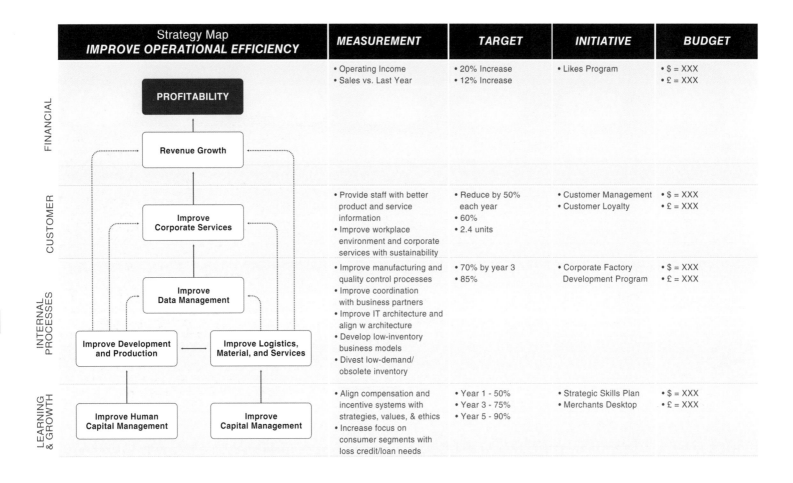

Strategy Map IMPROVE OPERATIONAL EFFICIENCY	MEASUREMENT	TARGET	INITIATIVE	BUDGET
FINANCIAL — PROFITABILITY → Revenue Growth	• Operating Income • Sales vs. Last Year	• 20% Increase • 12% Increase	• Likes Program	• $ = XXX • £ = XXX
CUSTOMER — Improve Corporate Services	• Provide staff with better product and service information • Improve workplace environment and corporate services with sustainability	• Reduce by 50% each year • 60% • 2.4 units	• Customer Management • Customer Loyalty	• $ = XXX • £ = XXX
INTERNAL PROCESSES — Improve Data Management / Improve Development and Production / Improve Logistics, Material, and Services	• Improve manufacturing and quality control processes • Improve coordination with business partners • Improve IT architecture and align w architecture • Develop low-inventory business models • Divest low-demand/ obsolete inventory	• 70% by year 3 • 85%	• Corporate Factory Development Program	• $ = XXX • £ = XXX
LEARNING & GROWTH — Improve Human Capital Management / Improve Capital Management	• Align compensation and incentive systems with strategies, values, & ethics • Increase focus on consumer segments with loss credit/loan needs	• Year 1 - 50% • Year 3 - 75% • Year 5 - 90%	• Strategic Skills Plan • Merchants Desktop	• $ = XXX • £ = XXX

Strategy Map **IMPROVE OPERATIONAL EFFICIENCY**	**MEASUREMENT**	**TARGET**	**INITIATIVE**	**BUDGET**
FINANCIAL				
CUSTOMER				
INTERNAL PROCESSES				
LEARNING & GROWTH				

Deliver on *Promise*

STEP 5

Align to prepare for

Strategy *Execution*

Step 9. Reward

In which the hero sees light at the end of the tunnel. Our hero's been through a lot. However, the fruits of his labor are now at hand — if he can just reach out and grab them! The "reward" is the object of knowledge the hero has fought throughout the entire journey to hold.

Once the protagonist has it in his possession, it generally has greater ramifications for the story.

Step 10. Return with the Elixir

In which the light at the end of the tunnel might be a little further than the hero thought. Now that she's seized the reward, the hero tries to return to the Ordinary World, but more dangers (inconveniently) arise on the road back from culture, change management resistance.

More precisely, the hero must deal with the consequences and aftermath of the previous act: the dragon, enraged by the hero who has just stolen a treasure from under his nose, starts the hunt. Or perhaps the opposing army gathers to pursue the hero across a crowded battlefield. All further obstacles for the hero, who must face them down before she can return home.

Step 11. Agent of Change

In which the last test is met.

Here is the true climax of the story. Everything that happened prior to this stage culminates in a crowning test for the hero, as the Dark Side gets one last chance to triumph over the hero. It is in this Final Battle that the protagonist goes through one more "rebirth" as he emerges as the agent of change.

Step 12.   Restore Order

In which our hero has a triumphant homecoming. Finally, the hero gets to return home. However, she goes back to a different person than when she started out: she has grown and matured as a result of the journey she has taken.

But we've got to see the hero bring home the bacon, right? That's why the protagonist must return with the "Elixir," or the prize won during the journey, whether that's an object or knowledge and insight gained to restore order.

The *superpower* received by the mentor to achieve <u>strategic</u> execution is:

1. **Set Direction and Context**
   - Review document and stakeholder deliverables sign-off
   - There is a clear view of what success looks like across the organization with relevant partners

2. **Establish accountability and performance metric**
   - Accountabilities are clear, key performance indicators and scorecards are balanced and cover both performance and health, and metrics cascade where appropriate
   - Targets stretch employees but are also fully owned by management, and they are supported by appropriate resources

3. **Design realistic budgets, plans, and targets**
   - Reporting gives a timely view of performance with appropriate detail, and it does not burden the organization

4. **Track performance management**

5. **Continuous delivery improvements**

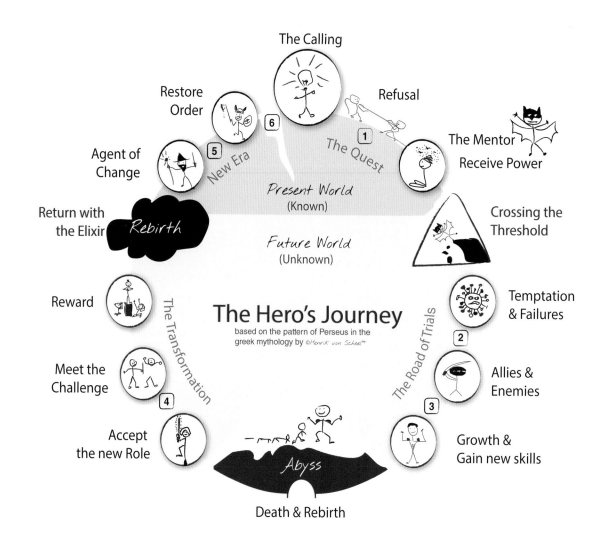

The Calling

Restore Order

Refusal

6

The Quest

The Mentor
Receive Power

Agent of Change

5

New Era

Return with the Elixir

Rebirth

Present World
(Known)

Crossing the Threshold

Future World
(Unknown)

Reward

The Transformation

The Hero's Journey
based on the pattern of Perseus in the
greek mythology by ©Henrik von Scheel™

The Road of Trials

Temptation & Failures

2

Allies & Enemies

Meet the Challenge

4

3

Accept the new Role

Growth & Gain new skills

Abyss

Death & Rebirth

Deliver Strategy Execution on Promise

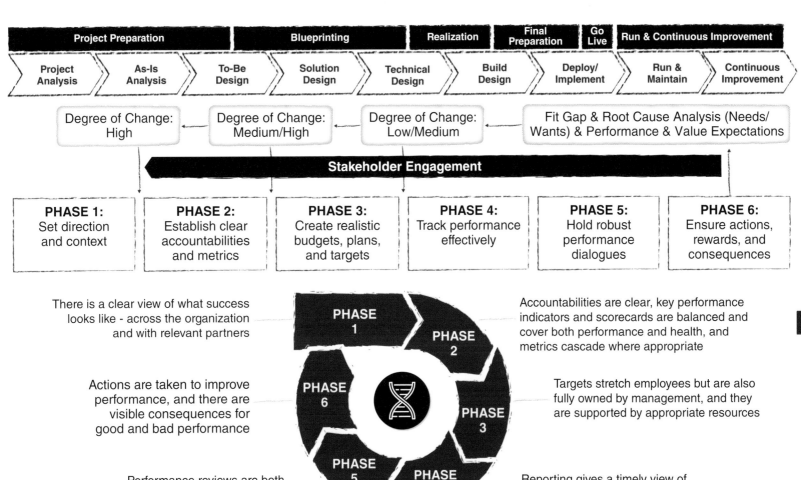

Project Preparation			Blueprinting		Realization	Final Preparation	Go Live	Run & Continuous Improvement
Project Analysis	As-Is Analysis	To-Be Design	Solution Design	Technical Design	Build Design	Deploy/ Implement	Run & Maintain	Continuous Improvement

Degree of Change: High ← Degree of Change: Medium/High ← Degree of Change: Low/Medium ← Fit Gap & Root Cause Analysis (Needs/ Wants) & Performance & Value Expectations

Stakeholder Engagement

PHASE 1: Set direction and context

PHASE 2: Establish clear accountabilities and metrics

PHASE 3: Create realistic budgets, plans, and targets

PHASE 4: Track performance effectively

PHASE 5: Hold robust performance dialogues

PHASE 6: Ensure actions, rewards, and consequences

There is a clear view of what success looks like - across the organization and with relevant partners

Accountabilities are clear, key performance indicators and scorecards are balanced and cover both performance and health, and metrics cascade where appropriate

Actions are taken to improve performance, and there are visible consequences for good and bad performance

Targets stretch employees but are also fully owned by management, and they are supported by appropriate resources

Performance reviews are both challenging and supportive, and are focused, fact based, and action oriented

Reporting gives a timely view of performance with appropriate detail, and it does not burden the organization

Step-by-step activities to deliver on promise

Phase 1: Set direction and context

Develop a foundation for delivery and establish a clear view of what success looks like – across the organization and with relevant partners.

- **Identify desired outcomes**

  - Capture purpose and goal (strategic intent)

  - Detect desire outcomes

  - Map stakeholders involved

- **Determine priorities**

  - Identify performance and value expectations

  - Understand implications and requirements

  - Evaluate risk involved

  - Determine priorities with stakeholders

- **Set targets/define success**

  - Determine measurements of success

  - Define executive accountabilities

- **Understand the challenge**

  - Evaluate past and present performance

  - Review the current state of delivery

- **Set direction and context**

Phase 2: Establish clear accountabilities and metrics

Define clear accountabilities, key performance indicators and scorecards are balanced and cover both performance and health, and metrics cascade where appropriate.

- **Establish metrics and trajectories**

  - Capture performance and value expectations

  - Priorities critical outcome with time-bound goals and trajectories.

  - Define key performance indicators and data source

  - Outline scorecards

  - Agree on routine scorecard review

- **Define clear accountabilities**

  - Establish clear accountabilities and metrics

  - Cascade performance metric to roles involved

Phase 3: Create realistic budgets, plans, and targets

Plan to deliver milestones, data, and trajectories. Understand the delivery chain. Build capacity at every level. Targets stretch employees but are also fully owned by management, and they are supported by appropriate resources.

- **Plan for delivery**

  - Specify the scope of delivery

  - Capture performance and value expectations

  - Gather high-level requirements

  - Develop a delivery plan with high-level activities, milestones, phases, and timelines

  - Chart methods used and systems impacted

  - Determine workload efforts, skills required, and roles involved

  - Define budget, performance measurements, and dependencies

Phase 4: Track performance effectively

Create routines. Reporting gives a timely view of performance with appropriate detail, and it does not burden the organization.

- **Build the delivery unit**

  - Establish a guide coalition and delivery unit

  - Understand the delivery unit challenges

  - Agree on delivery outcomes and metrics

  - Review delivery unit dependencies and risk

- **Delivery and track performance**

  - Put implementation plan into action

  - Set up performance effectively

  - Establish routines to drive and monitor

Phase 5: Hold robust performance dialogues

Solve problems as they arise. Performance reviews are both challenging and supportive, and are focused, fact-based, and action-oriented.

- **Robust performance management**

  - Put implementation plan into action

  - Review scorecard performance effectively

  - Establish routines to drive and monitor

  - Solve problems early and rigorously

  - Sustain and continually build momentum

  - Create an irreversible delivery culture

  - Build systems capacity all the time

Phase 6: Ensure actions, rewards, and consequences

Establish the right relationships. Persist and take action to improve performance, and there are visible consequences for good and bad performance

- **Continuous delivery improvement**

  - Routinely track delivery challenges

  - Identify performance gaps

  - Understand root cause

  - Define action required to improve performance.

  - Stakeholder communication of delivery

  - Communicate delivery status to the delivery unit

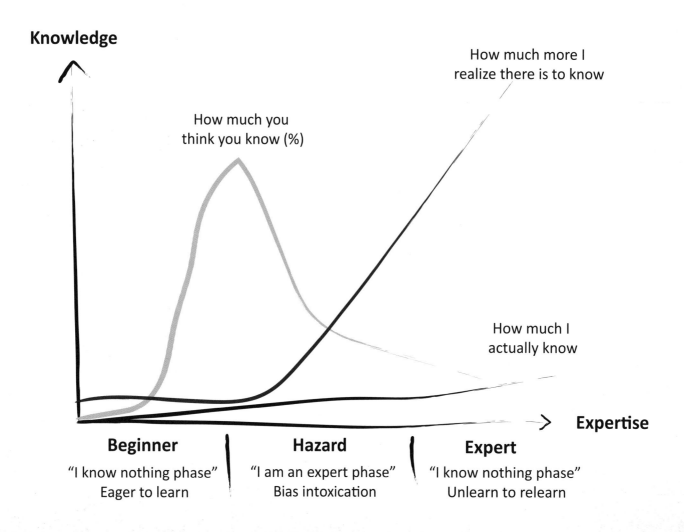

A modern visual interpretation of Socrates saying: "All I know, is that I know nothing."

Famous Last WORDS

Chapter Eight

Final words to the strategist

Failing by design
Strategy is a discipline that requires practice. Allow yourself to fail. Failure is not the opposite of success; it's success in progress if we learn from it.

I call this INTELLIGENT FAILURE.

DO IT. FAIL. LEARN from your mistakes, UNLEARN wrong biases, and RELEARN new principles. REPEAT.

On a personal note, my strategy work is applied to national economies, influences GDP growth, triggers global themes, and has shaped the performance of the fastest-growing companies. However, I have gone through many failures along the way in order to get to the successes.

The secret sauce.
The true value of strategy resides in the benefit of alignment. Align executives to see the company as it is, explore the unknown potentials together, and agree on what not to do, where to be different, and what to focus on to deliver impact.

The effect of aligning an organization on a common goal of performance and service delivery is the backbone of the organizational culture.

The core of the strategy is people

Put people before strategy. The core of any strategy is people. Companies are a sum of skills, capabilities, and competencies driven by people. They are the value of any company. Strategy is made by, delivered by, blocked by, and consumed by people. Any strategy should focus on how to get the best of the organization to create amazing profitable companies. There is no way around it. People before strategy.

Let us build a culture of strategy execution. Let us refuse to accept mediocrity. Let us think differently to create a better future.

One of the main objectives of strategy is to help understand the change and evolve the organization to adapt to the changes.

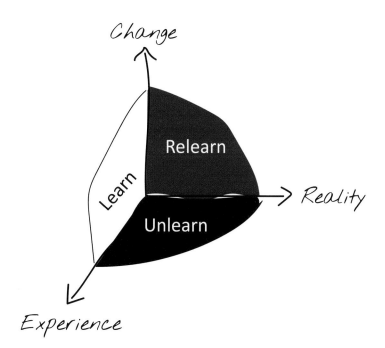

Common pitfalls to avoid with strategy

There are five common reasons why strategies are not succeeding on this journey.

Siloed implementation.

By pursuing strategy as a theoretical exercise, many companies unwittingly set up independent delivery teams that are decoupled from business leaders, operations managers, and central IT.

Others focus too much on replicating a single site experience, failing to appreciate wider network complexities.

Failure to adapt.

By deploying a one-size-fits-all approach, strategizers miss the opportunity to build in the customization and adaptation needed to leverage the unique circumstances, culture, and values of separate sites.

This is Straateeegyyyyyy!

Extract from a project manager in Strategy execution phase

When you make a choice to change certain things for the better, lots of old habits will try to win you over; the feeling of nostalgia kicks in slowly like poison.

In order for you to exterminate or exclude the poison, you have to consciously remake the decision to change over and over again until it replaces your old habit.

The power of change is not just simply to think differently but to act differently, the way you are with people but even more importantly the way you behave when you're alone, when no one is watching you, when you think no one is gonna judge you for what you do when you're alone.

* I can see what you are doing you know. *

Analysis paralysis.

Performing a full and deep up-front analysis of an entire network can leave an operation of steam before a transformation can get off the ground. Instead, robust, accurate-enough insights can be gleaned from a well-developed extrapolation methodology.

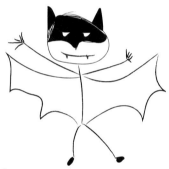

I am not saying, I am BATMAN.
I am just saying no one has ever seen me
and Batman in the same room together.

Technology-driven rather than value-driven.

A technology-first rollout means that solutions are deployed without a clear link to real value opportunities, business challenges, or capability requirements.

The result: undermining crucial buy-in from the people charged with making deployment work.

Letting the "perfect" defeat the good.

By waiting until a fully fledged, ideal-state data and IT/OT (information and operational technology) architecture is defined and implemented before rolling out Industry 4.0 solutions, operations lose out on the shorter time-to-impact made possible through a proven and pragmatic minimal viable architecture.

Death of the Genius

Three myths of creativity

There are myths of creativity and these myths are usually propagated by people who have romantic notions about heroes, romantic notions about eureka moments. And these myths of creativity keep people from collaborating and it causes them to be lone wolves. And the research says it causes them to fail.

So let me talk a little bit about those myths of creativity. In the business world, I battle against three myths.

Myth #1 Romantic notion of a hero

It's a romantic notion because we want to be heroes. We want to be empowered as heros. We want to think that we're the source and the genius. So this is how we tell the story.

Being a hero is a team sport

Myth number one, *the lone inventor*. This is very dangerous because there is no such thing as a lone inventor. As a matter of fact, there's a lot of historical research that has debunked Einstein. Specifically in terms of inventions, Henry Ford, not a lone inventor. A classic example: Thomas Edison. In the invention community, Thomas Edison is a brand. It stands for 14 people. Yes, there was a figurehead named Thomas Edison. His name is on 10,000 patents. He did not invent a single thing. He gathered people together and knew how to spot innovations and put people together like a creative soup, if you will.

Here's a classic example: Steve Jobs. You ask the average person, say a millennial who uses a lot of Apple technology, "Who's one of the greatest inventors of our time?" They'll say Steve Jobs. Steve Jobs once said, "I never created anything. All I did was notice patterns and put people together to finish projects." So think about it. If he did not have Wozniak, there is no original Apple, right? If he did not have Tony Fiddel, there is no iPhone. And the list goes on.

> **"** I never created anything. All I did was notice patterns and put people together to finish projects. **"**

Steve Jobs
Business magnate

Difference between being great or good

But until you believe that genius is a team sport, you will never give up control. And this is the problem for a lot of people in leadership and sales. They don't want to cede any level of control over their process to somebody outside of leadership or sales world because they don't value those voices enough. But this is the difference between good and great. The great will sell 20% more than their nearest competitor. The only thing they have in common is they've broken this myth and they understand that every deal is about rapid problem solving and no one person can solve the problem on his or her own.

Myth #2 – The eureka moment

Another myth of creativity that must be dispelled is the eureka moment. There is no such thing as a big idea that changes the world. I know this is another one of those hurtful facts, but very true based on empirical research points.

There are little ideas that combined with other little ideas that improve themselves into game-changing ideas. And I've experienced this personally on the creativity of digitalization and Industry 4.0. Industry 4.0 was a problematic strategy from the start on growth and productivity. The Industry 4.0 you see today was a thousand problems solved.

I rather want my things to be copied than me copying. I would feel ashamed!

Karl Lagerfeld
The Pimp Master

Hero is a team sport

Myth #3 No one is an expert

Finally, the third myth of genius or creativity that must be shattered if you want to be more collaborative is the myth of the expert.

Now I believe in involving people in a project who we think are experts on the problem space. But if you notice, I don't want experts on the solution space because most of the great solutions to fixing problems come from the edges of a domain.

You don't know water until you've left your fishbowl

People who don't know what they don't know are not limited by false constraints that hold people back who are in the middle of this subject. So the way I like to think about it is, if you could talk to a fish, if you could, if the fish could respond, if it could, and you walked up to a fish in a fishbowl and you asked the fish, "How's the water?" the fish would look at you puzzled and ask you, "What's water?" And that's the problem with experts.

Ideas can come from anywhere

People who are so steeped in a domain, they don't have the expansive perspective that allows them to recognize patterns and convergence because every invention, every solution is really about pattern or convergence recognition. And so it's really important for us to follow the following mantra in collaboration: Ideas can come from anywhere.

THINK OF SOME GOOD STUFF...GET IT DONE.

MASTER OF STRATEGERY

A hero evolves skills to see patterns

A really big part of what it means to be a hero or genius is to have a great deal of creative or novel thinking. Making these novel associations between ideas, having a lot of pattern detection. So it's not just about collecting a bunch of data and knowing a lot of facts, but it's making these novel connections between ideas.

A hero develops the ability to see patterns. Apophenia, also known as patternicity, is a very common phenomenon that every human has. Patternicity is the ability to see patterns in random events. It also applies when people deduce meaning from numbers, images, shapes, or any other objects that are truly random. To start on the journey of patternicity, I recommend viewing it from a lens of classification, categorization, and lifecycles.

Every human is in some sort endowed with the need to make things better, to invent things, to go beyond the borders. We're all pioneers; we're all fascinated with a frontier. I mean, why do we think we need to go to the moon or to Mars? It's because we're human and we wanna know what's on the other side.

When preparation meets opportunity

One of the things about genius, I think, is it's not just an individual or just a brain. It's about opportunity. In the words of Seneca: Luck is what happens when preparation meets opportunity. It's about somebody who is given the pathway to actually make a contribution. Think of our musicians. Most of us would consider Bach, Beethoven, and Mozart geniuses. These are people who were put in positions that allowed them to be creative. The creative spirit comes with many things other than just a brain. I think it comes with opportunity; it comes with resources; it comes with attitude.

Reusable work templates

Designed to make your own strategy

Templates

Copy Canvas prepare as

Work Templates

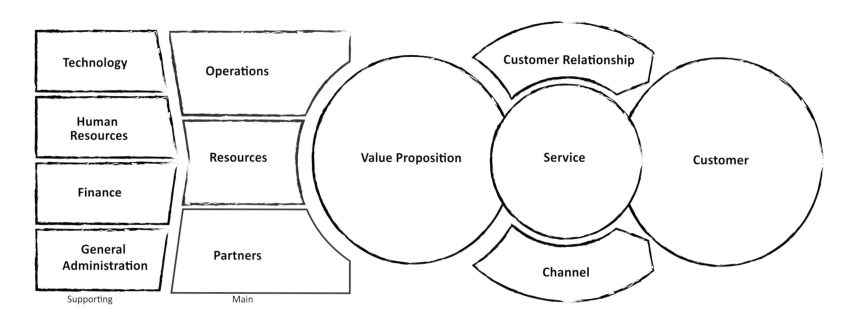

Technology

Human Resources

Finance

General Administration

Supporting

Operations

Resources

Partners

Main

Value Proposition

Customer Relationship

Service

Channel

Customer

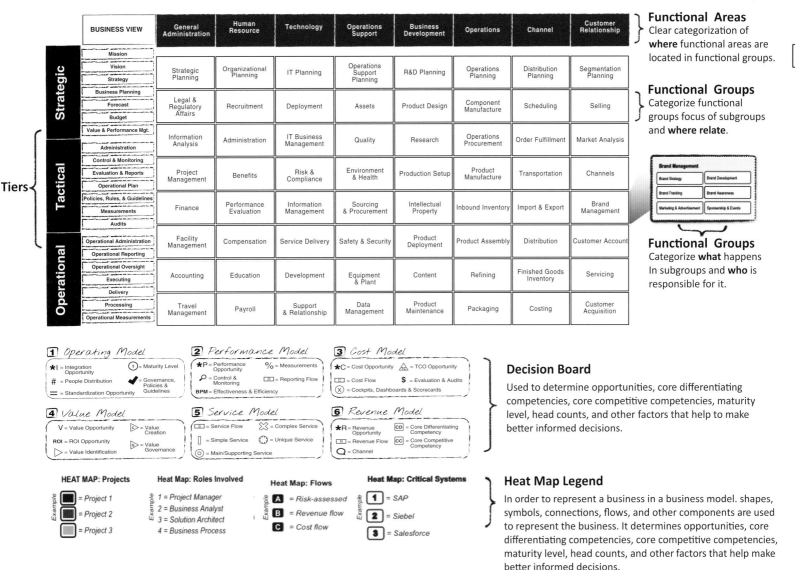

BUSINESS VIEW	General Administration	Human Resource	Technology	Operations Support	Business Development	Operations	Channel	Customer Relationship
Strategic — Mission / Vision / Strategy	Strategic Planning	Organizational Planning	IT Planning	Operations Support Planning	R&D Planning	Operations Planning	Distribution Planning	Segmentation Planning
Business Planning / Forecast / Budget	Legal & Regulatory Affairs	Recruitment	Deployment	Assets	Product Design	Component Manufacture	Scheduling	Selling
Value & Performance Mgt. / **Tactical** — Administration	Information Analysis	Administration	IT Business Management	Quality	Research	Operations Procurement	Order Fulfillment	Market Analysis
Control & Monitoring / Evaluation & Reports / Operational Plan	Project Management	Benefits	Risk & Compliance	Environment & Health	Production Setup	Product Manufacture	Transportation	Channels
Policies, Rules, & Guidelines / Measurements / Audits	Finance	Performance Evaluation	Information Management	Sourcing & Procurement	Intellectual Property	Inbound Inventory	Import & Export	Brand Management
Operational — Operational Administration / Operational Reporting	Facility Management	Compensation	Service Delivery	Safety & Security	Product Deployment	Product Assembly	Distribution	Customer Account
Operational Oversight / Executing / Delivery	Accounting	Education	Development	Equipment & Plant	Content	Refining	Finished Goods Inventory	Servicing
Processing / Operational Measurements	Travel Management	Payroll	Support & Relationship	Data Management	Product Maintenance	Packaging	Costing	Customer Acquisition

Tiers { Strategic, Tactical, Operational }

Functional Areas
Clear categorization of **where** functional areas are located in functional groups.

Functional Groups
Categorize functional groups focus of subgroups and **where relate**.

Brand Management — Brand Strategy, Brand Development, Brand Tracking, Brand Awareness, Marketing & Advertisement, Sponsorship & Events

Functional Groups
Categorize **what** happens In subgroups and **who** is responsible for it.

1 Operating Model
- ★I = Integration Opportunity
- ① = Maturity Level
- # = People Distribution
- ✓ = Governance, Policies & Guidelines
- = = Standardization Opportunity

2 Performance Model
- ★P = Performance Opportunity
- % = Measurements
- ◯ = Control & Monitoring
- R = Reporting Flow
- BPM = Effectiveness & Efficiency

3 Cost Model
- ★C = Cost Opportunity
- △ = TCO Opportunity
- CF = Cost Flow
- $ = Evaluation & Audits
- ✗ = Cockpits, Dashboards & Scorecards

4 Value Model
- V = Value Opportunity
- ▷ = Value Creation
- ROI = ROI Opportunity
- ▷ = Value Governance
- ▷ = Value Identification

5 Service Model
- S = Service Flow
- ✗ = Complex Service
- | = Simple Service
- ◌ = Unique Service
- ◎ = Main/Supporting Service

6 Revenue Model
- ★R = Revenue Opportunity
- CD = Core Differentiating Competency
- R = Revenue Flow
- CC = Core Competitive Competency
- ◠ = Channel

Decision Board
Used to determine opportunities, core differentiating competencies, core competitive competencies, maturity level, head counts, and other factors that help to make better informed decisions.

HEAT MAP: Projects
Example:
- ▪ = Project 1
- ▪ = Project 2
- ▪ = Project 3

Heat Map: Roles Involved
Example:
- 1 = Project Manager
- 2 = Business Analyst
- 3 = Solution Architect
- 4 = Business Process

Heat Map: Flows
Example:
- A = Risk-assessed
- B = Revenue flow
- C = Cost flow

Heat Map: Critical Systems
Example:
- 1 = SAP
- 2 = Siebel
- 3 = Salesforce

Heat Map Legend
In order to represent a business in a business model. shapes, symbols, connections, flows, and other components are used to represent the business. It determines opportunities, core differentiating competencies, core competitive competencies, maturity level, head counts, and other factors that help make better informed decisions.

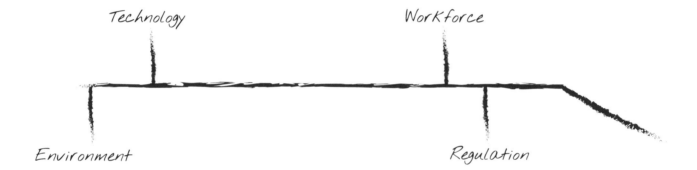

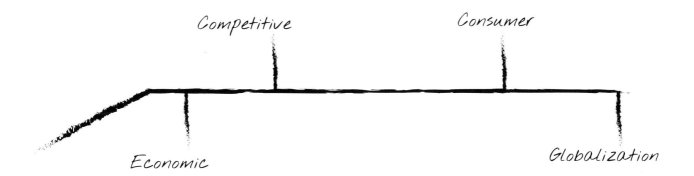

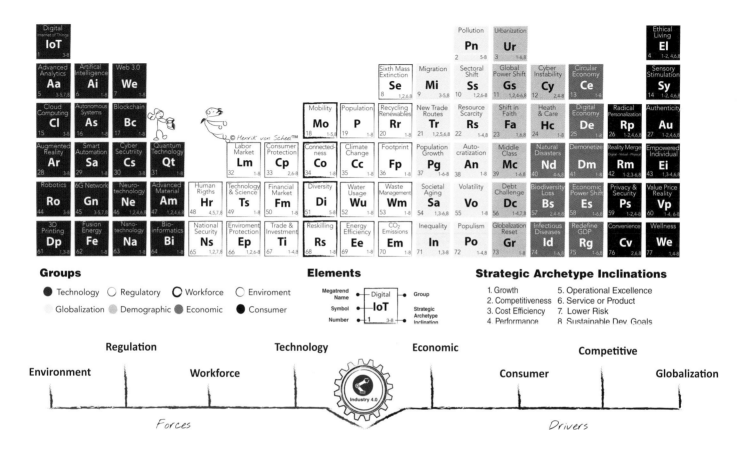

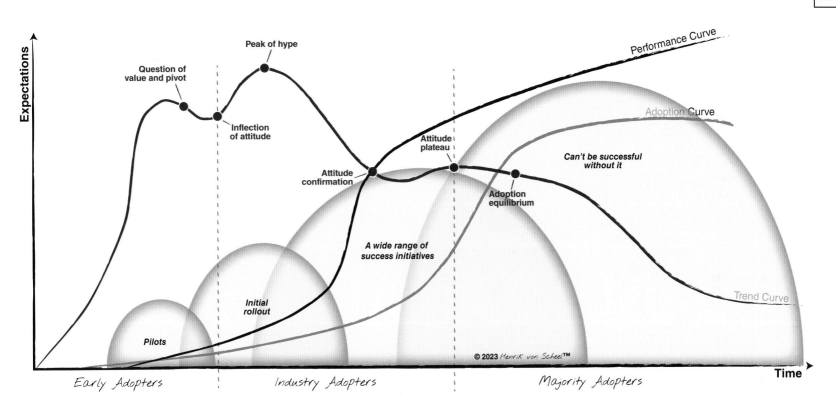

Expectations

Peak of hype

Question of
value and pivot

Inflection
of attitude

Attitude
plateau

Attitude
confirmation

Can't be successful
without it

Adoption
equilibrium

A wide range of
success initiatives

Initial
rollout

Pilots

Performance Curve

Adoption Curve

Trend Curve

© 2023 Henrik von Scheel™

Early Adopters

Industry Adopters

Majority Adopters

Time

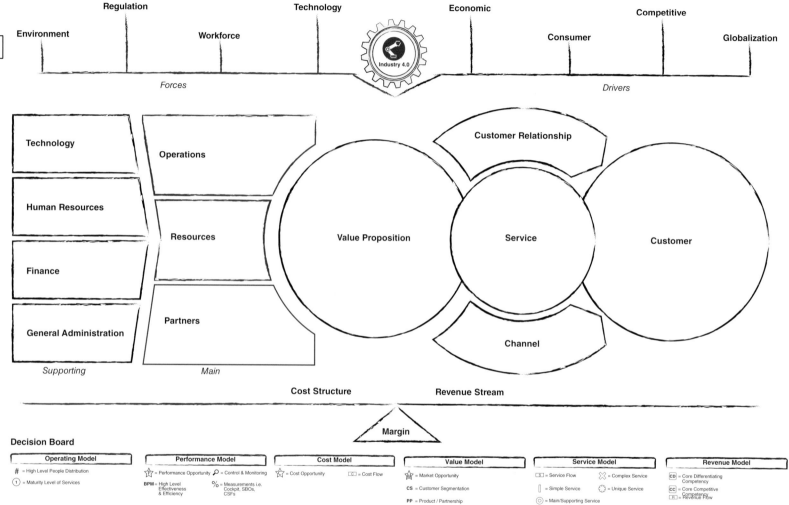

Environment   Regulation   Workforce   Technology   Industry 4.0   Economic   Consumer   Competitive   Globalization

Forces   *Drivers*

Technology

Human Resources

Finance

General Administration

Supporting

Operations

Resources

Partners

Main

Value Proposition

Customer Relationship

Service

Channel

Customer

Cost Structure   Revenue Stream

Margin

Decision Board

Operating Model

\# = High Level People Distribution

1 = Maturity Level of Services

Performance Model

☆ = Performance Opportunity   ⌕ = Control & Monitoring

BPM = High Level Effectiveness & Efficiency

% = Measurements i.e. Cockpit, SBOs, CSFs

Cost Model

☆ = Cost Opportunity   C = Cost Flow

Value Model

☆ = Market Opportunity

CS = Customer Segmentation

PP = Product / Partnership

Service Model

S = Service Flow   ✕ = Complex Service

| = Simple Service   ⊙ = Unique Service

⊙ = Main/Supporting Service

Revenue Model

CD = Core Differentiating Competency

CC = Core Competitive Competency

R = Revenue Flow

Strategy Map **IMPROVE OPERATIONAL EFFICIENCY**	*MEASUREMENT*	*TARGET*	*INITIATIVE*	*BUDGET*

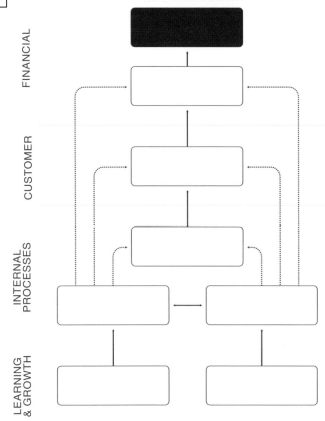

FINANCIAL

CUSTOMER

INTERNAL PROCESSES

LEARNING & GROWTH

Strategic Business Objectives	Critical Success Factors	Key Performance Indicators	Major Business Process and Performance Measures	Ownership	Activity and Performance Measures
			Process:		Process:
			M1.		M1.
			M2.		M2.
			Process:		Process:
			M1.		M1.
			M2.		M2.
			Process:		Process:
			M1.		M1.
			M2.		M2.
			Process:		Process:
			M1.		M1.
			M2.		M2.

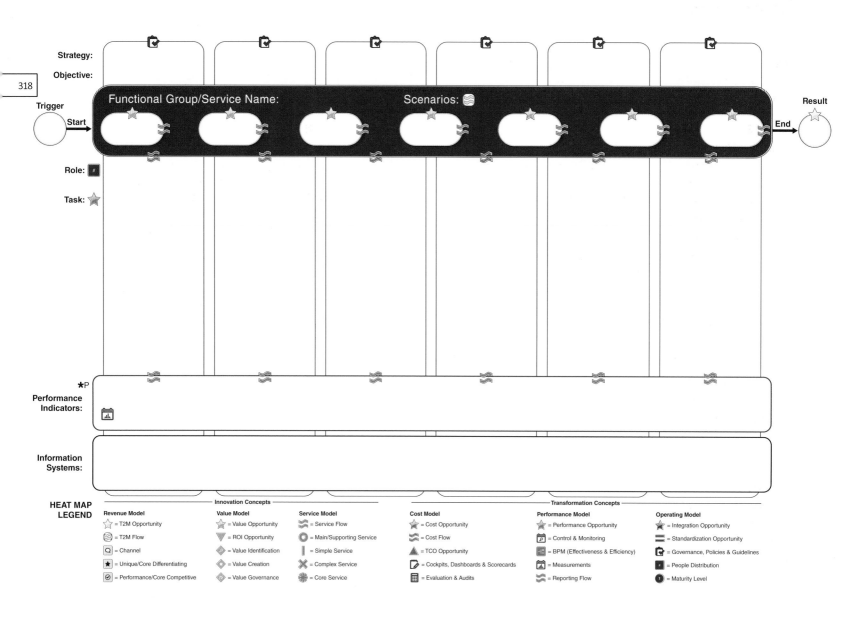

318

Strategy:

Objective:

Trigger

Start

Functional Group/Service Name: Scenarios:

Result

End

Role: #

Task: ☆

★P

Performance Indicators:

Information Systems:

HEAT MAP LEGEND

─ Innovation Concepts ─

Revenue Model	Value Model	Service Model	Cost Model	Performance Model	Operating Model
☆ = T2M Opportunity	☆ = Value Opportunity	≋ = Service Flow	☆ = Cost Opportunity	☆ = Performance Opportunity	☆ = Integration Opportunity
⬡ = T2M Flow	▽ = ROI Opportunity	⊚ = Main/Supporting Service	≋ = Cost Flow	▣ = Control & Monitoring	▤ = Standardization Opportunity
▢ = Channel	◈ = Value Identification	❘ = Simple Service	▲ = TCO Opportunity	▦ = BPM (Effectiveness & Efficiency)	▸ = Governance, Policies & Guidelines
★ = Unique/Core Differentiating	◈ = Value Creation	✕ = Complex Service	⬗ = Cockpits, Dashboards & Scorecards	▦ = Measurements	▪ = People Distribution
⊚ = Performance/Core Competitive	◈ = Value Governance	✳ = Core Service	▦ = Evaluation & Audits	≋ = Reporting Flow	❶ = Maturity Level

─ Transformation Concepts ─

References

Chapter 1

1. D. Clark, Average company lifespan of S&P 500 companies 1965-2030, Statista (2001).

Chapter 3

2. Michael E Porter, *Competitive Strategy: Techniques for Analyzing Industries & Competitors*, The Free Press, 1980.

3. Gary Hamel, & Prahalad, C. K., "The Core Competence of the Corporation," *Harvard Business Review,* May-June 1990, pp. 19-91.

4. Michael E. Porter, *The Competitive Advantage of Nations*, The Free Press, 1990.

Chapter 4

5. A Digital Agenda for Europe, European Union Communication (2010) 245 – EUR-LEX.

6. Michael E. Porter, *The Competitive Advantage of Nations*, The Free Press, 1990.

7. Angus Maddison, *The World Economy: A Millennial Perspective,* 2001, Table B-18.

8. Angus Maddison, *The World Economy: A Millennial Perspective*, Project Database 2010-2018.

9. Gregory Clark, *A Farwell to Alms: A Brief Economic History of the World*. Princeton University Press, 2008, p. 47.

10. World Bank, World Development Indicators, Employment by Industry chart, World Bank Database, 2019.

11. Paul Brassley, "Out and Technical change in Twentieth-Century British Agriculture," *Agriculture History Review* 48, no 1 (2000), p. 66.

12. Francois Bourguignon & Christian Morrisson, *Inequality among World Citizens 1820-1992*. American Economic Review 92: 731.

13. Johan Norberg, Progress: Ten Reasons to Look Forward to the Future. One World, 2016, p. 191.

14. UN Environment Program Protected Planet, World Database on Protected Areas, 1872-2003 data et al. Measuring the Extend and Effectiveness of Protected Areas as an indicator for Meeting Global biodiversity Targets, Figure B360 (2005).

15. Gale Pooley & Marian Tupy, The Simon Abundance Index. A New Way to Measure Availability of Resources. Cato Policy Analysis, no. 857, 2018.

16. Francois Bourguignon & Christian Morrisson, *Inequality among World Citizens 1820-1992*. American Economic Review, 92: 731.

17. World Bank, World Development Indicators: Water Productivity, Total GDP per Cubic Meter of Total Freshwater Withdrawal.

18. Xiao-Peng Song et al., Global Land Change from 1982-2016, *Nature*, 560, no 1. (2018), 639.

19. Our Nation's Air 2018. Comparison of Growth Areas and Declining Emissions, 1970-2018 US Environmental Protection Agency.

20. World Bank Database, Global CO_2 Emission 1960-2014 kilogram per 2010 dollar per Gross Domestic Product.

21. David Cutler and Ellen Meara, Changes in the Age Distribution of Mortality over the 20th Century. National Bureau of Economic Research Work Paper no. 8558, October 2011, p. 44.

22. World Health Organization, Ten Facts on Immunization, March 2018.

23. World Bank, World Development Indicators. Individual Using Internet and Mobil Cellular Subscriptions data indicators 2016.

24. Olga Basso, Reproductive Epidemiology in an Evolutionary Perspective. Why Bigger may not be Better. *Current Epidemiological Report* 1, no. 2 (2014), 98.

25. William D. Nordhaus, Do Real Output and Real-Wage Measures Capture Reality? The History of Lighting Suggests Not, in the *Economics of New Goods*, eds., Timothy F. Bresnahan and Robert J. Gordon. Chicago University Press (1996) p. 36.

26. World Health Organization, Cancer Death Rate Map 2017, Our world in Data. Cancer Factsheet, September 12, 2018.

27. Arnulf Grubler et al., A Low Energy Demand Scenario for Meeting the 1.5 C Target and Substantiable Develop Goals without Negative Emission Technology. *Nature Energy* 3, no. 1 (2018), 515-527.

28. W. Michael Cox & Richard Aim, Onward and Upward Bet on Capitalism – It Works. William O'Neil Center for Global Market and Freedom 2015-2016 Annual Report.

29. United Nations Statistics Division, Department of Economic and Social Affairs. Millennium Development Goal Indicators: Global access to improved drinking water source, 1990-2015.

30. FAOSTAT - Food & Agriculture Organization Corporate Statistical Database, Food Balance Sheet. UN Food and Agriculture organization, January 27, 2020.

31. Nicola Bulled & Richard Sosis, Examining the Relationship between Life Expectancy, Reproduction, & Educational Attainment. *Human Nature*, 21, no. 3 (2010), 276.

32. United Nations Development Programme, Human Development Reports, 2018, Table 2. Organization for Economic Co-operations and Development.

33. Monty Marshall & Gabrielle Elzinga-Marshall, Global Report 2017. Conflicts, Governance and State Fragility. Center for Systernic Peace. Vienna, VA. 27 Aug 2017.

34. United Nations Office on Genocide Prevention and the Responsibility to Protect, Definitions: Genocide.

35. World Bank, Population Living in Slums, Chart 1990-2024.

36. Thomas Szayna et al., What are the Trends in Armed Conflicts. RAND Corporation, Santa Monica, CA, 1998, p. 1.

37. United Nations, Department of Economic and Social Affairs. Population Division. World Urbanization Prospect: The 2018 Revision, File 2. Percentage of Population of Mid-year Residing in Urban Areas by Region, Subregion, Country and Area, 1950-2018.

38. World Bank Database, Global CO_2 Emission 1960-2014 kilogram per 2010 dollar per Gross Domestic product.

39. Robert Barro & Jong-Wha Lee, Educational Attainment for Total Population. 1950-2000, June 2018.

40. Jakob Pietschnig & Martin Voracek, One Century of Global IQ Gain. A formal Meta Analysis of the Flynn effect, 1909-2013. Perspectives on Psychological Science, 10, no. 3 (2015): 285.

Chapter 4 continued

41. Angus Maddison, Global Life Expectancy 1500-2016. *The World Economy*, Vol 1 (Paris OECD Development Centre, 2006), 33, table 1-5B.

Chapter 5

1. Louis V. Gerstner, *Who Says Elephants Can't Dance?* Harper Business, 2002.

2. Richard D'Aveni "The Empire Strikes Back – Counter Revolutionary Strategies for Industry Leaders," *Harvard Business Review*, November 2002, pp. 66-74.

3. Gary Hamel & C. K. Prahalad, "The Core Competence of the Corporation," *Harvard Business Review,* May-June 1990, pp. 19-91.

4. Chris Zook & James Allen, *Profit From the Core: Growth Strategy in an Era of Turbulence*, Harvard Business School Press, 2001.

5. W. Chan Kim & Renee Mauborgne, "Blue Ocean Strategy," *Harvard Business Review,* October 2004, pp. 76-84.

6. W. Chan Kim & Renee Mauborgne, "Value Innovation: The Strategic Logic of High Growth," *Harvard Business Review*, January-February 1997, pp. 102-112.

7. Daniel Goleman, "Leadership that Gets Results" *Harvard Business Review*, March-April 2000, pp. 78-90.

Chapter 5

8. Robert S. Kaplan & David P. Norton, "The Balanced Scorecard - Measures that Drive Performance," *Harvard Business Review*, January-February, 1992, pp. 71-79.

Index

" In a nutshell strategy is about making 3 choices: what not to do, where to be different, and what to focus on, in that order. "

Henrik von Scheel

The Art of Strategy in the age of disruption is a guided step-by-step handbook for anyone striving to master the building blocks of strategy by the leading authorities who ignited the Global Digital and 4th Industrial Revolution themes of today.

Highlights include

- Get the latest insight on the Industry 4.0 from the originator

- Discover the global megatrends that will disrupt everything

- Realize how to spot trends and thrive in uncertainty

- Learn the art of strategy in a guided step-by-step approach

- Uncover the latest management practices essential to manage the present and create the future

- Unveiling of Sun Tzu's modernized visual thinking models

- Benefit from reusable templates and visual memory effects

"The most influential management thinker of our times."
H.H. Sheikh Mohammed bin Rashid Al Maktoum
Ruler of Dubai

"He has influenced more executives and nations than any other business thinker."
Sam Palmisano, CEO of IBM

"One of the most pre-eminent strategists and advisors of his generation."
Eric Schmidt, Chairman of Alphabet

"Leading authority on strategy."
Financial Times

"Futurists of our century."
CNBC

ISBN 978-1-394-21026-8
53500

9 781394 210268